PASTORAL CARE IN THE CHURCH

PASTORAL CARE IN THE CHURCH

C. W. BRISTER

1817

HARPER & ROW, PUBLISHERS

NEW YORK, HAGERSTOWN, SAN FRANCISCO, LONDON

TO THE MEMBERS OF THE
BAPTIST CONGREGATIONS WHOM
I SERVED AS PASTOR AND WHO SHARED
WITH ME THE MINISTRY OF
PASTORAL CARE IN THE CHURCH

First Harper & Row paperback edition published in 1977.
ISBN: 0-06-061051-4
LIBRARY OF CONGRESS CATALOG CARD NUMBER: 64-19497

77 78 79 80 81 10 9 8 7 6 5 4 3 2 1

CONTENTS

[v]

PART II. *The Shape of the Church's Ministry*

PART III. *Procedures and Problems in Pastoral Care*

PREFACE TO

THE PAPERBACK EDITION

"Christ loved the church and gave himself up for her," wrote the Apostle Paul (Eph. 5:25). That single fact makes pastoral care in today's world possible and worthwhile. Creating the church was God's compelling purpose in the Incarnation, for "God was in Christ reconciling the world unto himself" (2 Cor. 5:19). Each local community of biblical people has been assigned the mission of sharing salvation's hope with a hostile, hurt, and wayward world.

Pastoral care is an intentional ministry carried out, not in isolation, but in the daily encounters, crises, mysteries, and decisions of God's people. True, each congregation is unique, and there are hundreds of thousands of ministers with varied theologies and work-styles. Their high resolve and heroic dedication would erode quickly, however, if they worked alone. The actual practice of ministry is *with*, as well as to or for, persons moving through life's passages and perils. Pastor and people, in "working together with God," transcend solitary struggles and powerful forces in order to advance his kingdom (2 Cor. 6:1).

The real stories of persons who are priests to each other are often stranger than fiction. Such case histories and the universal lessons they offer for pastoral practice lie at the heart of this volume. They have come from my years as a Christian pastor and teacher of ministers-in-the-making. My friendship with seminarians has become one of my cherished possessions. I have wanted my students to "make good" with God's people everywhere.

The parish pastor functions as a generalist and faces broad responsibilities. With the exception of large, wealthy congregations, he cannot select a favorite activity, like preaching, counseling, or administration, and specialize in it. To do so would be to neglect numerous duties and disciplines. The senior minister of a metropolitan church may be surrounded by able specialists. Still, they must each perform varied functions and diversify their efforts. Theological professors who write books, on the other hand, usually enjoy the luxury of a specialty: theology, church history, or pastoral care. Unfortunately, church leaders and educators do not always communicate clearly with each other.

That pastors and teachers may function on different wavelengths was demonstrated when I read the latest publications of a successful pastor and a noted professor the same weekend. The pastor's work was a public relations compendium of promotional tips for pushing a parish program. His church's Sunday school attendance had tripled in a ten year period, but the laws of growth he cited sounded egocentric, manipulative, and wearisome. The teacher had published a brief treatise on grief work in ministry. In style, he had adapted language from the health sciences that was technical and tedious. The pastoral specialist was highly idealistic about a parish minister's management of time. He assumed that counseling took priority over most other tasks. That reading was a revealing, though dismaying, experience.

Both writers did what their publishers had requested. They prepared small, inexpensive volumes for quick consumption by busy church leaders. It was, however, like receiving simultaneous signals from different planets. One wonders, can many tasks become truly unified in the life and work of one minister? I hope so. This book offers a pastoral perspective on all the work a minister does, with appreciation for the tensions created by his theological and ethical ideals in a pluralistic society.

So many things have happened since the first edition of the book was published. I will not attempt to catalogue all of them here, for time and space forbid that. *Pastoral Care in the Church* has received a warm welcome from readers on five continents and has been translated into other languages. It serves as a basic reader for theological students, of varied persuasions, in several countries. I believe its message is both timely and timeless.

Certain major trends will affect pastoral work in the final decades of this century. Patterns that are detectable in theological education, parish practice, and research publications deserve some notice here.

One, a new evangelicalism—rooted in biblical faith, extended toward world mission, and accountable in social action—pervades many churches, campuses, religious institutions, and publications. Personal and church renewal are *in* as persons grope for meaning, goals, and authenticity in an era of brutal violence and transient values. The ecumenical urge to merge institutions that followed World War II has waned, eroded by ecclesiastical politics, neo-nationalism, third world aspirations, Communist pressures, and stalemated wars. Fresh winds of God's Spirit have blown across denominational lines, however, diminishing the significance of religious labels. While organic union of all members of Christ's body seems far off, spiritual unity appears imperative.

Two, future ministers face intense social pressures and must help their people live with new realities. Struggles polarize around such issues as energy sources, environmental quality, heightened sexual consciousness, militant minority movements, crime and punishment, health care, the right to life, a guaranteed annual income, and responsible programs for aging and dependent citizens. Care must be given in a time of blurred boundaries between male and female roles, experimental family patterns, and unlicensed sexual therapies. Divorce has reached epidemic proportions. Ethnic consciousness-raising programs mushroom in the media, court actions, education, government, and industry. Displaced international communities have brought foreign mission fields to the church's front doorstep. Such issues require theological wisdom, moral clarity, and personal courage from concerned pastors.

Three, ministers who shape human values and share human suffering are becoming more discriminating in their use of secular theories and therapies. Furthermore, the human sciences have moved far beyond Freud, while remaining in his debt. Humanistic psychology, for example, takes account of a person's basic worth, aspirations, values, and peak expriences, not just his anxieties, neuroses, and psychoses. Developmental psychologists have focused upon states of individuation in adolescence and young adulthood, and upon transitions into middle age and aging, rather than upon infancy and childhood alone. Recent research encourages understanding, not only of pathologic infantile frustrations and adolescent disorders, but of normal adults moving through time and managing life's critical passages.

Group work has transcended the human potential movement's focus on intimacy, joy of sensory awareness, and meeting one's needs for survival, love, esteem, and self-actualization. Transactional Analysis (TA) offered family members new hope for game-free intimacy, and gestalt therapy, aimed at integration and wholeness, received new impetus from Frederick Perls and his colleagues. Pastors bringing a Christian perspective to such techniques will continue to enhance ego functioning and strengthen family life.

New group approaches have sacred and secular counterparts. *Life skills* groups vary in purpose: anxiety management, assertiveness training, communication skills, marriage/family enrichment, decision-making training, life/work planning, interpersonal competencies, and parenting skills. *Life theme* groups include areas like human sexuality, values clarification, self-esteem building, raising male/female consciousness, and so on. Examples of *life transition* groups include: young marrieds, new parents, the middle years, aging and retirement, grief and personal loss, and formerly marrieds.

Expanded vistas in counseling merit the minister's time and attention. Through reading, workshops, supervised practice, and continuing education seminars he will learn the techniques of micro-counseling, crisis intervention, behavior modification, transcultural therapies, life planning and career design, parent effectiveness training, reality therapy, and counseling older persons for retirement and death.

Four, clinical pastoral education (CPE) has entered its second half century. Acceptance of CPE is reflected in the almost universal membership by seminaries in the Association for Clinical Pastoral

Education (ACPE), and widely expanded programs. Clinical pastoral education is still concentrated in medical and institutional settings where adequate budgeting provides salaries for supervisors and stipends for students. New impetus has been provided, however, for CPE in settings like churches, campus ministries, and counseling centers.

Five, Doctor of Ministry (D.Min.) programs in numerous theological schools are geared to the actual practice of ministry. Some schools offer four-year, in-sequence curriculums for Master of Divinity and Doctor of Ministry degree students. Other seminaries require that doctoral level applicants demonstrate the promise of excellence in ministry through a minimum of two or three years of parish experience. Then, if approved by the faculty, they may become candidates for the professional doctoral degree.

Whatever the model of admission, a set of desirable competencies for pastoral practice guides most Doctor of Ministry programs. While allowing some specialization, the D.Min. is viewed as a generalist degree. It is designed for the study, practice, and evaluation of varied competencies relating to the ministry. Growing in popularity, the D.Min. is a professional, not a teaching, degree.

The circle of my indebtedness has widened immeasurably with the years. A roll call of names is impossible. I am grateful for Southwestern Baptist Theological Seminary's splendid sabbatical leave program, my publisher's commitment to long life for this volume, the Association of Theological Schools' generous fellowship a second time around, the work of translators, colleagues' and students' use of the book, and for family members' acceptance and encouragement.

C. W. BRISTER

Fort Worth, Texas

INTRODUCTION

When future church historians explore the data of mid-twentieth-century American Protestantism, they will be obligated to interpret at least four crucial movements on the contemporary scene. These include: (1) the renaissance of biblical study in schools and churches, (2) the ecumenical conversation within Christendom, (3) the laity's role in the mission of the church, and (4) the emergence of a responsible pastoral theology based on our new understanding of pastoral care. Theological education and discussion, the local church's ministry, and Christian communication with the world all find a growing edge in one or more of these historic concerns. The present discussion, while cognizant of these major theological currents, is designed to interpret Protestant pastoral care in a world come of age.

Since World War II, numerous volumes have appeared stressing some aspect of pastoral work: the hospital ministry, family counseling, group dynamics, and the interrelations of psychiatry and religion. Scores of counseling books, from representatives of varied disciplines, have been offered as pastoral prompters.[1] Chief justification for the present volume is the need in theological education and pastoral practice for a comprehensive interpretation of Christian pastoral care, and for clarification of some basic issues

[1] See, for example, volumes in the "successful pastoral counseling" series published by Prentice-Hall, Inc., under the general editorship of Russell L. Dicks.

in pastoral theology.[2] While pastoral care dates from religious antiquity and has advanced greatly through clinical study in recent years, the "new pastoral care" is as yet the skill of no more than an elite ministerial minority. The term itself refers to the employment of wisdom from theological disciplines and clinical experience in pastoral relationships. The "new pastoral care" has developed principally in this country as a result of the clinical pastoral education movement.

Certain points on a vocational compass are noted here in order to chart properly the course of this discussion and to restrict our sphere of investigation. In an effort to communicate with a varied audience this essay begins with some intrinsic foundations of pastoral care. Subjects in Part I, such as the pastor's identity, the church's caring task, Christian anthropology, and theological education are introduced, not in order to be discursive, but to be theologically discriminating. The early chapters will therefore lack novelty for specialists and schoolmen, but are included in this compendium as an essential context for a general pastoral audience. Part II traces the contours of Christian shepherding through the pastoral action of the local congregation. Part III offers clinical wisdom to those who share life's common ventures and crises as Christian helpers.

While pastoral care is embedded in relationships, and cases exemplifying certain aspects of pastoral ministry will appear throughout this work, the present volume is not designed as a counseling casebook. Clearly, one learns about pastoral preaching and counseling from the foibles and successes recorded ably by others.[3]

---

[2] More than a decade has elapsed since the publication of Paul E. Johnson's *Psychology of Pastoral Care* (Nashville, Tenn.: Abingdon Press, 1953). Nor has any basic work in pastoral theology appeared since Seward Hiltner's *Preface to Pastoral Theology* (Nashville, Tenn.: Abingdon Press, 1958), with the exception of Wayne E. Oates' *The Christian Pastor* (Philadelphia: Westminster Press, 1951; rev. and enlarged edition, 1964).

[3] Relevant pastoral preaching is well demonstrated in Charles F. Kemp (ed.), *Pastoral Preaching* (St. Louis: Bethany Press, 1963). For clinical guidance in pastoral counseling, see Newman S. Cryer, Jr. and John M. Vayhinger (eds.), *Casebrook in Pastoral Counseling* (Nashville, Tenn.: Abingdon Press, 1962), and Seward Hiltner and Lowell G. Colston, *The Context of Pastoral Counseling* (Nashville, Tenn.: Abingdon Press, 1961).

Using both clinical and academic research sources, I am trying to answer the broader question: "What is Christian pastoral care?"

While polemical writings in this rapidly developing field will certainly appear, this essay is apologetic in nature. It is designed to serve as a primer in pastoral work. The discussion centers upon

1. Pastoral functions *and* their theoretical basis,

2. Persons and the relationships between them, and

3. Christian doctrine as it functions in pastoral work.

Grateful pastoral counselors asknowledge their debt to the medical specialties, to social work, to the guidance movement, and to contributions from varied disciplines. Yet they seek professional competence as ministers, not as objective therapists. It is hoped that clergymen will share this and similar works with practitioners in medical and allied fields, thereby contributing to interprofessional colleagueship. Granger E. Westberg's *Minister and Doctor Meet* (Harper & Row, 1961) illustrates concretely how ministers may share their basic philosophy, goals, and methods with physicians at the community level. While this work is not addressed directly to the dialogue between psychiatry and religion, it assumes the reader's knowledge of such discussions.[4] Basic issues introduced here will provide lines of direction and cardinal points for discussion in the chapters that follow.

The theological situation. Historically, "practical theology" has included at least three major aspects of Christian ministry: (1) communiacting the gospel of Jesus Christ, (2) organizing the church for its work, and (3) caring for the souls of its members. We acknowledge the basic wholeness of ministry while respecting the integrity of each aspect or perspective of religious vocation. Preaching, teaching, and healing—the comprehensive ministry of Jesus Christ—emerge incarnate in the person and work of the Christian pastor today. Whatever his function, the modern minister is to embody a compassionate spirit and professional competence as he labors in Christ's stead.

[4] See, for example, the important essay by Albert C. Outler, *Psychotherapy and the Christian Message* (New York: Harper & Row, 1954). Cf. Simon Doniger (ed.), *The Nature of Man in Theological and Psychological Perspective* (New York: Harper & Row, 1962).

Pastoral theology as a critical study of the caring process and as a growing body of interpretative theory is coming of age in the latter half of the twentieth century.[5] There are some churchmen and theological schools in both Europe and America that have slept through this revolution and still view the practical disciplines in ancillary fashion. Paul Tillich has contributed profoundly to our understanding of the caring process—*listening love* he calls it. Yet he excludes the practical disciplines from the formal structure of theology.[6] Fortunately, this stepchild stigma is passing. Partly because of his pastoral background and the influence of his friend Eduard Thurneysen, Karl Barth has treated practical theology as indigenous, not auxiliary, to theology in his *Church Dogmatics.*[7]

The recent study of theological education by H. Richard Niebuhr, Daniel D. Williams, and James M. Gustafson notes that "the development of pastoral theology as a theological discipline is still in process."[8] The report suggests three areas of inquiry which are pertinent to this discussion, without proposing a formal definition of pastoral theology. "The student needs three contributions from his work in pastoral theology: first, an interpretation of the care of souls within the church and his pastoral office; second, an interpretation of the meaning of the data and scientific understanding in this field for Christian faith and theology, and third, growth in self-knowledge both as a person and as one who is to be a channel for the healing promised in the Gospel."[9]

---

[5] This may be demonstrated by examining materials in Charles F. Kemp, *Physicians of the Soul* (New York: The Macmillan Co., 1947) and John T. McNeill, *A History of the Cure of Souls* (New York: Harper & Row, 1951), in comparison with discussions by Hiltner, *op. cit.,* and Oates, *op. cit.,* in this country and by European theologians like Eduard Thurneysen, *A Theology of Pastoral Care,* trans. Jack A. Worthington and Thomas Wieser (Richmond, Va.,: John Knox Press, 1962), and Frederic Greeves, *Theology and the Cure of Souls* (Manhasset, N. Y.: Channel Press, 1962).

[6] Paul Tillich, *Systematic Theology* (Chicago: University of Chicago Press, 1951), I, 32-34.

[7] Translated by G. T. Thompson and Harold Knight (Edinburgh: T. & T. Clark, 1956). Barth's position is made clear in I, 2, 812-43 *et passim.*

[8] H. Richard Niebuhr, Daniel D. Williams, and James M. Gustafson, *The Advancement of Theological Education* (New York: Harper & Row, 1957), p. 122.

[9] *Ibid.,* p. 127.

Several implications appear in this statement, the *first* of which is the necessity for integrity in pastoral work today. Pastoral care and counseling, popularly conceived, have been abstracted from their theological-clinical roots and baptized with the activism of successful churchmanship. Ministers, encapsulated in the calendars of contemporary church life, feel compelled to include pastoral care (of some sort) in their portfolio of professional duties. Yet much traditional pastoral work has floundered in theological illiteracy and ministerial inadequacy. Before we offer the healing promised in the gospel to others we must first be made whole ourselves.[10]

Second, these schoolmen recognize that the pastoral task is essentially theological. The learning of functions or techniques, while essential to pastoral operations, has often supplanted fundamental theory in the education of ministers. When counseling is wedded to a fictional theology it remains superficial, and clerical functions are less than Christian pastoral care. Pastoral theology involves more than a proliferation of helps and hints for a successful pastorate. Its prior concern is the life of the soul before God. Thus the *substance* of pastoral theology is nothing less than *theology*. Who then are the pastoral theologians? Properly, ministers, laymen, and specialists involved in the shepherding process are best equipped to theologize about their task.[11] Such fundamental theory, developing from biblical wisdom and pastoral work, forms the substance of pastoral theology.

Also implicit in this statement is the cohesiveness of Christian faith and knowledge. The pastor's primary clues about God, man, the world, Christian experience, and his vocation are givens of the Christian faith rather than discoveries of empirical knowledge. Yet Christian experience demonstrates and validates the revelatory witness and timeless wisdom of scripture. Pastoral theologians employ resources from the Word of God, the research of men, and divine revelation in human suffering. Any contribution to the Christian

[10] See Chap. 3, "Preparation for Pastoral Care."
[11] Hiltner suggests correctly that all Christian helpers are to be creators of pastoral theology, *Preface to Pastoral Theology*, p. 39.

faith from inquiry considered to be *pastoral* should be viewed as a
part of the theological mainstream rather than as an independent
body of thought.

One further note from these schoolmen should prompt humility
in all Christian helpers and pastoral theologians. Because the development of pastoral theology is "still in process" through inquiry
into living relationships, our theological statements will be tenta-
tive, descriptive, and vulnerable. Robert McAfee Brown once suggested that the Christian's life should be marked by "finality of
commitment [to] the living God" yet by "tentativeness of statement" regarding our understanding of God and our existence before
him.[12] The true spirit of Christian ministers and theologians is not
a smug, stern dogmatism but a humble, teachable trust in the
heavenly Father. The pastor-theologian matures through his relationships and reflections upon them to the extent that he is
guided by God's Spirit and committed to his providence in human
experience.

The pastoral task. Knowledgeable ministers who move among
their fellows in daily life can testify from their experience to the
diversity of spiritual problems and the depth of human need. Students for the ministry are soon jarred out of their collegiate idealism and cultural folklore by the reality of human sin and suffering
revealed in field work or clinical assignments. Their specialized
theological jargon is invaded by the vocabulary of human tragedy,
moral aberration, spiritual rebirth, and hope. Clearly, whether he
is a novice or a veteran, a minister needs a comprehensive grasp
of his task, of resources available in his church and community,
and of the possibilities for growth and personal change open to
him and to his people.

Perhaps the place to begin in establishing a *definition* of the pastoral task is with a specific pastoral relationship. Rev. Paul Baker,
minister of a rural church, was notified that Danny Redd, two-year-
old son of one of his church families, had been fatally burned in a

[12] Robert McAfee Brown, *The Spirit of Protestantism* (New York: Oxford
University Press, 1961), p. 52.

home accident. The child's parents were members of the church and sent their two oldest children to Sunday school, but did not attend services regularly themselves. Pastor Baker had visited them often and remembered when word came of the tragedy that Mrs. Redd had at one time attempted suicide. He learned that Danny, one of four children, had gotten into some burning trash and suffered fatal burns before his mother and brother could rescue him from the flames.

The pastor called upon the grief-stricken family soon after hearing about the accident. When he arrived, Mr. Redd asked him to talk to the distraught mother, whose hands were bandaged from severe burns.

MOTHER (sobbing): I'm so glad you've come! We need you so much!

PASTOR: I am so sorry . . . I came as quickly as I could.

MOTHER: It was terrible . . . I don't know how he got into the fire. (Pause.) I was right there; we couldn't put it out. (Pause.) He was hurting so. Why did he have to hurt? He was so, so sweet and little. Why did he have to hurt? Why did Danny have to die?

PASTOR: Mildred, I am afraid I can't answer your question. Men all through history have asked "Why?" but did not always get an answer. Jesus even asked on the cross, "My God, my God, *why* hast Thou forsaken me?" Now, we cannot understand but we *can* trust God whether he gives us understanding or not.

MOTHER (weeping): I want my baby; I want to see my baby; I want to go to my baby! (Mr. Redd quieted her.)

PASTOR: Mildred, you cannot do that now. You must stay here and help Tom and the children. God has given you other children and they need their mother. Danny is with God. You must let God care for him while you care for the other children. (He listened as her grief poured out.)

MOTHER: I caused all this! Why didn't I watch him better? . . . Oh, Brother Baker . . . ! (A long silence.)

PASTOR: Surely you did what you could to save him. (Pause.) We must trust God now. Let us seek comfort and instruction in

God's word. (He read previously selected passages on God's care—Psalm 23; the resurrection—I Thessalonians 4:13-14; the stewardship of suffering—II Corinthians 1:3-7; and God's comforting presence—Isaiah 43:2.)

They prayed after he had read the brief scripture selections. The Redds asked the minister to be in charge of the funeral and left other arrangements in the hands of relatives and friends.

Even a casual reading of the pastor's report reveals his mishandling of the Redds' acute bereavement during this prefuneral visit.[13] As we shall see in Chapter 9, the psychological process of "grief work" has been studied intensively, beginning with Freud's preliminary essay "Mourning and Melancholia." The Christian pastor's understanding and support of those who mourn may be strengthened greatly by a knowledge of such studies. Pastor Baker "comforted" the Redds without undestanding the emotional import of their baby's death. His words, while tender, did not take seriously their feelings of confusion, bitterness, and disruption of their value system. The scripture selections, each appropriate for healthy grief work in its due season, actually repressed the parents' true feelings. He overlooked the father's dry-eyed numbness and the mother's guilt feelings for having neglected the child. Seeking to represent the "God of all comfort," his prefuneral ministry was repressive and insensitive to the Redds' deepest feelings.

While we have no record of the funeral sermon and service of interment, the pastor provided a summary of one follow-up call that transpired soon after the funeral. They thanked him for the "beautiful service for Danny," and the mother asked that he read I Corinthians 13, concerning "those things that abide." Pastor Baker reassured the Redds of the Christian's abiding home with his heavenly Father, of God's care of Danny and his concern for them and their surviving children. They were invited back to church services, since they had felt the strengthening support of Christian friends anew. Eventually the bereaved family members were able

---

[13] This and all other reports of pastoral relationships represent actual situations and appear by permission. Names and places have been changed to assure anonymity.

to resume their daily rhythm of life and to participate in church activities.

While we shall expand on shepherding functions during the crisis of grief in Chapter 9, what may be noted about the pastoral task from the foregoing case? Descriptively, we may observe that: (1) Spiritual oversight of God's flock implies a dynamic awareness of human development and behavior under stress. (2) Christian ministers and church members participate mutually in shepherding tasks, with due sensitivity to humanity's hurt and God's grace in time of need. (3) Pastoral care operates not only within the walls of a church building but in any relationships with the "least of these" who acknowledge God's presence in their midst (Matt. 25:31-46). (4) While such oversight involves specific functions, at a deeper level it is a spirit of concern nurtured through the faith, worship, and corporate life of the people of God.

How, then, shall we conceive pastoral care in the context of a shepherding community? Pastoral care has been viewed mistakenly in the past as superficial do-goodism; as a crutch for life's cripples; as God's psychiatry aimed at "peace of mind"; or as a form of faith healing which might save us from suffering, fear, and death. This is the mistaken, theologically incapacitated "shepherding" of some who have viewed Christianity as a potent anesthetic administered by clergymen to sufferers in crises. Again, pastoral care has been construed as *the pastor's* work, usually through a private conversation with an individual person. Such concepts fail to communicate the comprehensive shepherding ideal revealed in the New Testament.

Biblically and practically, *pastoral care is the mutual concern of Christians for each other and for those in the world for whom Christ died.* Protestant pastoral care views the church itself as minister and the pastor as a servant of servants. His role as leader, teacher, and example is fulfilled within the church's shepherding ministry. God's people care for hurt humanity as they incarnate his redemptive presence in life, where the real needs are (John 17:15-26). The church thus finds its life in the world by grappling with the evils, distress, and unanswered questions of men "for Christ's sake." Again, the caring church is true to its calling when it serves those within its fold as a community of identity, of relationship, of confession, of worship, of inquiry, and of hope. The following chapters interpret the pastoral functions of ministers and laymen who are participants in such a "company of the committed."

I

Foundations of Pastoral Care

CHAPTER 1

✶

PASTORAL CARE IN
THEOLOGICAL PERSPECTIVE

THE PASTOR who provides leadership, spiritual guidance, and encouragement to a congregation is the most nearly normative concept of the Christian minister in history. From the time Jesus Christ chose certain disciples and "appointed them that [they] should go and bear fruit" pastoral care has been a universal practice in the life and mission of Christian churches. All those who loved him were "to love one another," to strengthen each other in the faith, and to minister to those in the world for whom Christ died (John 15:12-17). Such care implies not anxiety, nor what Kierkegaard called "dread" concerning life's tragedies, but self-transcendent concern for others. This generous impulse, which can be accepted or stifled, employs the vocabulary of Christian compassion in all human relationships.

Paradoxically, our human tendency is to view wounded spirits from a safe distance. Man's natural inclination is to refuse aid to life's wounded and pass by on the other side. This is a day when self-realization and self-preservation have been exalted, when men and nations assist only those who can reciprocate in some measure, and self-denial for the sake of others is ridiculed. Responsible men have difficulty in appreciating, let alone serving, irresponsible and irreligious men. Prejudice closes doors to understanding, and fear of the "other" dictates a policy of caution, a defensive life-style,

[3]

rather than acceptant attitudes of helpfulness. Preoccupation with one's own concerns seals the eyes of good men to potential personal objects of care. And generosity has been stifled in the past by the avarice and hostility of some thankless recipients of Christian care.

It is not easy for contemporary man, lulled into indifference by "religion in general," to particularize his faith by identifying with another person's need. Yet God's concern for mankind manifested in the Incarnation remains irrepressible. The New Testament contrasts his rich generosity with our solicitous self-concern (cf. Rom. 5:6-8). Those who serve as instruments of God's hands and channels of his grace cherish the "other" for his or her own sake and for God's sake. In reality, it is not to churchmen that the world's sin-sick and embattled citizens turn, but to Christ, whom they hope to find through us or in spite of us.

This essay was introduced with the experience of a Protestant minister who, along with members of his congregation, shared one family's burden until the members were able to resume life's tasks again. I have suggested that pastoral care is the mutual concern of Christians for each other and for those in the world for whom Christ died. While the pastor has a unique social role and ecclesiastical office, he has no monopoly on the church's caring concerns. Rev. Paul Baker, the Redds' minister, confessed: "The Christian people of the community played a more important part in this case than did the pastor." With this in mind, let us explore some criteria for caring, the helper's true identity, and areas of Christian concern for others.

I. CRITERIA FOR THE PASTORAL TASK

In a Sprunt lectureship at the Union Seminary of Richmond, Daniel Day Williams said: "The pastoral task, as it comes to every minister and every Christian, is to respond to the wonder of God's care for the soul and to share with others such knowledge as he has of God's healing power."[1] There is profound wisdom here in

[1] Daniel Day Williams, *The Minister and the Care of Souls* (New York: Harper & Row, 1961), p. 147.

that (1) it is God's healing power that Christians offer to wounded persons; (2) divine love is the shepherd's motivating purpose, not human need; and (3) only those who have first been healed at God's hands function as true channels of his power. Furthermore, a desire to help must be matched by an informed understanding in order that our spiritual labors be not in vain. A physician whose son had proved a terrible disappointment reflected sadly: "Sometime parents think they are doing the best they know how to do, but their best isn't enough." Clearly, we need no new tinkers with souls nor clever manipulators of human destinies. Rather, persons who have come of age in a secular world require profound wisdom in those who would communicate with them about God's healing power.

We recognize that pastoral care of shattered folk like the Redd family is only one of a vast variety of ministerial tasks in contemporary church life. So strategic is shepherding *at the appropriate time*, however, that it deserves to be performed well. Like a skilled surgeon who must employ all his training and wisdom to suture the edges of a single wound, the Christian pastor must assume full theological and practical responsibility for his work. A modern minister needs to know *how* to fulfill his multifunctional role, *why* he is ministering, and *what* it is that he is doing. This presupposes technical skills, theoretical knowledge, and theological wisdom as well. Does it imply that those who fail to meet certain conditions of caring are thereby exempt from compassionate living? Not at all! It does suggest, however, that we examine basic criteria for pastoral work and for critical reflection upon that work, leading to pastoral theology.

1. *Motivation*

From the early church period to the present the reconciling and sustaining love of God has motivated spiritual service in Christ's stead (John 15:17; II Cor. 5:14, 19). The Apostle John declared: "We know that we have passed out of death into life, because we love the brethren. He who does not love remains in death. . . . By this we know love, that he laid down his life for us; and we ought to lay down our lives for the brethren. But if any one has the world's goods and sees his brother in need, yet closes his heart against him, how does God's love abide in him? . . . Let us not love in word or speech but in deed and in truth" (I John 3:14-18). Every Christian, not merely those who are ordained, is to participate in the church's mission of reconciliation and soul care. Christ calls his people to care and simultaneously beckons those in the world to respond to their concern. The motives of giving and receiving are operative together.

Rev. Paul Baker *might* have shared the Redd family's brokenheartedness out of a sense of duty, through force of habit, because the community expected him to officiate at all funerals, because of private vows or ecclesiastical expectations, or by personal request of the family and friends. Primarily, however, the pastor and lay folk served in tender response to humanity's hurt. Members of the Christian community were sensitive to suffering and available to help when a pastoral opportunity presented itself. They became instruments of God's grace and peace for a specific time and need (Heb. 4:16).

Christian love is the primary generating environment of true pastoral labor. Fear cautions against such activities, operates in order to save the self, and thereby rejects the "other." Love, which transmutes our human incapacities, tunes our care to the inner tempo of people's spiritual needs. Pastoral care and counseling are not engaged in as an escape from other demanding ministerial obligations. Neither do we counsel men and women in order to gain control over dependent personalities or to satisfy an insatiable appetite for the secrets of their souls. The "healer" whose erotic stirrings are satisfied in close encounters with others is himself in need of healing. Constrained by Christ's love, the minister's heart is open constantly to the stresses of life and the dimensions of his people's need.

Someone has suggested that we interpret the story of the Good Samaritan (Luke 10:30-37) in the light of our own experience. Life thrusts us, at times, into each of the roles filled by the parable's characters. Do we need the reminder that Christians are not above falling to the spoilers and landing injured on life's high-way? A theological student once offered transportation to a hitch-hiker late at night. In a matter of moments the recipient of his generosity leveled a pistol at his head, demanded his wallet and his keys, beat him in the face with the gun, then pushed him from his car and drove away. The would-be "helper" was himself left literally stunned and half-dead on the roadside. Suffering knows no partiality. It invades the privacy of the just and unjust alike. Again, there are specific occasions when, like the priest and the Levite, church people pass life's wounded by. Through ignorance, indifference, insecurity, emotional instability, fear, or preoccupa-tion with private burdens, many religious folk leave life's injured bleeding and alone. There is the happy opportunity occasionally to be the Samaritan, a good neighbor, ready and generous to aid those in distress. Some kindly folk are innkeepers who receive hurt persons into a place of temporary refuge and healing. The role of Christian physician, school counselor, social worker, and hospital personnel parallels that of the ancient innkeeper. Help is sometimes given; at other times received.

Pastoral care thus arises both out of the *push* of the pastoral calling and the *pull* of human need. The shepherd's heart—Christian response to humanity's hurt—is a gift in some people. It must be cultivated by others. But, as Christ reminded Simon Peter, such a ministry can be sustained only by mature love (John 21:15-17).

2. *Theological Responsibility*

A glance at the dialogue in the Introduction indicates that the questions the Redd family asked their minister after Danny's death were basically theological.

1. Why do the innocent suffer? Why does man have to die?
2. Is the stewardship of suffering a Christian possibility?
3. How can life move beyond grief to responsibility again?
4. Can we believe in the resurrection of the body and a place called heaven?
5. How can Christian parents cope with feelings of failure or guilt regarding their responsibilities?

Earlier we noted the importance of the process of grief which must be worked through as a principle of pastoral care of the bereaved. Obviously, Rev. Paul Baker did not take the psychodynamics of the grief process into account. In relating the Word of God to the Redds' situation, he sensed no revelatory element in religious experience. Doubtless he did all that he knew to do. Clearly, the generating center of his pastoral care was focused in the Christian faith.

Integrity in pastoral work presupposes theological and clinical wisdom as well as a loving heart. Preachers, for example, are to understand both hermeneutics and the psychology of audience participation in worship. Church administrators must be skilled in economics, ecclesiology, and group dynamic processes. And pastors are also theologians when they reflect upon God's ways with man and upon the life of man before God. This is the realm of *pastoral theology*—discriminating reflection upon pastoral relationships in the light of the Christian faith.

Theology presupposes God's self-revelation; he makes himself known to man. Yet divine revelation through the Word of God anticipates consequences in human experience.[2] Each doctrine growing out of biblical revelation and historic Christian interpretation has its parallel in human experience. Ministers will discover mistaken views of God, of sin, of the Incarnation, of guilt and forgiveness in their pastoral conversations. Such erroneous ideas may indeed serve as a growing edge for corrected concepts as profound questions are faced through reading, preaching, or counseling. Occasionally, a church member amazes his pastor with his quiet wisdom about the church's mission, some aspect of family life, or the daily providence of God. Thus, our knowledge of God develops both from biblical study and from personal experience.

To theologize, to frame a theology, is every Christian's privilege and obligation. With due respect for all who have witnessed to their faith in the past, each Christian is to articulate his own faith reverently before God (Rom. 14:12; I Pet. 2:9). Biblical truth does

[2] See John Baillie, *The Idea of Revelation in Recent Thought* (New York: Columbia University Press, 1956), pp. 83-85.

not change. Man's *understanding* of God, the universe, and his own existence before God does change. *God himself is the absolute truth* rather than man's statements about God in the form of theological propositions. Every Christian minister, therefore, has both a practical and a theological vocation. He must know whereof he speaks and possess a "ready answer" for the hope resident in his heart (I Pet. 3:15). A corresponding responsibility rests upon each community of believers—the church—to reflect upon its faith, life, and ministry, and to articulate the content of its faith to those in the world.[3] Meanwhile, God transcends and judges man's partial knowledge and all religious systems. Through the illumination of the Holy Spirit, he desires to lead his people continually "into all truth" (John 16:13).

The criterion of theological responsibility in pastoral work refuses to halt at the halfway house of those who consign the practical disciplines to the technical status of mechanics. The Anglican Martin Thornton reflects such a limited perspective by proposing that "pastoral theology may now be defined as applied dogmatics . . ."[4] Thus his recent work stands with the nineteenth-century Continental point of view rather than with our contemporary understanding. James Smart is nearer the truth when he writes in *The Rebirth of Ministry* that pastoral theology should bring "the whole of theology to a focus upon [the] one point in the church's life where it attempts to deal with human beings not in the mass but as individuals or intimate groups, family or otherwise."[5] Such a focus of theological wisdom in pastoral work requires more than a rigid application of certain techniques in mechanical fashion. Careful attention must be given to the process of pastoral care and counseling and to principles which will strengthen personal relationships. In the method of pastoral work introduced here, ultimate

[3] I am indebted to James Leo Garrett, professor of Christian Theology, the Southern Baptist Theological Seminary, for this observation through personal communication.

[4] Martin Thornton, *Pastoral Theology: A Reorientation* (London: S.P.C.K., 1956), p. 7.

[5] James D. Smart, *The Rebirth of Ministry* (Philadelphia: Westminster Press, 1960), p. 109.

human concerns are illuminated by Christian convictions as well as by clinical conclusions.

3. Methodology

A theology of pastoral care both fashions and is fashioned by an acceptable methodological orientation. Without a comprehensive *method* of work the pastor struggles through his days ill-equipped, often crushed by the demands of his office. Such a man feels inadequate for the slippery ground of some desperate counseling situations, keeps few pastoral records, and seldom reflects upon his shepherding relationships. Clearly, action in another's behalf is the vanguard of pastoral work, while reflection upon one's ministry follows subsequently. By such a dualistic process of action and reflection pastoral theology is formed.

The clinical pastoral education movement has addressed itself to the need for a responsible method of pastoral work and has contributed greatly to our understanding of pastoral theology in this century. The pioneering research of Anton T. Boisen, reported in *The Exploration of the Inner World* (Harper & Row, 1936; new ed., 1952) and *Religion in Crisis and Custom* (Harper & Row, 1955), has been a shaping influence in pastoral ministry for a generation. Among those who have taken Boisen seriously and used his "first principles" in the formulation of a responsible theology of pastoral care are men like Seward Hiltner, Paul Johnson, Wayne E. Oates, and Carroll A. Wise. The thrust of Seward Hiltner's *Preface to Pastoral Theology* is that pastoral work, properly examined, has valid implications for the Christian faith. His perspectival approach of focusing the shepherding spirit upon *all* the operations of the church and functions of the minister represents a major contribution to pastoral methodology. Hiltner demonstrates through case-examination a method by which a systematic pastoral theology— healing, sustaining, and guiding—may be constructed.[6] This he

---

[6] In his serious attempt to reformulate pastoral theology, Hiltner affirms the necessity of roots in the "eternal verities of the faith" (*Preface to Pastoral Theology* [Nashville, Tenn.: Abingdon Press, 1958], p. 51), yet gives scant attention to these verities in his methodology. Hiltner does not deliberately snub biblical categories. He presupposes them, then bypasses them in an effort

rightly calls a preface, which anticipates further investigation.

We are all in debt to these precursors for valuable prolegomena in both pastoral theology and psychology of religion. Yet much basic research in these fields remains to be done. What method, then, shall guide pastoral service today and theological investigation in days to come?

Negatively, we should note that (1) while pastoral care may be isolated *for* specialized study it should not be isolated *from* classical theology. We cannot erect a complete doctrinal structure on insights from pastoral practice alone. Again, (2) the church's mission in the world will not permit a minister or congregation to spend full time with ecclesiastical housekeeping, thereby neglecting those for whom Christ died. Theologizing must parallel Christian service, *not* replace it. (3) Reflection upon one's pastoral relationships which takes the narrative form of *anecdotes only* is not to be construed as theological pursuit. Cases of pastoral counseling

---

to assimilate the contributions of contemporary personality sciences "into a theological context" (p. 7). While he appreciates the traditional branches of theology, Hiltner proposes "another kind of branches of theology, whose focuses are a particular perspective upon operations" (p. 21). He perceives three "operation-centered" branches of theology: communicating, organizing, and shepherding, which are to be developed as cognates to traditional theological categories by "critical and discriminating inquiry" (p. 21).

His proposal "brings the shepherding perspective to bear upon all the operations and functions of the church and the minister, and then draws conclusions of a theological order from reflection on these observations" (p. 20). For clinical wisdom he examines the pastoral records of Rev. Ichabod Spencer, a Presbyterian minister in Brooklyn in the mid-nineteenth century, and extrapolates theory from them. This admittedly is a narrow empirical base for such extensive conclusions. It should be noted that this approach to theology has historic precedent. Schleiermacher, the nineteenth century German theologian, held that "the proper study of [pastoral] practice would illuminate theological understanding itself (pp. 46-47, 225). His method is akin to Paul Tillich's correlational theology in that "studying shepherding in the light of theological questions and returning with theological answers, can take full account of psychology" and thus remedy the present bifurcation of theology and psychology (p. 26).

As a clue to his method, Hiltner writes that "the basic clue to the systematic construction of this author has come from Boisen" (p. 51). Anton T. Boisen's unique study of "living human documents" in the Elgin (Ill.) State Hospital as a source of theological understanding may be found in *The Exploration of the Inner World* (New York: Harper & Row, 1936; new ed. 1952) and *Religion in Crisis and Custom* (New York: Harper & Row, 1955).

are preserved, not like enemy scalps or trophies from expeditions into the no man's land of grief, mental illness, or disbelief, but in order that they may become instruments of learning. Another man's pastoral work is inspected, not out of idle curiosity, but as an avenue to self-awareness and improvement as a minister.

Positively, Christian shepherding should be guided by theological presuppositions which grow out of a threefold process. Note that the first two stages are of a different order than the third.

1. Pastoral care anticipates a relevant employment of basic theological understanding in pastoral work.

2. Pastoral care requires a skillful employment of contemporary cultural disciplines in pastoral work.

3. Pastoral theology, conclusions of a theological order revealing the content of pastoral work, emerges from critical reflection upon one's encounters with "living human documents."

This method was first suggested by Boisen, expanded by Hiltner, and is illustrated in Edward Thornton's *Theology and Pastoral Counseling* (Prentice-Hall, 1964) and in recent clinical research. While one recognizes the validity of investigating the content of pastoral interviews with theological questions in mind, the thrust of the present volume is more functional than theoretical. It seeks to describe the comprehensive process of pastoral care and counseling, including systematic appraisal of the content of individual conversations.

The purpose of this chapter is to underscore the theological basis for Christian shepherding. When pastoral practice is squared and plumbed with an adequate biblical theology, notes Wayne Oates, "we can avoid creating a 'gnosis' kind of theology that will use the same words current in classical theology without regard to the historical rootage of meaning in Biblical revelation."[7] Thus we need to appreciate certain motifs of ministry in scripture, as well as the historic caring concerns of Christian churches. While pastoral care presupposes Christian theology in its *modus operandi*, it is dependent upon cultural disciplines as well. The subconscious

---

[7] Wayne E. Oates, *Protestant Pastoral Counseling* (Philadelphia: Westminster Press, 1962), p. 92.

dimensions of personality, dynamics of religious conversion, significance of symbolism in worship, components of guilt and hostility,
and soul care of desperate persons caught in the twisted existence
of our culture, all require of today's ministers skilled knowledge.

The method of pastoral work outlined in subsequent chapters
employs findings from both the behavioral sciences and the theological disciplines. As ministers employ man-science resources in dealing with persons, it is not to be construed as a "theological invasion
of anthropological territory."[8] Rather, biblical anthropology (which
has a past, present, and future of its own) engages in dialogue with
cultural disciplines which have provided new ways of thinking
about persons in communities and new modes of working with
them. Psychological dimensions of human reality cannot be overlooked; yet neither are they the center and circumference of existence. Clergymen are to view "cultural manifestations with Christian
eyes," notes Emile Cailliet, appreciative of scientific penetration into
the depth of reality and the fresh information disclosed thereby.
He writes: "It would be a strange thing to deal with culture without ever learning anything from culture. . . . The knowledge of
faith is no substitute for that of the specialist in his field, or of the
man of culture in his cultural circle."[9]

There is need for a mutual exchange of information between
theologians and scientists in an atmosphere of mutual respect. Do
we need the reminder that the revelation of God in his Word does
not invalidate scientific research and new understanding? Science,
correctly viewed, can become the servant rather than the enemy of
the Christian faith. God's design is that science, like every human
discipline, should become a divine service. Scientific findings, while
immensely helpful, cannot be absolutized into a new faith, for
they are descriptive and proximate, not ultimate and absolute.
What is true of theology is also true of science; *all* of man's partial
wisdom falls under the judgment of God. While science's highest
achievements have corrected our misconceptions and enriched our

[8] Theodore O. Wedel, *The Gospel in a Strange, New World* (Philadelphia:
Westminster Press, 1963), p. 34.
[9] Emile Cailliet, *The Christian Approach to Culture* (Nashville, Tenn.:
Abingdon Press, 1953), Preface, n.p.

lives, science alone can never sustain life in its eternal dimensions. This is the realm of faith.

The third aspect of methodology noted above is the Christian helper's theological task. Through reflection upon his pastoral contacts, in which he has sought to employ both divine and human resources, theological wisdom accrues to him and others. This was illustrated above in the area of grief work, but is applicable in any area of Christian shepherding. Let us be warned, however, that while certain aspects of religious experience may be investigated, the process does not yield what William James once called empirical or scientific theology. Samuel H. Miller has wisely noted that "religion can never be reduced to clinical conditions, for the profound reason that God is free."[10] God's love, grace, and justice are not test-tube phenomena. But while the content of the Christian faith transcends all human attempts to capture and explain its profound mystery, it is possible to develop reliable knowledge about faith's function in life.

In this connection it may be helpful to distinguish, as did P. T. Forsyth in *The Person and Place of Jesus Christ*, between "theology which is a *part of the Word*, and the theology which is a *product* of it."[11] This is akin to Paul Tillich's distinction between original and dependent revelation. He writes: "An original revelation is a revelation which occurs in a constellation that did not exist before . . . There is continuous revelation in the history of the church, but it is dependent revelation."[12] The Bible as "original revelation" stands as the unique and unrivaled record of God's redeeming activity in history. This is the *truth* of the Word. Theological wisdom which generates from Christian life and work, under the Holy Spirit's illumination, is a *product* of the Word. Such "dependent revelation" is the area of continuous inquiry of pastoral theologians and students of religious experience.

[10] In Hans Hofmann (ed.), *Making the Ministry Relevant* (New York: Charles Scribner's Sons, 1960), p. 74.
[11] P. T. Forsyth, *The Person and Place of Jesus Christ* (New York: Eaton and Mains, n.d.), p. 15, emphasis supplied.
[12] Tillich, *Systematic Theology* (Chicago: University of Chicago Press, 1951), I, 126.

With certain criteria for caring and theologizing established, it is necessary to raise and answer two questions, significant for this theological perspective. First, what is the minister's essential theological identity? Second, in the light of biblical theology, what are to be the caring concerns of the modern Christian congregation? Christian pastoral care needs a normative orientation in the light of diverse views concerning the church and its ministry in our time.

II. BIBLICAL MOTIFS OF MINISTRY

There are some observers who think that biblical motifs are far removed from what modern people can understand. One has noted, for example, that the shepherd and sheep imagery in scripture fails to convey the reality of the contemporary pastor-parishioner relationship. "Some want to revive the concept of the pastor as the shepherd of his flock," says Hans Hofmann. "It is hard to believe that modern people either want to or ought to follow their normally poorly educated minister without reservation."[13] Admittedly, members of Christian congregations are not mere sheep; but neither are they patients or clients! Modern ministers are not superior shepherds overseeing helpless flocks; but neither are they psychotherapists or Madison Avenue executives.

There is a timelessness and truth of infinite worth in certain biblical motifs which represent initially God's care for his creation. Some of these are fragmentary, illuminating a single aspect of spiritual concern. Other motifs rise like mountain peaks as dominant themes, indicating salient features of the pastoral calling. Amid all the confused questionings, bewildering doubts, and per-

[13] Hofmann, *op. cit.*, p. 11. Paul Tillich holds that a shortcoming of all religions, including Buddhism and the like, is that their symbols are far removed from the thought patterns of modern man. W. Lloyd Warner's recent inquiry into the "sacred symbolic life" of our culture, *The Family of God* (New Haven: Yale University Press, 1961), serves as a reminder that religious symbolism cannot be ignored by those who search for and seek to communicate the full meaning of spiritual reality. He states that in America "the family is becoming increasingly significant as an emotional matrix for the . . . symbolic life of the group" (p. 19).

plexities that beset the modern minister, some truths stand fast and offer stability to his calling. Once instructed and inspired by these themes, the modern pastor should be able to labor with greater certainty and joy.

Underlying such occasional word pictures as "salt," "light," and "branches," which illuminate some facets of Christian concern, are three central motifs of ministry in scripture—servant, shepherd, and sonship. The servant or steward had a dynamic relationship to his lord as one rendering loving service to or for his master. The faithful pastor today shares uniquely in the work of the Great Shepherd and Bishop of our souls. And the true son of God, including *all* believers, is a potential brother to all for whom Christ died. None of these aspects of ministry seeks an imperialism over the others. Yet the order in which they are presented has meaning. One who serves (redemptive activity) in the work of the Great Shepherd (representative role) participates in the family of God as a brother-man to persons and as a son to the heavenly Father (the pastoral relationship).

1. *The Servant Motif*

Priests, prophets, and kings were viewed in the Old Testament primarily as instruments or servants of God. Jesus Christ referred to himself frequently as God's servant or son, and as the good shepherd, embodying Old Testament themes and enriching them with new meaning. Writers of the New Testament noted carefully that the Son of God walked among men "as one who served" (Luke 22:27). When men misunderstood him and would have made of Christ an earthly monarch, he clarified his role as that of a suffering servant: "The son of man came not to be served but to serve, and to give his life as a ransom for many" (Matt. 20:28). When the disciples argued about their potential places of honor in the future kingdom which they expected Jesus as the Christ to establish, he admonished them to humility and warned them of trials to come (Luke 22). At the Last Supper he "girded himself with a towel" and "began to wash the disciples' feet" as an added demonstration of the nature of his office as God's servant (John

13:4-11). Small wonder that the Apostle Paul expressed the Savior's Passion thus: Christ "emptied himself, taking the form of a
servant" and "humbled himself and became obedient unto death,
even death on a cross" (Phil. 2:7-8).

It is not surprising then that *diakonia*, the Greek word for ministry, was employed by New Testament writers characteristically as
"the most favored way of referring inclusively to the church's
workers and their work."[14] Each follower of Christ had his own
task to perform, emboldened by Jesus' assurance: "As the Father
has sent me, even so I send you" (John 20:21). As Jesus commis-
sioned the twelve disciples to a ministry of preaching and healing
he gave them "authority over unclean spirits" and power to "heal
every disease." He reminded them of the costliness of their caring.
They were to love him above their own parents and families, to
serve at personal risk, to be faithful even if they fell into unfriendly
hands, remembering all the while that "a servant is not above
his master" (Matt. 10:1-39). Some of those who received salvation
and healing from Christ were invited into his service, to "go and
tell others" what the Lord had done for them (cf. John 4:7 f.;
Mark 5:19). Christ himself became the model upon which their
service was patterned; their work was conceived as a continuation of
his ministry.

The constituency of the early churches performed "varieties of
service" as they were endowed by the Holy Spirit, without thought
for the prestige of office. In their earliest development the churches
knew "nothing of the distinction between priests and laymen," as
Emil Brunner has suggested.[15] Theirs was a common priesthood
(I Pet. 2:5, 9) in which all were active and in which each sought
to serve faithfully as a minister of reconciliation (II Cor. 5:18; Col.
1:7). Paul indicated that the authority granted to certain leaders
of the primitive churches arose not out of their superiority but out

---

[14] John Knox in H. Richard Niebuhr and Daniel D. Williams (eds.), *The
Ministry in Historical Perspectives* (New York: Harper & Row, 1956), p. 1.
Cf. also pp. 1-26.

[15] Emil Brunner, *The Misunderstanding of the Church*, trans. Harold Knight
(Philadelphia: Westminster Press, 1953), pp. 59-62. See also Eduard Schweizer,
Lordship and Discipleship (Naperville, Ill.: Alec R. Allenson, 1960), pp. 20-21.

of their serviceability (I Cor. 16:15 f.). While *diakonia* came to be used in a particular sense for the office of deacon, John Knox affirms that "its original more inclusive sense was never completely lost."[16]

The priesthood of the early believers was not obviated by the appointment of bishops and deacons as the growth and orderly functioning of the churches made a more formal or institutional ministry necessary (cf. Jas. 5:14; Heb. 13:7, 24; I-II Tim.; and Titus). Clear expositions concerning the informal charismatic (or grace-gift) offices may be found in I Corinthians 12:27-30, Romans 12:6-8, and Ephesians 4:11-12. The Apostle Paul indicated that God had "appointed in the church" ministries, such as those of teacher, prophet, miracle-worker, healer, helper, and administrator. Clearly these offices, while informal, were less than the total number of members. The Ephesian passage suggests that the purpose of such divinely appointed helpers was for the equipping of all "the saints for the work of ministry" and for "building up the body of Christ." Those who were "strong" spiritually were admonished "to bear with the failings of the weak" in order to "edify" or strengthen their neighbors (Rom. 15:1-2).

What bearing does this servant motif have upon contemporary pastoral care in Protestant churches? (1) It clarifies the *pastoral nature of the church* and its corporate responsibility for caring. All who belong to Christ are committed to a life of loving service, whatever their particular occupations may be. (2) Pastoral care is to be viewed within the context of the *central redemptive mission* of the church. That interest in persons which omits their relationship to God may be supportive, even therapeutic, but it is not pastoral care in the fullest Christian sense. (3) The basic role of the pastor is seen to be that of a *servant of servants*.

Spiritual care may be rendered on an official level by a church's minister, but it may also be rendered unofficially on a personal level

---

[16] Knox, *op. cit.*, p. 1. Prof. Knox insists that the terms "bishop" and "deacon" referred originally to *functions* and are not to be mistaken for the formal *offices* which appeared later. Cf. p. 10. He notes correctly that the ministry was both "charismatic" (Spirit-given) and "institutional" in that its intent was the growth and proper functioning of the churches.

by any capable Christian. The pastor serves as a consultant to his congregation, as an example to the inept, as a coach instructing those whose zeal outruns their skill, and as a participant-observer in the life and ministry of the congregation. The term "Christian pastoral care" refers not to benevolent activity by one in an over-position of power but to a redemptive ministry of personal or social service. The Bible thus clarifies both the instrumental identity and operational activity of the true minister and other Christian helpers.

2. *The Motif of Shepherd*

In the literature of pastoral theology entire books have been devoted to the shepherd theme, and pastoral theological systems have been built upon it.[17] This has been true no doubt because the character of God himself has been viewed supremely as that of a shepherd—a firm hand leading, feeding, disciplining, and protecting his people (Isa. 40:1-11). The shepherd symbolism pervades the imagery of the Scriptures. The psalmist viewed God as the Great Shepherd—restoring the soul of a distraught man, leading him in goodly paths, protecting him from the Evil One, and supplying nurture for body and spirit in his eternal goodness (Ps. 23). Those who labored in God's behalf were viewed as undershepherds and warned to be faithful (Ezek. 34:2-10; Jer. 23:1-4; Zech. 13:7-9).

We have seen that this shepherd motif has become a stone of stumbling for some moderns who resent the idea of being viewed as part of a dumb flock, driven by herd instinct or maneuvered by a strong paternalistic leader. When we recover the biblical perspective, however, we discover that the most familiar figure of Palestine was the shepherd. And sheep were esteemed, not despised, in that ancient economy. They provided a livelihood, wool for clothing, and were the shepherd's friends through the long days and nights on the Judean hills.

[17] This is in effect what Seward Hiltner has done in his *Preface to Pastoral Theology.* Cf. footnote 6, above. See also his *The Christian Shepherd: Some Aspects of Pastoral Care* (Nashville, Tenn.: Abingdon Press, 1959), and Charles E. Jefferson, *The Minister as Shepherd* (New York: Thos. Y. Crowell Co., 1912).

The Eastern shepherd was characterized by his skill in guiding and protecting his flock. His life was very hard. He was concerned for *all* the sheep and had an eye for the green meadow, the quiet water pool, and the cool resting place. His strength was tested in fighting marauding beasts which attempted to plunder the flock. He was noted for tenderness in caring for new lambs and for restoring the lost and strayed. Faithfulness marked his daily companionship with the sheep. A true shepherd never forsook the flock. George Adam Smith has noted that the shepherd of Judea was at the forefront of his people's history. This suggests the experience supporting the concept of God as a shepherd and his people as his flock (Ps. 23:1, 79:13, 100:3).

In the New Testament, Jesus called himself "the good shepherd" who knew his sheep by name (John 10:11, 14). Of all the self-descriptions he used—light, bread, door, way, truth—the motif of shepherd was evidently most prominent in Jesus' thinking. "When he saw the crowds, he had compassion for them, because they were harassed and helpless, like sheep without a shepherd" (Matt. 9:36). He conceived his mission "to the lost sheep of the house of Israel" as costing him his very life's blood (Matt. 15:24). One sheep that went astray required more time, skill, and devotion than ninety-nine safe on the hillside (Matt. 18:12-14).

Jesus devoted much time to the preparation of his "little flock" who would continue his work following his death (Luke 12:32). It was Jesus' last command to Peter to feed his lambs and his sheep (John 21:15-19). Small wonder that Simon Peter exhorted his fellow elders to "tend the flock of God . . . not as domineering over those in your charge but being examples to the flock." He assured them that "when the chief Shepherd is manifested you will obtain the unfading crown of glory" (I Pet. 5:2-4). The spirit of the true shepherd, then, is not superiority but comradely care.

Central to the shepherd motif in scripture is the idea of sacrificial service. The writer to the Hebrews claimed in his benediction for his readers that Christ, the shepherd king, had indeed become God's sacrificial sin offering (Heb. 13:20-21). Christ both judged and cleansed man from sin, thereby unifying the law of the Old

Covenant with the grace of the New. Thurneysen has reminded us correctly that "the concrete practice of pastoral care consists in the true ordering of gospel and law, of justification and sanctification."[18] G. B. Wurth speaks of Jesus' unique synthesis of the demand and the promise of God. "His pastoral care and his cross were not two independent things . . . Behind his shepherding lay his cross . . ."[19]

We find anchorage here at two points in biblical thought. (1) Jesus' pastorship speaks to a central concern in contemporary pastoral care and counseling—the proper relationship between persuasiveness and permissiveness, between law and gospel, and between confrontation and consolation. Clearly, Christian shepherding both includes and transcends the concept of "tender solicitous care." The New Testament shepherd-sheep relationship is that of one *leading and nurturing* those given to his care, of one *guiding* with righteous discipline, *guarding* with loving concern, *sharing* the life of his comrades, even *sacrificing* his life if need be for his people. (2) In scriptural imagery "sheep" represent sensitive persons, created in God's image, who "labor and are heavy laden" (Matt. 11:28). These were persons from all races and classes of mankind who were "fainting" and "scattered abroad" (Matt. 9:36-37). They filled the city streets, thronged the market places, and walked the dusty roads of Palestine. Pastors today need to feel the pull of the people upon their own personalities after the manner of the great Shepherd, Jesus Christ.

3. *The Motif of Sonship*

The family relationship was very strong in the faith and life of ancient Israel and was carried over into Christianity. Jesus the Son of God claimed those as his family who did his will. There came a time in the sequence of relationship with his disciples when Christ called them his brethren. "No longer do I call you

[18] Eduard Thurneysen, *A Theology of Pastoral Care,* trans. Jack A. Worthington and Thomas Wieser (Richmond, Va.: John Knox Press, 1962), p. 255.
[19] G. Brillenburg Wurth, *Christian Counseling in the Light of Modern Psychology,* trans. H. de Jongste (Grand Rapids, Mich.: Baker Book House, 1962), p. 9.

servants, for the servant does not know what his master is doing;
but I have called you friends, for all that I have heard from my
Father I have made known to you" (John 15:15). Even as Jesus
structured this brother-man relationship with his followers, he
announced that soon he would be with them no more. They would
be compelled to serve in his stead (John 15:16-27). His friendship
was linked to their obedience in a shared ministry. These first
followers proclaimed that Jesus' ministry as Son consummated
God's redemptive purpose and would be continued through the
church's life and work. By faith all God's sons are to be devoted
to *the* Son's saving mission.

The Apostle Paul frequently expressed this spirit of sonship. "We
are children of God, and if children, then heirs, heirs of God and
fellow heirs with Christ . . ." (Rom. 8:16-17). He linked the idea of
a Spirit-led life with sonship and suffering for Christ's sake, yet
did not limit this to those in formal church offices. God has
promised this new relationship (Gal. 3:29), which would free those
who were in bondage "to the elemental spirits of the universe" (Gal.
4:3). He reminded the capricious Galatian Christians: "Through
God you are no longer a slave but a son, and if a son then an heir"
(Gal. 4:7; cf. Eph. 3:6 and Titus 3:7). Simon Peter reminded
husbands and wives that they were "joint heirs of the grace of
life" (I Pet. 3:7), within the family of God.

Those adopted into God's family had a unique brotherly relationship and responsibility to one another. They were to "bear one
another's burdens, and so fulfil the law of Christ" (Gal. 6:2), even
as each Christian had his own work and had "to bear his own load"
(Gal. 6:5). The spirit of this passage lies at the heart of the mutual
pastoral care exercised within the family of God. The individual
had his own regular load to carry like a soldier's personal pack.
But when a brother or sister in Christ was overpowered and immobilized by temptation, or grief, or any distress, the "spiritual
ones," those who were mature spiritually and secure emotionally,
were to "restore him in a spirit of gentleness" (Gal. 6:1).

Pastoral care is considered to be the task of the entire church
family wherein an individual's burden is lifted temporarily or

shared continuously by the group. Ideally, the group bears the burden until the individual is able to assume his own load once more. Thereby, the whole church family is made strong once again. Frederic Greeves notes that there is "really only one vocabulary that suits this relationship—it is that of family relationships. By God's grace, any one of us may become a spiritual 'father' (or 'mother') to another human being, but it is as brethren that we meet."[20] The fact that all members share the church family's pastoral spirit and activity does not invalidate the institutional office of pastor, however. The pastor serves redemptivevly as a shepherdly representative of God and is related as a brother-man to persons in his ministry of pastoral care.

III. CARING CONCERNS

The discussion thus far has introduced criteria for pastoral work and called into dialogue biblical insights of ministry. Now we are to analyze four specific realms of caring in the church. The term *care* is employed, neither in the sense of apprehensiveness and burdensomeness nor that of sentimentality and acquiescence. That care which distinguishes a true church of the living God from cults, esoteric sects, and other social groups is the profound concern for the total range of man's existence which pervades its life. Unlike some institutions of the community which are concerned with limited aspects of existence—education, health, welfare, and so on —the Christian congregation cherishes man in the totality of his life because an opportunity is given. The church's ministry is personal and social, ranging from individual salvation and guidance to mutual support and social welfare. Let us examine these concerns.

1. *The Ministry of Reconciliation*

The Christian ministry of reconciliation is addressed to all men everywhere who dwell in spiritual darkness, estranged from God, from the universe, and from the human community. Consider some

---

[20] Frederic Greeves, *Theology and the Cure of Souls* (Manhasset, N. Y.: Channel Press, 1962), pp. 174-75.

of the ways in which persons experience lostness in life. Jean-Paul Sartre's *No Exit*, a one-act play in the setting of the hell of religious eschatology, mirrors the horror of human relationships without the saving quality of grace. One man and two women, trapped in the sleepless abode of the damned, ultimately reveal why they were sent to hell. Each stares through lidless eyes at the others' shame in a forced fellowship of disgrace, disgust, and distrust. Expecting the judgment of red-hot pokers and torture chambers, the characters try to justify their past, only to discover that "Hell is—other people!"[21] They must experience each other's shame helplessly for "*all* time."

From Sartre's perspective the ultimate sadness remains. The characters crystallize in a fixed, anguished hostility. Is this portrait, drawn by an atheistic, existential philosopher, unlike our human situation apart from divine grace? Against such a dark background the "beginning of the gospel of Jesus Christ" is good news indeed (Mark 1:1)! The Gospels convey God's action to save man from rebellion, estrangement, and the bondage of sin through the reconciler—Jesus Christ. Paradoxically, God used the cross and resurrection to bridge sin's chasm, offering humanity himself again. The first Christians perceived their salvation experience in terms of a new relationship with God (II Cor. 5:18-20; Eph. 2:16; Col. 1:20; Heb. 2:17). It is inconceivable that Jesus' reconciling ministry could have been accomplished apart from persons. Through this ministry Christ called the church into being and commanded his followers to incarnate love in all their relationships.

Pastoral care which is theologically sound must concern itself with the demonic forces and deceitful idolatries of man's existence. Chaucer's Man of Lawe reminds us that "Sathan, that ever us waiteth to bigyle" is an ancient enemy who still delights to engage man in mortal combat. Christian pastors must grapple earnestly with the final mysteries and verities of existence in order to exercise pastoral ministry with integrity. Thurnysen is correct at this point: "True pastoral care does not rest until it has carried the forgiving

---

[21] Jean-Paul Sartre, *No Exit and the Flies*, trans. Stuart Gilbert (New York: A. A. Knopf, 1947), p. 61.

Word into these depths in the strength of the Spirit and of prayer
and has really . . . brought man again under the healing power of
grace."[22] Man, who experiences his lostness in an immoral society,
is reconciled to God, to himself, and to others in the Christian
community of true believers.

Reconciliation is or should be shared most intensely in family
experience. Despite this ideal, however, fathers of every age eat
"sour grapes, and the children's teeth are set on edge" (Jer. 31:29-
30). Often the family circle fails to be an agent of reconciliation
for one or more of its members. A young man seeking insight into
feelings of being his family's black sheep once shared his spiritual
pilgrimage with a Christian friend.

> I grew up on a farm. My father always assigned more chores
> to us than we were able to do. But he worked hard along with
> us in order to make a living. In fact, he could outwork my brother
> and me any day in the week.
> Dad was a stern taskmaster. I never remember him saying
> that I had done anything well . . .
> One day, he and mother and I were working in the garden.
> I did something wrong . . . displeased him somehow. Dad cut a
> tree limb and beat me with it. His words cut me to the quick:
> "Boy, can't you do *anything* right? Someday, you're gonna turn
> out to be a no-good, or a criminal, or something!" It was the last
> beating he ever gave me.
> That was the day I decided to leave home; I was fourteen
> at the time. And, when I left, I never went back as long as dad
> was alive. I did go to his funeral though . . . I wonder what he'd
> think if he knew me now. . .

Gratefully, he told of God's grace effecting his salvation and new
life direction. Yet, wistfully, he longed to have his earthly father's
approval of his spiritual resurrection and new life. But that was
not possible. There was no waiting father for this prodigal son
(Luke 15:11-32). Our sympathies are stirred immediately by this
account, for have not we also experienced misunderstanding at
family hands? From the New Testament's viewpoint, a person is
not *right* with God, that is in full fellowship with him, until he is

[22] Thurneysen, *op. cit.,* p. 67. See also the excellent discussion of the relatedness of therapy and salvation in Daniel Day Williams, *op. cit.,* pp. 11-29.

right with his brethren (Matt. 5:23-24; I John 2:9, 4:19-21).

If the church as a whole implements its ministry of love for the burdened, rejected, disturbed, and shattered folk of the community, its care must be carried from a formal place of worship into the human arena.[23] In this life, where else is one to be reconciled except in family, educational, economic, recreational, and civic relationships? A gospel which will not *work* in life is no gospel at all! While it looks at man's potential wholeness from the perspective of salvation, the church must also consider man's potential wholeness from the perspective of physical-emotional health. God's design for man's wholeness challenges churchmen to recover their sense of personal mission—to incarnate God's good news in *all* human relationships.

2. The Ministry of Righteous Discipline

While noting the breadth of the church's concern for all persons for whom Christ died, there is a more restricted obligation to be noted also. Discipline presupposes membership in the body of Christ, or has this membership as its purpose (Matt. 18:15-35, 28:19-20). The ministry of righteous discipline involves both teaching new believers to "observe all things" and restoring those who have been drawn away. The relationship between those rendering and receiving this pastoral care thus occurs within the context of the church.

The word *discipline* is derived from the Latin *disciplina*, which means "school" and is rooted, along with the word "discipleship," in the Latin verb *discere*, "to learn." James L. Garrett has written that the "motif of responsible discipline in the Christian community has been repeatedly emphasized during Christian history."[24] Its practice has involved meaningful instruction, brotherly admonition, public penitential discipline, private confession and remission, and

[23] See Eduard Schweizer, *Church Order in the New Testament*, trans. Frank Clarke (Naperville, Ill.: Alec R. Allenson, 1961) for an instructive study of the ministry of the church.

[24] James Leo Garrett, Jr., *Baptist Church Discipline* (Nashville, Tenn.: Broadman Press, 1962), p. 9. Cf. Frank Stagg, *New Testament Theology* (Nashville, Tenn.: Broadman Press, 1962), pp. 273-76 for an incisive statement concerning church discipline in the New Testament literature.

in extreme instances banning by the congregation or excommunication by ecclesiastical officials. Banning, while extreme, was viewed by at least some of the Protestant reformers as redemptive in intent, purifying the fellowship and prompting repentance in the offending brother. The scriptural intent was to gain a brother, not to destroy him. Once censured, if the party truly repented, he was restored to the Christian fellowship in a spirit of loving forgiveness.

While the Protestant reformers exposed the Pharisaic legalism of discipline as conceived and administered in medieval Roman Catholicism, they did not abandon its practice or righteous intent. Calvin conceived discipline in the church as the ligaments which connect and unite the members of the body. Luther conceived discipline, in the form of personal conversation, as being joined with the public ministry of "Word and Sacrament" in an effort to extend God's forgiveness of sins to the individual. The very nature of the church as the people of God required the discipline of confession and forgiveness, according to Luther. His pastoral concern was directed toward the individual who had become guilty of sin. Calvin's concern was to preserve the integrity of the Christian community, as well as to lead the individual to repentance.

The practice of classic church discipline went into an eclipse in the centuries subsequent to the Reformation. It has been ambiguously conceived and practiced sporadically by various confessions but has claimed renewed attention in contemporary Protestantism. There is accumulating evidence of interest in a committed, disciplined churchmanship in both Europe and America.[25] While specific cases of discipline will be noted in Chapter 8, the statement of certain principles is in order here.

[25] This claim is demonstrated by the wide interest shown in such discussions as that by Dietrich Bonhoeffer, *The Cost of Discipleship*, trans, R. H. Fuller (2d ed.; New York: The Macmillan Co., 1959, paperback); D. Elton Trueblood, *The Yoke of Christ* (New York: Harper & Row, 1958); Franklin H. Littell, *The Free Church* (Boston: Starr King Press, 1957); and Geddes MacGregor, *The Coming Reformation* (Philadelphia: Westminster Press, 1960). Unique experiments by communities of disciplined Christians are being conducted in America and abroad, such as the Iona Community in Scotland, the Taizé Community in France, and the Faith and Life Community, Austin, Texas. Also, a few churches, such as the Church of the Saviour, Washington, D.C., and the Aldersgate Methodist Church, Cleveland, Ohio, are conducting experimental fellowship groups and reporting their findings.

Positively and preventively, churches should do more than merely offer new members a brief, formal acceptance into fellowship. Instruction should be provided for all ages of persons in discipleship groups as well as in church school groups. Conducting baptism or offering prayer for new members *one* Sunday, while significant, misses the point of positive instruction in the history, faith, and life of the church. Negatively and therapeutically, when a church chooses to censure someone who has selected secularism as a way of life, properly "the church does not exclude [a person]; it simply recognizes that he is not one of them."[26] He has already excluded himself from a proper Christian style of life. Discipline addresses the major growth problems of the Christian life, including theological illiteracy, ethical failure, and spiritual immaturity. Discipline's objective is spiritual maturity within the fellowship of Christ.

There are a number of perils and problems involved in establishing a disciplined church membership, such as individualism, moralism, and judgmentalism. In evangelical Christianity it is the congregation proper, not an individual officer, member, or group, which conceives and administers discipline in keeping with its polity or constitution. While aspects of discipline may be exercised by members of the church for each other (such as prayer or confession), those who discipline represent the congregation, not merely themselves.

3. The Ministry of Mutual Encouragement

There has been a tendency in some discussions of the care of souls to conceive the pastor's role as a crisis ministry, a sort of crash program for the accident victims of life.[27] From a theological perspective, the crisis approach is only a part of the truth. The Lord's care of his people, described in Ezekiel 34:15-16, places the church's

[26] Stagg, *op. cit.*, p. 275.
[27] Some readers of Wayne E. Oates' *The Christian Pastor* (Philadelphia: Westminster Press, 1951) adopted uncritically his "crisis ministry" approach in Chap. 1. They thereby missed the import of his valuable discussion of various levels of pastoral care in subsequent chapters. Oates' position has been clarified in a revised edition (1964) of his classic introduction to the pastoral office.

caring concerns upon a broad base. "I myself will be the shepherd of my sheep . . . says the Lord God. I will seek the lost, and I will bring back the strayed, and I will bind up the crippled, and I will strengthen the weak, and the fat and the strong I will watch over; I will feed them in justice." The full ranges of humankind, both beyond and within the confines of the Christian fold, are included in God's concern. We are reminded of Christ's conception of his ministry, which reflected deep concern for man's common ventures as well as life's crises (Luke 4:16-19; cf. Isa. 61).

John T. McNeill in *A History of the Cure of Souls* examined certain classic documents on *Seelsorge* (soul care) in the Reformation tradition. He refers to the work of the Strasbourg reformer Martin Bucer (d. 1551), *On the True Care of Souls,* as "the outstanding early Protestant text on the subject" of pastoral care.[28] Bucer's writing reflects a concern for man in his full range of existence, including the strong, devoted Christian who occasionally needs encouragement and praise, as well as prayer support. While the English Puritan pastor Richard Baxter (d. 1691) began his discussion of "oversight" in *The Reformed Pastor* with evangelism, he also summarized duties for building up the converted. His practice in the Kidderminster community included conferences with every family of the parish, eight hundred in all, at least once each year.[29] Baxter's appeal and influence, because of the breadth of his concern, skilled ministry, and careful reflection and writing, needs to be restudied by modern ministers.

Mutual encouragement refers to a Christian's loving interest in and concern for what matters much to others. This includes the ministry of friendship, like that of David and Jonathan, which "strengthens one's hand in God." Most people stand in need of encouragement at least occasionally. Such care includes (1) the sharing of burdens (Gal. 6:1-5); (2) speaking a word in season to

[28] John T. McNeill, *A History of the Cure of Souls* (New York: Harper & Row, 1951), p. 180. Cf. pp. 177-81.

[29] Richard Baxter, *The Reformed Pastor,* ed. with a preface by Samuel Palmer (London: J. Buckland, 1766), cf. Part II, "A stated minister's duty with respect to his people." A paperback edition of Baxter's work is now available (Richmond, Va.: John Knox Press, 1963).

one perplexed or distressed (Prov. 15:23); (3) extending hospitality to an embattled Christian who feels himself suddenly to be a stranger in the earth (Rom. 12:13; I Tim. 3:2; I Pet. 4:9); (4) visiting the sick and imprisoned (Matt. 25:31-46); (5) praying for the captives from life's conflicts (John 17; I Cor. 14:15; Jas. 5:16, etc.); (6) comforting the bereaved (Rom. 15:4; II Cor. 7:13; I Thess. 4:18, etc.) even as God comforts those who are cast down; (7) and extending skilled counsel to those who seek light on some decision, relationship, or problem (Prov. 12:20; Ps. 55:13-14; Prov. 11:14).

While laymen are motivated to support one another, they will look to their minister as a skilled model in the ways of encouragement. The church's supportive ministry must extend beyond the confines of four walls and formal meetings. As early Christians perceived their daily living to be a continuous act of worship, so caring is to be incarnated in the home, in educational circles, in social justice, in work and play. This looks toward the Christian ideal of life as a "living sacrifice . . . acceptable to God" (Rom. 12:1).

4. *The Ministry of Social Welfare*

The profound concern felt by God's people for the welfare of others, beginning with Christian conversion, proceeds along a continuum of obligation which includes all man's welfare. Following the lines of Christ's summary in Matthew 25:31-46, which obviously relates divine judgment to Christian social concern, churches have extended their pastoral ministries in institutional fashion through the ages. Jesus' great interest in the welfare of the widow, the orphan, the outcast, the sick, the poor, the demonic, and the dispossessed has stimulated this extension of his ministry.

To speak of building up the church or of extending the worldwide mission of the church, without due concern for the shape of man's bondage and suffering, would be a travesty indeed! The majority of the Master's miracles were related directly to relieving a specific person's need: blindness, handicap, demon possession, chronic physical ills, hunger, acute illness, and bereavement. Widowed persons and fatherless children were some of God's special protégés in both Old and New Testament times. The jobless, expecting Christ's imminent return and history's denouement, were admonished to return to their tasks by the Apostle Paul (I Thess. 4:11; II Thess. 3:10). Labor was honorable; occasions for work were to be provided, and the workman was to receive due compensation for his labor (Matt. 20:8; Col. 4:1; Jas. 5:4). Employment and the mutual relations of employers and employees is a spiritual, not merely a secular, concern. The just treatment of servants, esteemed by the prophets, was magnified by the apostles. A classic document in first-century pastoral theology is Paul's letter to Philemon in behalf of the runaway slave Onesimus.

A number of Jesus' parables are laden with pastoral social concern. The importunate widow, the good Samaritan, the laborers in the vineyard, the prodigal son, the rich fool, the talents, and the rich man and Lazarus are examples. Those who take the church's ministry seriously can ill afford to overlook the social realm of obligation and service. Wayne Oates has commented upon the atrophy of caring ministries in some American churches and the resulting relegation of such functions to nonchurch agencies.[30] He warns that a subtle process of secularization occurs as churches shift their responsibilities to community agencies and to professional helpers who feel little or no responsibility to the church.

This does not minimize the "pastoral" responsibility of persons and agencies in the community charged with the welfare of all citizens. The claim of Christian doctrine which impinges upon the pastoral ministry, however, requires practicing responsible social welfare. Pastoral care thus has its personal and small-group dimension, and a measure of social obligation as well. Provision for a community's underprivileged, aging, jobless, and ill citizens is individual and institutional. The fact that churches establish schools, hospitals, and benevolent institutions does not obviate the obligation of God's people to render personal care in their own communities. Again, interest in the salvation or healing of the religionless individual is to be matched by Christian justice for all persons in the social order.

[30] Oates, *Protestant Pastoral Counseling*, p. 52

CONCLUSION

Based upon the timeless witness of scripture and the corporate experience of Protestantism, these pastoral concerns are relevant in every age. Such patterns of ministry suggest guidelines for the church's mission in a secular world. The comprehensiveness and cohesiveness of Christ's ministry challenge the partial and superficial concerns of many congregations. Pastoral care anticipates a universal interest in all persons without distinction of race, sex, social class, age, or religious condition. Care for one's neighbor should permeate all levels of life: personal, vocational, family, church, and social relationships. In the church, each aspect of ministry—preaching, evangelism, administration, and education— is to be viewed *pastorally*. The minister's first concern is the spiritual well-being of his people, not a success-oriented program. Christian churches cannot withdraw into shallow pietism, rational humanism, or specious moralism which might preoccupy their energies but would prevent their communicating with real people in a demanding world.

The incarnational shepherding introduced by Jesus Christ, who became our "neighbor," sensitizes each Christian to his fellow man. I have said that pastoral care is Christian response to humanity's hurt. If we follow this clue it will be necessary to establish appropriate answers to the *right* question: "Who is my neighbor?" The nature of man for whom Christ died is the theme of the next chapter.

SUGGESTED READING

Clebsch, William A. and Jaekle, Charles R. *Pastoral Care in Historical Perspective.* Englewood Cliffs, N.J.: Prentice-Hall, 1964. Pictures the chief functions, varied rituals, and twenty-one exhibits of the history of the pastoral art. A major work.
Hiltner, Seward. *Preface to Pastoral Theology.* Nashville, Tenn.: Abingdon Press, 1958. (Chaps. 1, 2, 4.) A perspectival approach to the theological understanding of the minister's chief functions.
McNeill, John T. *A History of the Cure of Souls.* New York: Harper &

Row, 1951. (Chaps. 1, 4, 5, 15.) A comprehensive account of the poetic-prophetic history of pastoral care from biblical times to the present.

Oates, Wayne E. *Protestant Pastoral Counseling*. Philadelphia: Westminster Press, 1962. (Chaps. 1, 2, 6.) An exposition of counseling principles by a free church theologian from within the categories of the Christian faith.

Thurneysen, Eduard. *A Theology of Pastoral Care*. Translated by Jack A. Worthington and Thomas Wieser. Richmond, Va.: John Knox Press, 1962. (Chaps. 1, 2, 12, 16.) A systematic presentation of principles and processes of pastoral care from a Continental theologian's viewpoint.

Williams, Daniel D. *The Minister and the Care of Souls*. New York: Harper & Row, 1961. (Chaps. 1, 6.) A theological interpretation of pastoral work by one skilled in the wisdom of the behavioral sciences.

CHAPTER 2

⚜

PASTORAL CARE AND
THE NATURE OF MAN

IT IS very easy for the contemporary program-oriented congregation to assume that its organizational machinery is geared to serve humanity. The ultimate sadness is that a person or family can come into the life of a church, get caught up into the swing of things, and still fail to experience the "power of the personal" within its institutional structure. Persons are also subtly depreciated in those religious communions which seek to become the body of Christ by denying the essential humanity of persons. Herein lie two extremes in ecclesiology. The former is a quasi-realized eschatology, in which the church exists by and for its own spiritualized objectives. It is deeply conditioned by its temporal existence within history. The latter is evidenced in esoteric sect-groups requiring mystical "second blessings" of members and seeking to transcend temporal existence by denial and escapism.

The testimony of a convict's spurious childhood "religious experience" once stabbed a church's conscience into greater awareness of actual human needs. A layman had heard about the prisoner and asked him to recount his spiritual pilgrimage to a small church group. In essence, the man said that he had joined his parents' church as a lad in dutiful conformity to their expectations. However, his formal identification with the church was not corroborated by personal acceptance from the congregation nor by an inner awareness of God's Spirit. As he grew older he drifted into indifference and immoral behavior, and was eventually caught and convicted for a criminal act. While awaiting transfer to the state prison he experienced what he interpreted as a genuine spiritual conversion. His plea for human forgiveness, acceptance, and a chance once he was free from prison evoked both shock and shame from those present. Had regeneration come too late or would there be a chance to help this man *here* as well as *hereafter*?

One of the most significant services rendered to the churches by the social and behavioral sciences has been to restore them to a rightful mind about man's worth in God's work. A corollary gift is the reminder of the social, historical nature of the church as a human community of God's people. Jesus once said of religious observance, "The sabbath was made for man, not man for the sabbath" (Mark 2:27), implying that the church exists for man's good as well as for God's glory. To admit that the church is a human, social community may be for some churchmen initially a stone of stumbling. Yet, it was not unto angels that the Son of God was revealed, but to sinful men (Matt. 9:13; cf. Luke 15).

The burden of this discussion is of James M. Gustafson's persuasion that the church is a divine-human community: of belief, of memory, of language, of understanding, and of action. While his *Treasure in Earthen Vessels* analyzes primarily the continuities which the church has in common with other human communities, it refocuses the particularity of the individual within the community of faith. "Wherever the Church is gathered some of man's natural needs are met," such as his need for social interaction, approval, new experiences, appropriate personal development and conduct, self-extension, and preservation. Indeed, the personal and social needs of individuals are the "ingredients in the life of the Church without which it could not exist."[1]

The Christian pastor's profound concern is to relate the gospel of Jesus Christ to every need and condition of men. To this end, the contemporary minister must know his people and understand

[1] James M. Gustafson, *Treasure in Earthen Vessels: The Church as a Human Community* (New York: Harper & Row, 1961), pp. 15, 28.

their concerns. His knowledge of human nature from personal experience may be superficial and his gains from theological study may be ambiguous. While the church's first concern is man's spiritual welfare, it is possible to oversimplify his religious situation. The Christian faith is concerned with all aspects of man's life before God in the world. While a pastor cannot dictate the sociological situation, cultural climate, psychological health, and economic well-being of his people, his work will be influenced by these crucial dimensions of human existence.

1. THE PRIMACY OF PERSONS

Those charged with the spiritual oversight of the people of God will remember that his steadfast love was revealed because of the primacy of persons in the divine economy. God's care has always been tailor-made, fashioned to each man's particular condition. Pastoral care acts upon the basis of this principle of particularity— love conforming to the concrete needs of a specific person or group. Attentiveness to persons *in depth* is the hallmark of true pastoral care. One's view of man is the tacit and crucial correlate of this principle. Eduard Thurneysen has reminded us that "all confusions in pastoral care have their root in a distorted or false understanding of man."[2] One's concept of man is crucial in pastoral practice for numerous reasons.

1. *The minister is a member of the* laos—*the people of God—and is to relate to them redemptively.* The persons who form the congregation, the church committees, the diaconate, the teachers— these are the people with whom the minister and his family share a common life under God. What needs shall his preaching focus? What responses does his presence in a group evoke? What channels of service does he illuminate with the Christian gospel? What word of hope shall he speak to those in despair? Moreover, pastoral care implies a reciprocal relationship between the pastor and his people. They are both subjects and objects of mutual care one for

[2] *A Theology of Pastoral Care,* trans. Jack A. Worthington and Thomas Wieser (Richmond, Va.: John Knox Press, 1962), p. 66.

the other, and the common object of God's gracious care. The pastor cannot relate impersonally or remain aloof and at the same time express genuine concern for and communicate with persons. He and his family are persons, too, with human drives, doubts, and desires for life-in-community.

Occasionally his views will clash with those of some person or church group. Painful estrangements may disrupt their life together. Yet his lot is cast with the common humanity for whom Christ died. When people experience their minister's love, the majority will relate to him in like manner, warmly and responsively. Together, they will seek to express God's love in mutual support, to announce his concern for those outside the Christian fold, and thereby to advance the kingdom of God.

2. To understand man's nature and need is imperative *because of the crucial place of the doctrine of man in one's theology and pastoral practice.* To quote Frank Stagg: "One must correctly understand the biblical doctrine of man in order to understand its doctrine of sin or salvation. . . . *In the doctrine of man one stands at the crossroads for his theology.* The road he chooses here determines the balance of his theology."[3] The Bible speaks of God's creating man in his image for fellowship with himself and of ordering a way of life for him which was best for man (Gen. 1:26 f., 2:7 f.). God designed the family for human perpetuity and community and placed man and woman in the world for a responsible existence (Gen. 2:15-24). When man rebelled against his ordained existence as the creature of God, he selected a way of life different from God's way, and was fully responsible for his decision.

The ingress of sin and man's resulting bondage can be understood only in terms of his rejection of God's companionship and decision to live apart from God (Gen. 3:1-10). Once Adam and Eve exercised their freedom and made their fatal choice they experienced shame and were estranged from God and from each other (Gen. 3:11-12). As man fled God's face and blamed woman

[3] Frank Stagg, *New Testament Theology* (Nashville, Tenn.: Broadman Press, 1962), p. 31, emphasis supplied.

for beguiling him, love degenerated into fear. He lost the life he prized and was driven from the garden into the tragic plight of sinful existence. Thus man became guilty of sin and destructively related to God, to himself and his family, and to his world (Gen. 3—4).

Biblical history is the story of man's fall from a loving relationship into the estrangement of sin and of God's free gift of a new life— a new relationship—through the grace of our Lord Jesus Christ. The Apostle Paul wrote concerning this new humanity: "In Christ Jesus you who once were far off have been brought near. . . . For he is our peace, who has made us . . . one, and has broken down the dividing wall of hostility, by abolishing . . . the law of commandments and ordinances, that he might create in himself one new man in place of the two, so making peace, and might reconcile us both to God . . . through the cross, thereby bringing the hostility to an end" (Eph. 2:13-16). Those once "not a people" were thus enabled to become "God's people" by his mercy (I Pet. 2:10). Through the Atonement God made true selfhood possible for man in that his Son reconciled "all things to himself . . . by the blood of his cross" (Col. 1:20). Christ enables each person to face his own sinful history with courage and forgives each person who faces the cross with trust and true repentance. For a person honestly to face the cross is like facing death himself—the death of the old self. The cross focuses the particular shape of each person's sin, frees the person from his bondage in sin, restores him to a rightful mind, and gives him power to become a true son of God (John 1:12).

Redeemed man is viewed biblically as both a new *being* and as a "babe," *becoming* through processes of personal development. Such a new man in Christ may be unable to assume the full risks and responsibilities of mature service immediately. Those who admire the Christian example of the Apostle Paul tend to overlook the quiet years following his conversion experience which he spent in Arabia, Damascus, and Tarsus, before joining Barnabas for the first missionary journey (Gal. 1:17-18; Acts 9:30, 11:25-26). Paul was not pressed into immediate service by God's Spirit, but was led into quiet places for meditation, spiritual development, and new resources. This dynamic view of salvation recognizes man's responsibility for growth as well as God's transforming touch upon his life.

Christian selfhood develops in terms of one's personal history, mental capacity and training, relationship patterns, body image, emotional stability, and cultural milieu. Accordingly, man's essential humanity and continuing needs require pastoral insight and proficiency. It would be preposterous to assume that one who has experienced Christian conversion is thereby encapsulated in a protective vacuum, isolated from the vulnerability of human existence. Fortunately, the Christian approaches life from a new point of view, reinforced by the resources of God's Holy Spirit. He affirms with the apostle: "By the grace of God I am what I am" (I Cor. 15:10).

3. One's view of man is crucial in the sense that *the principles of personality drawn from the Bible and life are not to obscure the object of the church's concern, namely man himself and persons in dynamic relationships.* Gordon W. Allport, who has contributed much to contemporary understanding of personality patterns, has exposed the tendency of some to espouse theories rather than to cherish persons. He warns against any view of man which is so preoccupied with presuppositions that it loses sight of the person's individuality, his "uniqueness of organization."[4] In this respect, many ministers are less loving and have less insight than they themselves imagine. Manifestly, it is possible to have a correct theology and a proper psychology and still be relatively ineffective in a Christian ministry to persons.

4. Man's true nature clamors for consideration because *the individual has become obscured in what David Riesman calls "the lonely crowd."* In America, we have become accustomed to thinking of men in mass groups and to communicating with the masses impersonally in bulk form and broadcast fashion. A man is easily distorted into a stereotype or a caricature, where he is cartooned rather than characterized. A person is in great danger of becoming

[4] Gordon W. Allport, *Becoming: Basic Considerations for a Psychology of Personality* (New Haven: Yale University Press, 1955), p. 21.

merely a number or an obscure statistic, lost in the group: a family, a social class, a political party, a racial minority, a labor union, a potential sales market, a professional organization. Our eyes have become accustomed to the populace. It takes great effort to see a face in the crowd. It was once observed about a famous American pulpiteer that he loved everyone in general so much that he loved no one in particular. In contrast, our Lord is pictured in the Gospels as moving among persons with a masterful capacity to view them as individuals and not en masse. Jesus "knew what was in man" and thus knew how to relate appropriately to persons (John 2:23 f.). This sensitivity to the underlying situation in the other person is essential in pastoral practice today. Good intentions and pious protestations are poor substitutes for facing "the intricate perplexities of human life."[5]

II. A CASE IN POINT: WHAT IS IN MAN?

A counseling situation in a church setting focuses the matter of human complexity for us. The case in point arose when a teen-age girl, popular with her age group at church and at school, approached the church's youth minister. All that he knew about her before the counseling contact was that she was from a fine Christian home, had one brother, was an outstanding high-school student, and was considering a church-related vocation. The young lady, whom I shall call Jill, made an appointment, indicating that she wanted to share something that was bothering her.

Jill arrived in the minister's office for the appointment promptly. After a brief greeting, she related a series of incidents from the previous fall which had given rise to her perturbed state. After a football game, she and a few girl friends had entertained the team, their dates, and several others at her home. They danced, cut up, ate refreshments, and were having a good time until some of the boys brought in some beer. With agitation and some hesitance, Jill related how her pleasant party was spoiled by a few hoodlums

[5] Paul E. Johnson, *Psychology of Pastoral Care* (Nashville, Tenn.: Abingdon Press, 1953), p. 25.

who became quite rowdy. She rebuked them, requesting that they not bring beer into her home again.

The story became more complicated as news of the affair spread at school the following week. But it deepened in intensity in terms of a symbolic interpretation assigned to Jill's experience on the day after the party. The conversation with her minister reflected her vivid memory and sensitive spirit.

JILL: The next morning after the party, my girl friend and I were cleaning up the den and I came across a picture that my brother had painted on a small block of tile that had come loose from the ceiling. I just glanced at it and saw that it was a crazy picture of a goofy-looking fellow. I put it back in place in the ceiling. Then I stepped back and took a good look. Oh, it was awful! All at once it changed! It had a horrible-looking face and a look in the eyes that I'll never forget.

MINISTER: What did the face look like?

JILL: Oh! It was horrible! (She began weeping.) It looked like Satan! (She wept softly.) I'm sorry I cried but I just can't get that face out of my mind.

MINISTER: Did anyone else see the picture?

JILL: Yes, my girl friend saw it and it looked horrible to her, too. She said it made her feel as if she were going to die. I felt that way, too.

Following this acknowledgment of what to Jill was a painful experience even after several months, the minister asked if her parents knew anything about her feelings.

JILL: Oh, no! They would think I was crazy. I took the picture and turned it over and put it back in the ceiling. It scared me so much. (Pause.) What do you think caused it?

MINISTER: Do you have any idea of why the picture changed and frightened you so?

JILL: No, I just feel that God is trying to punish me in some way, but I don't understand why.

Rather than yielding to her plea for an immediate explanation (which he did not have), the minister assured Jill of God's love, of his desire to understand and to forgive her. "You have trusted him for the answer to many other problems," he said, "and with his help we will work this one out." He asked for the privilege of thinking about the matter and talking to her again later. After a word of praise for her courage in sharing her burden with someone, they turned in confident prayer to God for cleansing and direction. In the next few weeks they talked further of Jill's Christian convictions clashing with her conduct at certain parties and of the conflicts of conscience which this moral turbulence had provoked.

They determined together that the face of Satan which she had seen in the "funny face" was in a sense a distortion in her own soul. The "Satan face" was a symbol of her own feeling of evil, of being cut off from her devout parents, of being punished by God, of even momentarily wanting to die. And in a sense her experience was a dying and rebirth to a new relationship of trust in God and in herself. Following confession of her real guilt and feeling true forgiveness, she affirmed: "I believe with God's help I can forget the whole thing. It is so good to know that he will help me in this matter." In a follow-up contact the counselee reflected that a load had been lifted from her shoulders and that she was functioning happily in life's activities again.

Following this experience of confession, involving an underlying psychic situation, the minister determined to get some clinical training in pastoral care. He perceived that there were some psychic phenomena at work in Jill's distorted "Satan face," but he was ill-prepared to grasp the symbolism involved. He discovered empirically the profound truth noted by Daniel Day Williams: "Every human relationship embodies a mystery, and our Christian ministry participates in the deepest mystery of all, the life of the soul before God."[6] He saw that a vivacious girl in a stereotype was just another "hairbrained teen-ager." But, viewed as a sensitive person before God, Jill had deep feelings about her conduct and needed a pastor's understanding in order to realize true forgiveness.

III. PASTORAL UNDERSTANDING OF PERSONS

A well-intentioned Christian helper may actually become a stumbling block rather than a servant to those in need. We recall

[6] *The Minister and the Care of Souls* (New York: Harper & Row, 1961), p. 13.

Paul's admonition to loving, wise, and circumspect behavior on the part of the mature Corinthians in their relationships with weaker brethren. He warned: "By your [lack of] knowledge this weak man is destroyed, the brother for whom Christ died" (I Cor. 8:11). It is at the high risk of costly failure of both God and man that the contemporary pastor remains uninformed about persons.

Ministers have often been guilty of a kind of reductionism in thinking about individuals, using appellations such as sinful, neurotic, lonely, depraved, paranoid, or compulsive to describe personality in an oversimplified concept. "Personality is far too complex a thing to be trussed up in a conceptual strait jacket," warns Allport.[7] There are varied perspectives for approaching man which may be perceived by some as being mutually exclusive. Yet considered judgment indicates that the several approaches furnish mutual support to understanding persons-in-relationship. Accordingly, it should be instructive to examine several sources of wisdom about man's nature and needs.[8] These perspectives upon personality include: biblical revelation, speculative reason, scientific research, and pastoral reflection.

1. Biblical Revelation

The Christian minister is urged to define a biblical anthropology before *fully* exploring various other views of personality. In light of their specialized interests and education, ministers should be disciplinary (theological) prior to becoming interdisciplinary (perspectival) in dealing with persons. This reasoning about sequence lay behind the elucidation of the Christian doctrine of man at the outset of this chapter. While that doctrinal statement need not be repeated, one additional emphasis should be made here. *Man's true identification resides in the heart of God and was reflected in the face of Jesus Christ.* The Incarnation demonstrated God's con-

---

[7] Allport, *op. cit.*, p. vii.

[8] I am indebted to Denison M. Allan, *The Realm of Personality* (Nashville, Tenn.: Abingdon Press, 1947), pp. 17-55, and to Karl Barth, *Church Dogmatics*, trans. Harold Knight *et al.* (Edinburgh: T. & T. Clark, 1960), II, 2, 22-27, for helpful discussions at this point. See also T. K. Penniman *et al.*, *A Hundred Years of Anthropology* (2d ed. rev.; London: Gerald Duckworth & Co., 1952), pp. 13-23 *et passim*.

cern to be known and desire that man should come to himself through life in the Son. Jesus Christ is viewed in scripture as the second Adam (I Cor. 15:45), through whom man may become what God intended him to be (Heb. 2:8-9). Before God opened the conversation with man through his Son, sinful man was humanity's only measure of itself. True or essential man was impenetrably veiled by distorted, sinful man. "The mystery of the Incarnation," writes James I. McCord, "wherein the divine entered human history and identified himself with human nature disclosed to us our true humanity."[9] Biblical anthropology is thus grounded in (though not limited to) Christology.

In Hebrew-Christian thought, man is essentially a unified and relational, rather than an atomistic, being. Amid all the prevalent models of man and partial views of personality in ancient thought, the biblical writers saw the promise of his wholeness inherent in the essential wholeness of God. At last, "the self was seen in its true light: as not the opposition of body and soul, nor the opposition of the natural and supernatural, but as the creature of the Creator, alienated by sin but capable of reconciliation."[10] In Christ, human forgiveness was not merely promised but accomplished. Man becomes a new creation by accepting Christ's love as the focal center of his new identity.

Since man's true identification resides in the heart of God and was made effective in the work of Jesus Christ, what is a Christian person to be in this modern world? After all, that is the layman's question! One has put it this way: "How is a Christian existence possible in this world when one, in both his work and pleasures, shares in its culture, its tasks, and its worldly goods?"[11] The theological perspective reminds us that *ought-ness* precedes *is-ness;*

[9] James I. McCord, "Know Thyself: The Biblical Doctrine of Human Depravity," in Simon Doniger (ed.), *The Nature of Man in Theological and Psychological Perspective* (New York: Harper & Row, 1962), p. 23. See also K. J. Foreman, *Identification: Human and Divine* (Richmond, Va.: John Knox Press, 1963).

[10] Wayne E. Oates, *Christ and Selfhood* (New York: Association Press, 1961), p. 213.

[11] From Rudolf Bultmann's preface to the new edition of Adolf Harnack, *What Is Christianity?* (New York: Harper & Row, 1957), p. xi.

that God has a design for man unlike that of the world's fashion. We have been designed "after the mode of heaven" with guidance for life's directions and grace to help in time of need. Man's plight is to be perceived, not as some pessimistic existentialists and optimistic humanists claim, but in the full light of God's will for man and his gracious action in man's behalf. Realism envisions not only the darkness of man's present predicament but also the Light shining inextinguishably in the darkness (John 1:5). With sympathetic insight, the Christian minister enables people to perceive the difference Christ makes in their lives.

2. Speculative Reason

Pastoral understanding of persons is rooted not only in doctrinal thought but in man's measure of man, which has been long in the making. Poets, philosophers, dramatists, political and economic theorists, and some scientists have slowly evolved a speculative anthropology through the centuries. Reinhold Niebuhr has suggested that all modern views of human nature are adaptations and varying compounds of primarily two distinctive views of man: the biblical view and that of classical antiquity.[12] The latter view belongs to the speculative sphere of thought and has been very influential upon religious concepts of man even to the present day.

Speculative anthropology has generally developed in the context of a world-view wherein reason and enlightened self-interest have served as a substitute religion. Socrates urged his fellow Athenians toward one pursuit: "Know thyself!" Beginning with Platonic, Aristotelian, and Stoic conceptions, the classic view of man might be called *transcendental*. The ancient Greeks viewed man as a hierarchy of matter, life, mind, and spirit, in an ascending order of values. They held wisdom to be life's supreme value and concurred generally that the wise man would be virtuous. The matter of man's growth and education was most significant for Plato, Aristotle, Spinoza, Leibniz, Kant, Hegel, and John Dewey in this

[12] For a trenchant analysis of the classical view of man in contrast to the Christian view, see Reinhold Niebuhr, *The Nature and Destiny of Man* (New York: Charles Scribner's Sons, 1949), I, 5-12. Cf. C. Kerenyi, *The Religion of the Greeks and Romans* (New York: E. P. Dutton & Co., 1962), pp. 177-260.

century. Man's perfectibility was thus approached through gaining wisdom. Yet the Greeks in ancient times experienced a growing sense of tragedy as the truth became apparent that there was no straight path to human self-realization and fulfillment. The classic view of man was pervaded by pessimism, primarily because of the brevity of life, the Greeks' cyclical concept of history, and doubts about human perfectibility.

Transcendental speculations have afforded a meeting ground for educators and artists; poets and playwrights; for metaphysical theists such as J. E. Boodin and Alfred N. Whitehead; ethical idealists such as R. A. Tsanoff and W. M. Urban; and philosophers such as Ernst Cassirer, Henri Bergson, and John Dewey. Romanticism and the liberal optimism about man of the nineteenth and early twentieth centuries had their antecedents in speculative anthropology. These ancient concepts have given impetus to modern studies of the age—character levels of personality development which are quite significant for pastoral understanding of persons.

Numerous *naturalistic* personality theories arose during the Enlightenment among philosophers and researchers who examined man as a natural creature. Rather than seeing him as a person created in God's image, observers like Hobbes, Darwin, Nietzsche, and Bertrand Russell viewed personality as a phenomenon of the natural order. Religion was treated by such thinkers, not as a reality, but as an epiphenomenon in the life of man. Like a train casting a shadow as it speeds along the rails, life was observed in most cultures to cast a religious shadow which these theorists felt compelled to consider. The stimulus-response theories of John B. Watson (*The Ways of Behaviorism*) and those of the Russian Pavlov are of this naturalistic order.

Most speculative personality theorists had only partial views of man. He was divided into components of reason, will, instinct, feeling, body, mind, and soul. He was bifurcated into essence and substance; reduced to a chain of ideas, a mass of protoplasm, a creature of values, a mechanistic stimulus-response organism, unrelated to a Supreme person.

The chief contribution of the mid-nineteenth-century existentialist Soren Kierkegaard toward a proper understanding of selfhood was his insistence that man be viewed wholly. He wrote: "The self is the conscious synthesis of infinitude and finitude . . . whose task is to become itself, a task which can be performed only by means of a relationship to God."[13] He viewed selfhood paradoxically in terms of its possibility and necessity. Becoming a self was "eternity's demand" upon man, said Kierkegaard, who viewed man's being in eternal dimensions. For him, man was both an existential and a teleological being—forced to venture in life, subjected to anxiety and dread, yet directed toward an ultimate destiny.

While the Christian minister cannot just write off all speculative thinking about man, neither can he uncritically weave its many threads into the tapestry of his thought. Wayne Oates suggests appropriately that an historical wisdom about man which is at the same time both related to and different from contemporary psychological estimates of him is "necessary for a Christian understanding of personality."[14] Christian anthropology is rooted in biblical faith, yet remains in polarity with this residual body of observation about man.

3. Scientific Research

A whole new arc of light illuminates pastoral understanding of persons as a direct outgrowth of the scientific investigation of the phenomena of man's conscious and unconscious existence. In the present century, more fully developed scientific criteria have been applied to the study of man than ever before. Admittedly, the central passion of scientific personality research is descriptive objectivity. The behavioral or social scientist generally examines man as man or man-in-community and excludes himself from participation in man's value systems. As a scientist, the psychologist is obligated to postulate his findings on the basis of impersonal data-examination. It is necessary to appreciate the perspective of

[13] Soren Kierkegaard, *Fear and Trembling and The Sickness Unto Death*, trans. Walter Lowrie (Garden City, N.Y.: Doubleday & Co., Inc., 1954), p. 162.

[14] Wayne E. Oates, *The Religious Dimensions of Personality* (New York: Association Press, 1957), p. 277.

such empirical observers, if we are to profit from their research, or indeed if we are to conduct true research ourselves.

Some personality scientists insist upon dealing with man in abstraction from his relationship to God. Such observers cannot do more than present partial observations of the essential realities of human nature. Gordon Allport claims that "as a science, psychology can neither prove nor disprove religion's claims to truth." Yet psychology can be pressed into the service of religion. It can examine religion's diverse claims and interpret the course of human religious development to its ultimate frontiers of growth. Cautioning his scientific colleagues, Allport warns that *a psychology that impedes understanding of the religious potentialities of man scarcely deserves to be called a logos of the human psyche at all.*[15]

Depth psychologists have made certain findings available about the rich dimensions of personality which are indispensable for the modern Christian's synoptic understanding of man. Influenced by the monumental efforts of the Viennese psychoanalyst, Sigmund Freud, ego psychologists have looked into human motives, memories, values, emotions, and feelings at unconscious levels of existence. Freud, a Jew by birth, wrote much about religion and its influence in the lives of his patients but was essentially a humanistic interpreter of it.[16] Following a genetic-biological model, he carried out research into the developmental phases of childhood, including influences aiding and impeding healthy development, during almost a half-century of psychoanalytic practice.

Christian pastors have not escaped the pervasive influence of the psychoanalytic approach to man. Freud's contemporary Carl Jung and others succeeded in linking man's religious strivings with the theory of cultural archetypes.[17] These theorists and their suc-

[15] *Op. cit.*, p. 98.
[16] See the Modern Library edition of *The Basic Writings of Sigmund Freud,* trans. and ed. A. A. Brill (New York: Random House, 1938). Cf. also Freud's *The Future of an Illusion* and *Moses and Monotheism,* both available in paperback. The reader may be interested in the provocative discussion by a British psychotherapist, Arthur Guirdham, M.D., *Christ and Freud* (London: George Allen and Unwin, 1959).
[17] Carl G. Jung's views may be found in *Modern Man in Search of a Soul,* trans. W. S. Dell and C. F. Baynes (London: Paul, Trench, Trubner & Co., 1933), and in two volumes of the Bollingen Series XX: *Collected Works,* Vol.

cessors traced man's neuroses directly to his unconscious, unassimi-
lated experiences of childhood and offered therapy for such conditions. Thus, psychoanalysis is not just a view of man, his drives
and frustrations; it is a method of healing. Once a person's repressed psychic conflicts were brought to the surface in a therapeutic relationship with an analyst, Freud observed that the patient
"recovered." He or she might be viewed as "getting worse" by
family and friends, for Freud's goal was freedom from unconscious
conflicts imposed upon the *id* by the *superego*. Psychoanalysis,
accordingly, is a backward look into one's developmental history,
rather than a cross-sectional examination into present conscious
concerns or an orientation toward life ahead. Its goal, akin to
that of religious faith, is increased ego-strength.

Modern Freudians have sought to correct Freud's limited model
of dynamic mechanical determinism. Harry Stack Sullivan, Karen
Horney, Erik Erikson, and others have conducted extensive studies
in self dynamisms, interpersonal relations, and cultural anthropology, as well as in psychic conflicts. These therapists have sought
to enable their patients to gain insight into conflicts and to achieve
freedom of relationships in the process of *becoming*.[18] Several
psychoanalytic schools of thought now operate in Europe and
America. Wilhelm Reich has observed in *Psychoanalytic Theories
of Religion* (Vol. 1) that psychoanalysis is not merely a body of
research and a technique of therapy; it is also a philosophy of life
for its proponents. Christian ministers will be wise to observe these
distinctions.

Psychology's services to human kind are being increasingly recognized and utilized. Personality scientists have developed varied
instruments for data-measurement, for testing, for exploring the
development and the fragmentation of personality. Influential
gains have been made in medicine, the guidance movement, education, industrial psychology, work with trainable (retarded) chil-

---

VII, *Two Essays on Analytical Psychology*, trans. R. F. C. Hull (New York:
Pantheon Books, 1953), and Vol. XI, *Psychology and Religion: West and East*,
trans. R. F. C. Hull (New York: Pantheon Books, 1958).

[18] See H. S. Sullivan, *The Interpersonal Theory of Psychiatry*, ed. Helen S.
Perry and Mary L. Gawel (New York: W. W. Norton Co., 1953).

dren, psychotherapy, and the rehabilitation of former mental patients. Studies are being conducted clinically in areas of mutual interest to theology and psychology, such as: responsibility, anxiety, guilt, hope, gratitude, and the will.

While clear distinctions exist between theology and psychology at abstract, theoretical levels, the two disciplines converge on the applied level of their mutual concern—man's life before God and in the human community. Interaction between members of the helping professions in rendering service to those who need it is essential. Some theologians, like Karl Barth, urge caution in this regard. Others, however, sense the usefulness of learning about human nature from scientific inquiry. Emil Brunner writes: "There is a psychology . . . a knowledge of facts about man which the Christian must weave into his picture of man like anyone else, if his picture is to be true."[19] In addition, psychology of religion exists as an autonomous discipline *within* theology and deserves careful study by churchmen.[20]

With the contributions from ego psychology in mind, what factors of human development profoundly influence pastoral relationships with persons?

1. *Persons tend to relive early, primary group (family) experiences in all later relationships.* Personality scientists have demonstrated that behavior patterns are learned much like habits, though often unconsciously. Each person is motivated by unique feelings and emotions, which are expressed in life's developing stages. This complicates the pastor's task of communication and ministry, for he is usually unaware of a person's self-system and dynamic behavior patterns in the past. While the brother-man relationship of pastor and people is appropriate in Protestant churches, some persons may distort this ideal or relate to ministers according to their unresolved conflicts. For example, a minister may become the

[19] Emil Brunner, *The Christian Doctrine of Creation and Redemption: Dogmatics*, trans. Olive Wyon (Philadelphia: Westminster Press, 1952), II, 46-47. Cf. Barth, *op. cit.*, p. 23.
[20] The best general survey of the literature of psychology of religion is that edited by Orlo Strunk, Jr., *Readings in the Psychology of Religion* (Nashville, Tenn.: Abingdon Press, 1959). See also the systematic introduction by Walter H. Clark, *The Psychology of Religion* (New York: The Macmillan Co., 1958).

object of one person's affection, of another's dependency, and of another's aggression. Rather than react defensively—meeting his own needs—the pastor should seek to understand why the person uses him as he does. Along with seeking a creative, realistic relationship with such persons, ministers should encourage the "transference" of their feelings to God, who understands.

2. *We have been encouraged to understand that all behavior is purposeful, when viewed in depth dimensions.* This was demonstrated on one occasion when a child crawled under a church pew and would not come out with a mother's coaxing. When the child failed to respond to her soft words, the pastor saw the mother pull him forcefully from under the pew and spank him. As things turned out, it was promotion Sunday, and the child did not want to go into a new church school department. The four-year-old youngster, accustomed to being in a nursery-type group, feared a new situation. His belligerence was a façade for basic insecurity. Had the mother prepared him adequately for the transfer, it might have precluded his acted-out fear of the unfamiliar.

The episode reminds us that pastoral ministry must be tuned to the inner tempo of people's lives. Those in special need may manifest attitudes which are difficult for Christian workers to accept. Their actions may be contrary to the teachings of scripture. As the pastor recalls his own spiritual autobiography, he will "speak the truth in love" and relate flexibly to persons in varying religious experiences. He does not wish "that any should perish" (II Pet. 3:9).

3. Accordingly, *ministers should relate to persons according to identifiable clues in their relationship rather than through the use of prefabricated responses or pre-set techniques.* This takes into account the personal resources and limitations of both pastor and parishioner under God. A person may not recognize the deepest reasons for his feelings of being driven by ambition to achieve, of needing approval, of being withdrawn, feeling rejected or insecure with others. One pastoral technique will not work on all individuals. It is first necessary to assess factors underlying a person's behavior, then to relate to him accordingly. The depressed person, for instance, may appear in the community as a potential

suicide or as a problem drinker. His drinking may be a "way to be found out" in his dark night of the soul *before* he actually takes his life. It may be a call for help, a clue for care, not a reason for rejection. The suspicious child may be a fighter at home and a troublemaker at school or church. The right question may be "Why is he suspicious of others?" not "How shall he be punished?" The girl who feels rejected at home or school may act out her resentment by a premarital pregnancy, though she may not love the baby's father at all. Leontine Young's study, *Out of Wedlock*, reflects such internal causes of sexual delinquency.

After hearing a broken-hearted girl's story of an out-of-wedlock pregnancy, a forced marriage, and an early separation, a minister replied: "I am experiencing you now, Mildred, as a girl who is starved for real love." She sat, weeping and nodding her head silently. She felt understood! Years before, her father had been placed in a mental hospital and her life had lacked male identification and support. Her sexual experiences and spurious marriage relationship had failed to satisfy her deepest need for male understanding and help. A Christian minister, exemplifying God's love and forgiveness for such a girl, will seek to meet her spiritual needs as a pastor: where she has known only guilt and shame and betrayal, he will help her to *realize* self-understanding and forgiveness and trust, so that she may learn to live again.

This reminds us that the pastor's concern will not lie in flippant emotional flashes or temporary changes in counselees, induced by religion used as a superficial aid or palliative. Christian faith is not "rubbed on" wounded spirits; it must be experienced to be authentic. Significant change in *character*, produced by the gracious love of God and insight of the person, is the pastor's primary concern. Alterations in *conduct* will follow, rather than produce, character change. Knowing these deeper phases of human selfhood, the pastor will be able to penetrate to the heart of them.

4. *Pastoral Reflection*

Pastoral theology, it was indicated earlier, focuses an informed theological understanding upon the church's ministry to persons, families, and groups. Reflection upon one's ministry, in turn, should enrich pastoral understanding and inform his pastoral practice. In the past, ministers have experienced intense relationships with persons, succeeded with some and failed with others, without noting carefully what was happening. Periodic review of pastoral relationships will yield clues to man's nature and supplement the pastor's understanding of his task. Case histories are helpful,

The verbatim interview and contact report methods of teaching pastoral care and counseling confront student ministers with the possibility and necessity of perceiving the substance of their contacts with persons. The student records the significant verbal and emotional content of his contact with a parishioner and is asked to interpret what occurred between them and what course of action he will pursue in the future. Pastoral records and reflection upon relationships, in the light of the Christian faith, enable the minister to "bring out of his treasure what is new and what is old" (Matt. 13:52). Let us return to the counseling situation with Jill, the teen-age girl mentioned earlier, and state certain theological observations in the light of these criteria.

1. *A person under stress uses as "minister" a Christian who is available, who is understanding, and who can be trusted.* Such a ministering person may or may not be *the pastor* per se. Jill's capacity to trust and decision to entrust even the deepest secrets of her soul to her youth minister has significance for pastors. After all, entering into the initial experience of eternal life is a matter of basic trust, of committing oneself to God in faith for life. When persons come to the pastor or to a fellow Christian in a motive of trust, the minister will do nothing to injure that trust and will seek to point the person's trust beyond himself to God.

2. *Note how shame for one's attitude or actions brings the matter of one's identity sharply into focus.* Helen Merrell Lynd's *On Shame and the Search for Identity* illuminates this concept. Jill's approach to her minister was in part a quest for an answer to the basic question of her existence: "Who am I?" Her confession was an affirmation of her own basic Christian identity.

3. Closely related to identity is *the effect of guilt on one's sense of community*. What Jill perceived as sinful behavior cut her off from some of her peers, whose friendship she cherished; from her parents, who might think that she was "crazy" for feeling as she did; and from God, whom she felt she had offended. Her face-to-face meeting with God's minister was a desire to meet once again with God, to know his companionship, and to be one of the people of God.

4. *Confession to God through a priestly person and the assurance of God's eternal and gracious forgiveness lifts the load of guilt which one has carried for so long*. After several burdened months of pretense, Jill "came clean" to herself and to God, dropped her defensive mask, and found that God had indeed in Christ already forgiven her. Each step she took in the right direction strengthened her purpose to know, do, and love the will of God afresh.

5. *God is demonstrated as being active in the heart of things; in fact, in every area of life*. Meaningful life, according to Karl Menninger's *Love Against Hate,* involves the satisfactory experiencing of faith, hope, love, work, and play. It was in a leisure-time experience that Jill mismanaged things, along with the others, and felt God's punishment. Play was made right again after her decision to live up to her Christian ideals for herself. In America, where so much free time is available from educational and vocational tasks, there is need for a careful examination of the stewardship of leisure and of ways used by Americans to achieve relaxation.

6. *We should note, too, that the grace of God was made available to Jill and to her counselor by the Holy Spirit*. While the youth minister felt some anxiety because he did not have all the answers, he certainly felt himself to be dependent upon God's Spirit. Jill was strengthened despite her minister's human limitations. In their encounters and the intervals between conversations, the Holy Spirit served as their mutual counselor. God himself bore the burden of the relationship, shedding his love abroad in troubled hearts through the Holy Spirit. It is unnecessary to extrapolate further upon the theological dimensions of this one pastoral experience. The importance of incisive, prayerful reflection upon one's pastoral

practice has been adequately demonstrated. This forms the growing edge of pastoral theology from age to age.

CONCLUSION

The Christian pastor investigates these various perspectives for thinking about man, not as a specialist but as a general practitioner. Investigations in each area of wisdom about human selfhood will cast new light on the hidden treasures of the Christian faith. Too, such studies reveal in unexpected ways the universality of human need which that faith alone can meet. While the minister's technical knowledge is limited, he understands that other professional persons also have their limits. After all, it is not to the latest theories that he is devoted, but to God and to persons. In that devotion he seeks every possible level of knowledge, human and divine, about the life of the soul.

SUGGESTED READING

Allport, Gordon W. *Becoming: Basic Considerations for a Psychology of Personality.* New Haven: Yale University Press, 1955. Paperback ed., 1960. A "self" theory stressing development as an open-ended *becoming* in which values play a major role.

Doniger, Simon (ed.). *The Nature of Man in Theological and Psychological Perspective.* New York: Harper & Row, 1962. (Chaps. 1-4, 18, 19.) Selected essays by representatives of varied disciplines.

Gustafson, James M. *Treasure in Earthen Vessels: The Church as a Human Community.* New York: Harper & Row, 1961. A profound study of the life and ministry of the church in terms of social theory.

Oates, Wayne E. *Christ and Selfhood.* New York: Association Press, 1961. A psychological study of Christology in terms of Christ's sense of identity, vocation, and destiny, with important implications for Christian personality theory.

Roberts, David E. *Psychotherapy and a Christian View of Man.* New York: Charles Scribner's Sons, 1950. (Chaps. 1, 4, 8-10.) A study of man's paradoxical nature, guilt, and salvation in light of thorough-going interaction between theology and psychotherapy.

Sherrill, L. J. *The Struggle of the Soul.* New York: The Macmillan Co., 1952. A pioneer correlational study of human development.

Williams, D. D. *The Minister and the Care of Souls.* See above, p. 33. (Chaps. 3-4.)

CHAPTER 3

❦

PREPARATION FOR
PASTORAL CARE

EXPERIENCE in the ministry, as in other vocations, is usually an eloquent, often painful teacher. A young minister and his wife once related to a former theological professor their disillusionment about working with people in the church. Rev. and Mrs. Joe Wells visited the seminary following two years of service in a small church on the West Coast. While in school the couple had done field work in an inner-city mission. Once away, however, they felt ill-equipped to cope with the varied pressures of life in a western mill town. The lumbermen did not live up to their hopes and dreams of a sophisticated, urban congregation. In turn, they were too cultured for their unpolished, blue-collared parishioners.

The people often asked Joe Wells what he did during the week. Some suggested that he should do manual labor alongside them at the mill—"something with his hands." Meeting in an inadequate building, living on less salary than they had anticipated, and facing opposition to their suggestions for improving the church, the Wellses tired and finally resigned. "Why didn't somebody tell us these things?" Joe implored. Mrs. Wells asked, "Will people feel that Joe is a failure?" The teacher sought to reassure them; the chief problem was their own feeling of having failed.

The young couple had called it quits and moved two thousand miles back to their home state. Clearly, they did not wish to quit the ministry. They were not doubting God's will; rather, they were perplexed about themselves. How had they escaped certain *threats* in school which they came to dread out in the church? Joe Wells sought answers to questions about *who* a minister is in modern life, how *his* authority differs from that of any other church member, and who a minister's *pastor* might be in future crises far from a seminary campus. The Wells had become very lonely in two years. They felt cut off from other ministers, from their people, even from God. Additional formal classroom training was not what Joe Wells needed, but clinical experience, security in relationships, and competence in dealing with people. The Wellses consequently determined to spend a year in clinical pastoral education before returning to a full pastorate once more.

Such experiences might be multiplied many times. Ministers return to theological campuses, or go to centers for continuing education, *more* teachable after practical church experience. One graduate expressed a common feeling thus: "I knew a whole lot more when I came here seven years ago than I know now, after four years in the pastorate."

The present discussion is a response to some chronic problems of ministers.

1. How is a minister to resolve the tension between the pull of his own humanity and his pastoral calling?

2. Is there any resolution of role conflict (pulled-apartness) among Protestant clergymen?

3. With what resources may ministers face the emotional, ecclesiastical, and ethical hazards of their high calling?

4. What preparation is essential for a pastoral ministry in our "brave new world?"

We shall consider some threats to contemporary clergymen and some learning problems and educational possibilities for an effective ministry in an age of stress.

I. The Ministry and Contemporary Threats

At the turn of this century American ministers were serving their churches about as their ministerial predecessors had done for several generations. There was little opportunity of securing a professional education for those who lived away from the East. The minister in the mid-West and the South often supported himself and his family as a farmer or craftsman six days a week, then conducted worship services for his fellow citizens on the Lord's day. This was about the extent of his ministry, except for a crisis such as a death in the community. There were few books beyond a Bible in such a man's meager library. The pastor's place in the social order was generally well-defined and well-regarded. In many instances, a minister with a seminary education was a town's first citizen by virtue of his calling and training.

The matrix in which the modern pastor's life is set is vastly more complex than the simple agrarian culture of the nineteenth century. This is true regardless of the societal situation and geographic location of his church. Urbanism has become America's way of life. Science and technology are leading a costly search into the unknown. Civilization appears poised on tiptoe awaiting the latest word from the scientists, rather than from the theologians. "Curiosity and not security," notes one observer, appears to be "the clue to a better future."[1] Times have indeed changed!

The Protestant minister is no longer viewed as a repository of absolute answers for life's imponderable questions—if this were ever the case. His voice is only one among many heard by his parishioners. Neither is he seen as an inherently superior person binding up the wounds of inherently inferior persons in Good Samaritan fashion. His work as a prophet of social righteousness is being superseded rapidly by the role of the politician. Some critics have found fault with the quiescence and disparateness they observe in leaders of America's "religious establishment." "Protestantism," accuses sociologist Peter L. Berger, "has little to say that would be of relevance to the mighty transformations through which American society has been passing."[2] Clearly, the Protestant minister is con-

---

[1] Hans Hofmann (ed.), *Making the Ministry Relevant* (New York: Charles Scribner's Sons, 1960), p. 12.
[2] Peter L. Berger, *The Noise of Solemn Assemblies* (Garden City, N.Y.: Doubleday & Co., 1961), p. 35.

fronted with some major threats as he seeks to make the transition from horse-and-buggy days to the space age.

1. The Threat of Ambiguous Identity

The threat of ambiguous identity demands an answer to the problem of who the minister actually is in modern life. Viewed from a functional perspective, the images of *who* a minister is and *what* he does appear labyrinthine in their intricacy. Is he a preacher, counselor, administrator, theologian, teacher, representative churchman, or simply lost in the maze of passageways of a "perplexed profession," as stated in a recent report?[3] Readers may recall the analysis of the minister's ideal and actual role functions, "The Minister's Dilemma," given by Samuel W. Blizzard in *The Christian Century* of April 25, 1956.

Research of "integrative roles" of Protestant ministers, conducted by Blizzard and George A. Lee, reveal three trends among ministers. Some are general practitioners, who are carefully discriminating as they seek to effect a balance of several roles. The vast proportion of men surveyed revealed a preference for one specialized traditional role, perceived broadly as: believer-saint, scholar, evangelist, liturgist, and father-shepherd. A third trend was indicated by those who were oriented to a more contemporary conception: the interpersonal relations specialist, the parish promoter, the community problem-solver, the educator, and so on.[4] While much role ambiguity is indicated by such research, it also challenges ministers and theological educators to move beyond role-functional conflict into a comprehensive concept of the ministry as a profession.

Specialists who tell the minister how to be an evangelist, or a skilled preacher, counselor, or theologian, often elevate his anxiety by adding another function to his overburdened conception of him-

---

[3] See H. Richard Niebuhr, *The Purpose of the Church and Its Ministry* (New York: Harper & Row, 1956), pp. 48-57.

[4] Samuel W. Blizzard, "The Protestant Parish Minister's Integrative Roles," in *The Minister's Own Mental Health* (Manhasset, N.Y.: Channel Press, 1961), pp. 143-55. Dr. Blizzard plans to publish a full report of his research in a book tentatively entitled, *The Protestant Parish Minister—A Behavioral Science Interpretation.*

self. The more he reads in the ministerial specialties the more inept he feels and the more threatened he becomes. In an effort to ameliorate this anxiety and to avoid a merely functional approach, the present discussion views the minister's task as a whole from a *pastoral perspective*. While other perspectives dominate his activities at times, as Seward Hiltner's *Preface to Pastoral Theology* has demonstrated, the present discussion is limited to the pastoral dimensions of ministry. All of the minister's proximate images should focus upon the ultimate goal for pastor and church: "the increase among men of the love of God and neighbor."[5]

2. The Threat of Lost Authority

From the time of Christ, men have asked by what authority the ministry has been performed (Mark 1:22, 27). Desciples like Peter and John testified what had happened, what they had seen and heard as eyewitnesses of Christ's majesty (Acts 4:20). The apostles had companied with the risen Lord and "spoke the word of God with boldness" because they were strengthened by his Spirit (Acts 4:31). This was the authority of an authentic witness. The Apostle Paul conceived himself to be ministering "in Christ's stead," with an imputed authority (II Cor. 5:20).

Various kinds of authority have been activated at different periods of the church's history: biblical, social, personal, and institutional. This century has witnessed a gradual weakening of the authority of the Protestant minister. In a day of general education, literary criticism, and scientific achievement, men do not give as much weight to the words of ministers as in the past. Consequently, some ministers have sought substitutes for true authority, such as popularity, prestige through visible success, and authoritarianism which "lords it" over people but does not minister to them. This is not to imply that all successful clergymen lack integrity and authenticity. It should warn those, however, who would deify themselves (cf. Acts 10:25-26; I Cor. 1:12-17). Any minister can join the casualty list of castaways

[5] Niebuhr, *op. cit.*, p. 31. In this connection, Wilhelm Pauck writes that "the Reformers customarily spoke of the minister as pastor" (H. Richard Niebuhr and Daniel Day Williams [eds.], *The Ministry in Historical Perspectives* [New York: Harper & Row, 1956], p. 116).

who have lost their reason for being.

Some young ministers imagine that when they are older they will be accorded authority by old and young persons alike in any community. Others, who lack professional training, feel that when certain ministerial techniques are mastered or academic degrees earned, then their ministry will be genuine. To base one's authority on age or any other social situation such as wealth or education is illusory indeed! Some depend upon prayer and piety, hoping that their lives will be infused with power and that men will be moved by the sheer force of their words. Still others use ecclesiastical officials and pressures for personal status and church promotions.

Many ministers find their authority in the "thus saith the Lord" of the Bible. It should be remembered that any biblical passage is available to every person of the community, not merely to ministers! Also, how an interpreter uses the Scriptures is influenced by his own religious experience, by practices in his particular denomination, and by various interpretations made through the centuries. Biblical authority is inextricably connected with such factors as the Holy Spirit's illumination, interpretation by one's religious community, the limits of reason, and the power of conscience. When the minister consults commentaries, expositors, and trusted friends and discovers contrary interpretations, where is he to turn? "What the situation calls for is a deeper and more active faith in God himself. *God alone is the ultimate source of authority*."[6] Thus, the minister is led to the humble admission that the authority which accrues to him as "an official witness to divine authority is neither under his nor the Church's control."[7] Pastor and church alike live under divine authority and grace.

If a minister cannot claim special power and privilege above any other Christian, wherein does his authority of office lie? Acknowledging God's ultimate authority, the minister offers to men, not simply a set of authoritative spiritual facts, but himself in a relationship which embodies both spirit and intent of the Christian

[6] Leonard Hodgson *et al.*, "God and the Bible," in *On the Authority of the Bible* (London: S.P.C.K., 1960), p. 8, emphasis supplied.

[7] Niebuhr, *op. cit.*, p. 67.

gospel.[8] The minister's authority, humanly speaking, is acknowledged as he demonstrates his authenticity as a Christian person
and pastor. He is accepted as a Christian minister to the extent
that he both perceives man's spiritual plight and makes God known
to him in his situation (Rom. 10:14-15). Those who bear in their
bodies *the marks of the Lord Jesus* serve as living images of his
love for men. The authentic minister, who can put others in touch
with the living God, has authority both *in* and *beyond* himself.

3. The Threat of Professional Competence

Possessing a ready answer for the hope resident in his heart
presses the Lord's servant to the limit as he moves like a weaver's
shuttle through the tangled threads of people's lives. The Word
of God must be related to persons in their situation in life. Yet the
face of a parish is a thousand faces. It is not an easy thing to
speak words which keep men and women on their feet when there
is little ground to stand on. Mr. Interpreter's task and dilemma are
very great.

Moreover, a minister to students, a military chaplain, or a missionary has to become a specialist with new breeds of beings, learn
new languages, and master new cultures if he is to function redemptively. Responsible laymen who spend their lives among persons who reject organized religion find that they must become
"all things to all men" in an effort to win some. Again, there are
varieties of unbelief embedded in the secularism and scientism
of modern life with which churchmen must be prepared to deal.
Karl Heim suggests that if "Christianity is not to allow itself to
be relegated to the ghetto," then "upholders of the Christian faith"
must call secularists and scientists into serious dialogue.[9] Was
Jesus merely employing the language of paradox when he proposed
that ministers be as "wise as serpents" and as "innocent as doves"
(Matt. 10:16)? From a human point of view, there is something of

[8] See Ernest E. Bruder, "The Minister's Authority in Pastoral Care," *Pastoral
Psychology*, XIII (October, 1962), 17-24. Also, cf. Daniel Day Williams, *The
Minister and the Care of Souls* (New York: Harper & Row, 1961), pp. 30-51.
[9] Karl Heim, *Christian Faith and Natural Science* (New York: Harper &
Row, 1953). Torchbook series, 1957, p. 5.

the quality of an impossible possibility about trying to become "all things to all men."

There is yet another side to this thorny matter of competence. Some men dread what they conceive to be an inevitable by-product of professional competence: that is, growing cold and indifferent in a dull professionalism. Ministers, like others in the helping professions, can become perfunctorily repetitious, even calloused, in their pastoral work—visiting the sick, counseling the discouraged, and burying the dead. Some pastors are ground down by life's abrasive pressures. Such weariness in well-doing cannot be charged to professional training and competence, however! It is possible for any minister to be overcome in the monotony of his routine, to succumb to the depressing drain upon his own physical and emotional resources. For such a man, life is no longer a mission but a drudgery.

In his book of plays, *The Devil and the Good Lord*, Sartre imagines a scene in the town of Worms, Germany, at the time of the Peasant's Revolt and the Lutheran Reformation. A poor woman pursues a tired priest, Heinrich, who tries to elude her. When he discovers that she wants information and not food, he pauses to hear her question. The sequence reads:

WOMAN: I want you to explain why the child died.
HEINRICH: What child?
WOMAN: My child. Don't you remember? You buried him yesterday. He was three years old, and he died of hunger.
HEINRICH: I am tired, my sister, and I didn't recognize you. To me, all you women seem alike, with the same face, the same eyes. . . .

He tries to explain to the grief-stricken, starving woman that "nothing on earth occurs without the will of God."

"I don't understand," she replies. The weary priest limps along with the pathetic figure at his side as he admits that he does not understand either. But, almost desperately, he admonishes: "We must believe—believe—believe!"[10] We see ourselves speechless

[10] Jean-Paul Sartre, *The Devil and the Good Lord* (New York: Vintage Books, 1962), p. 10.

in the presence of such deep hurt. Yet even when there is little to *say* or *do*, the minister must still *be* a minister to his people.

The man of God realizes that life is never transformed from quantitative existence into qualitative experience by itself. As a catalyst accelerates a chemical reaction, so the skilled minister in the midst of persons induces changed lives, by the power of the Holy Spirit. Yet, like the catalyst, he himself is vulnerable, subject to change, and needs renewal in the process of pastoral work. "Who," he ponders occasionally, "is sufficient for these things" (II Cor. 2:16)? Even with the finest training, the minister knows that, ultimately, his sufficiency "is from God" (II Cor. 3:5).

4. *The Threat of Human Existence*

With a sense of pastoral identity secured, recognizing God's ultimate authority, and gaining professional competence, the minister is still threatened by the fact of his own humanity. He, too, is a member of the human race and must face the problem of evil and experience the mystery of suffering in his finite existence. Each member of the minister's family is subject to the temptations, stresses, and hurts which are common to humankind. Yet some clergymen cherish endurance more than personal change. A Christian counseling center once received a "request" referral from county juvenile officials—a Protestant minister's son who had been arrested for auto theft. As things turned out, the youth complied with the legal authority's request for counseling *despite* his father's protest! His parents resented their son's arrest and preferred self-avoidance to substantial change in family patterns.

The minister is linked to what Arthur O. Lovejoy once called "the great chain of being." Like other men, he requires inner renewal in a perishing universe (II Cor. 4:16). The pastor labors in the faith that healing is available for human woe and divine grace is present in time of need. Yet his is not a blind faith requiring that *all* problems have *final* solutions. At least, from man's viewpoint they do not! I recall a conversation with a Christian layman who had suffered long from an incurable neurological condition. "It may take death to cure me," he admitted quietly one day in his hospital room.

Sometimes the minister's allegiance to God is the last nail that holds his own life together. A sensitive German preacher during World War I pondered this riddle of human existence in a sermon, "Concerning the Hidden and Revealed God." He had visited the wounded in a military hospital in 1916, and recalled the contacts with those brave men who had fallen under enemy fire. "My thoughts went out to those who still stood outside in the peril of battle," he said, those for whom "the rays of the sun cast no light." God seemed hidden temporarily in the chaotic smoke of the conflict. Yet, he concluded, when "the contradictions of life threaten to break our hearts, we will still give thanks in humility and reverence that nothing has been spared us. . . . Never before have we been so permitted to gaze into the depths of God!"[11]

These poignant testimonies from literature and life have let us inside the minister's skin. These two confessed what every religious guide learns ultimately—that God instructs the heart, not merely with facts and propositions but by pains and contradictions. Such experiences explain why some ministers are threatened by the intimacy of pastoral care. Their clay feet are exposed; they become vulnerable and are subject to human limits. Intimate contact places one's own personality at stake. A pastor once burst into tears in the presence of a colleague and his wife whose lives had been temporarily crushed. Their sorrow broke his heart, too; yet he was not ashamed to cry. True pastors should rest their defenses and reveal their hearts when they walk through the shadows with their people.

Why should the man of God resent his creatureliness and dread to reveal his own clay feet? After all, giving oneself to others is central in the Incarnation! That is what Christianity is all about— God risking himself to bring new life to his creation. Robert Frost has surmised:

[11] Rudolf Bultmann, *Existence and Faith*, trans. Schubert M. Ogden (New York: Meridian Books, 1960), pp. 24, 29-30.

> But God's own descent
> Into flesh was meant
> As a demonstration
> That the supreme merit
> Lay in risking spirit
> In substantiation.[12]

When he is tempted to shrink back from life's risks and relationships, the pastor should recall that Jesus Christ "emptied himself" and took "the form of a servant" in order to bring about human redemption (Phil. 2:7).

5. *The Threat of a Lost Heritage*

American ministers who have been involved deeply in the behavioral sciences and in the practice of pastoral counseling have tended to become isolated within theological circles. This loss of fellowship and process of specialization has occurred despite due warning against developing a "priesthood within a priesthood." Since the tendency of some leaders in the counseling field has been to truncate theology and pursue psychology, a departure from the pastor's classic heritage was inevitable. Certain teachers and pastors became identified with the medical profession, behavioral scientists, and mental health leaders to whom they turned for resources and as professional models.

It comes as no surprise that a European observer would accuse some American ministers of "secularizing the care of the soul entirely." This critic claims that pastoral counseling, which emphasizes adjustment by insight rather than justification by faith, is central in much American pastoral care. His challenge that "the care of the soul and the ministry of the divine Word have nearly ceased to go together" cannot be taken lightly.[13] Frederic Greeves, a British pastoral theologian, noted upon visiting this country and communicating with numerous clergymen that some American

---

[12] Robert Frost, in the Frontispiece of *In the Clearing* (New York: Holt, Rinehart & Winston, 1962), p. 7. Used by permission.
[13] G. Brillenburg Wurth, *Christian Counseling in the Light of Modern Psychology*, trans. H. de Jongste (Grand Rapids, Mich.: Baker Book House, 1962), p. 43.

ministers "are primarily consulted as psychologists" rather than as pastors.[14]

While such criticisms are extreme, they challenge ministers to jettison shallow syncretisms of theology and psychology and to inquire anew into their classic pastoral heritage. "Deep minds," Goethe once noted, "are compelled to live in the past as well as in the future." Accordingly, a look at these threats leads into a consideration of theological education. The fabric of a minister's thinking and the fashion of his selfhood are impressed indelibly through his education for a pastoral ministry.

II. EDUCATION FOR A PASTORAL MINISTRY

The serious theological student enters his professional community of learning with a bifocal desire: he desires to continue his personal development and to achieve some degree of professional competence. He is not a novice as far as the foregoing threats are concerned. Their shadows have in some way been cast across the lines of his existence. Yet he is not defeated by them. During his training, the student usually shapes a workable rationale as to his motivation for the ministry. When he considers varied motivations, such as those in the Niebuhr report, he is forced to define his deepest promptings for becoming Christ's minister.[15] Also, the shape which his own particular ministry will take is formed—the pastorate, missions, chaplaincy, journalism, teaching, and so forth.

A seminarian's personal and professional learning tasks proceed in dialogue through new insights, temporary defeats, and determined pursuit. His concept of his master role is influenced by biblical motifs, pastoral models, cultural images, and his personal participation in the life of a Christian congregation. The student's self-concept generally parallels his developing conception of the raison d'être of the church. The church's ministry and his own are

[14] Frederic Greeves, *Theology and the Cure of Souls* (Manhasset, N.Y.: Channel Press, 1962), p. 18.

[15] H. Richard Niebuhr, Daniel Day Williams, and James M. Gustafson, *The Advancement of Theological Education* (New York: Harper & Row, 1957), pp. 146-59.

indissolubly linked. Thus his training is at a deeper level than learning tasks alone, important as skills are. The theologue must fashion a consistent self-concept, develop resources and ego-strength, and acquire the professional style of life which will sustain his ministry anywhere through a lifetime. Conversely, *even as the seminarian receives, he must learn to give up some things.*

Facilitating the student's concerns for competence and character becomes a prime requisite of American theological schools. The seminary's imperative task is to create a balanced and mutually edifying environment of theoretical and practical studies. The design of its curriculum, chapel services, contacts among students and faculty, clinical education, and field work assignments should stimulate the student's love for God and service for humanity. Penrose St. Amant has written: "The chief purpose of a seminary is to provide the kind of professional education . . . which roots the skills needed by the minister as preacher, teacher, and pastor in theological, biblical, and historical depth. The techniques which the theological student needs to acquire—and which he sometimes is inclined to regard as unworthy of his serious concern—should be implemented through clinical training in the seminary and should be permeated with profound Christian concern in classroom and chapel."[16] This statement of purpose deserves incarnation in every theological community. With such needs in mind, what elements should characterize education for the demanding tasks of ministry in our dynamic world?

1. Learning as Quest and Commitment

A student minister carries his religious, cultural, and emotional background, as well as his physical and intellectual equipment, with him to theological school. If he is married, as many seminarians are today, there are added economic pressures and child-rearing concerns. His vocation as a student must be shared and stretched to include the vocations of family man and provider. These givens, along with his preferences, prejudices, study habits, and capacity

[16] Penrose St. Amant, "The Private World of Theological Students," *Religion in Life,* XXXI (Autumn, 1962), 504.

for critical inquiry and creative thinking, color his teachability.

The typical student is characteristically *atypical.* Some are meditators; others are activists; others are bookish. Some have a sense of humor, are flexible and sociable; others are severely serious, rigid, and isolated. Some are radiantly winsome and outgoing; others appear to be preoccupied and withdrawn. The common denominator for the majority of students is their *spirit of concerned quest and devoted commitment.* Within three years, the student's original intent to obey God usually becomes clarified, refined, and informed. He has been challenged to look at himself and his faith, and to do something about what he sees. He has been stimulated to see a shockingly real world approximately as it is and to relate himself to persons redemptively in their stations in life.

In the course of his theological training, the prospective minister is subjected to a rigorous "shaking of the foundations." This is not due to a deliberate attempt on the faculty's part to shatter and confound him. Far from it! Generally, his struggle of soul is prompted by his own stirrings of heart and mind, desire to be a real person, and ambition to learn and to serve. Most seminarians are thrown back upon the ultimate resources of their existence as they tread the deep waters of theological disciplines. These years of mind-stretching and soul-searching have divine and human dimensions. Humanly speaking, sympathetic faculty members, fellow students, churchmen, and family members are all involved directly or indirectly in the student's quest and commitment. Yet the student needs a *referent beyond himself* for the ordering of his life, and God is this referent.

As he works, the seminarian learns the merit of working together with God. To gain Paul's perspective is a great blessing: "I worked harder than any of them, though it was not I, but the grace of God which is with me" (I Cor. 15:10). The ministry is God's work before it is man's work! Learning to rely upon the strength and guidance of his Spirit is more than an intellectual proposition. Faith must become the vocabulary of the minister's existence. All his intellectual pursuits, service tasks, leisure activities, and human relationships must be undergirded by his relationship to God. Moreover, neither diligent study nor devoted worship is an end in itself. Both point beyond themselves to a life of obedient service. This counterbalancing process of quest and commitment is both preventive and therapeutic, challenging all human idolatries of the academic community. God takes human aspirations, flaws, and breakings of the heart and hallows them for his purpose. The man "thoroughly furnished unto all good works" will love the Lord with heart and soul, mind and strength as he serves as an instrument of his grace.

2. Learning to Communicate in Depth

The minister's most compelling idea of vocation may be stated simply: proclaiming Jesus Christ as Lord and living this truth out in the human community. To proclaim that Christ is Lord involves incarnating his sovereignty within every area of one's own life first, then asserting his lordship within the world. Living by the certainty of God's sovereignty, all Christians are called to be communicators of their faith. Thereby they recognize the gospel's priority in the church's life. The *koinōnia* is thus the bearer of God's good news, both in proclamation *and* in personal relationships. *The pastoral perspective of ministry cherishes proclamation as central and precious and challenges churchmen to communication in depth.* Preaching and teaching employ public address as their primary mode of communication. Technical training is provided for seminarians in an effort to perfect their sermonic style and quality of sermon delivery. Beyond preaching and teaching, moreover, students for the ministry must recognize other significant levels of address. Dynamic communication operates during all the lived-out experiences among persons, seven days a week. A careful vocational analysis reveals that the pastor's primary mode of address is the *relationship language* of the interpersonal encounter. The lines of his ministry are drawn primarily, but not exclusively, along person-to-person contacts and person-with-group encounters.

Distinguishing these two modes of address—public speech and personal dialogue—appears at first either artificial and unnecessary or arbitrary and impossible. Yet the minister embodies this distinction in the functional dimensions of his role and relationships. The church's leader should be capable of both *proclamation* in the celebration of worship and *dialogue* in the conversation of pastoral care and counseling. Depth communication is indigenous to the pastoral perspective of worship, evangelism, education, and administration in the church. The clergyman is as much a "steward of the mysteries of God" when he meets with his official boards, conducts a funeral service, or makes a pastoral call as when he is preaching on Sunday!

Pastoral communication occurs at multiple levels, verbally and nonverbally. Findings of Jurgen Ruesch and Weldon Kees demonstrate that nonverbal communication actually precedes and supports spoken language.[17] Ministers thus encounter persons and groups with specialized theological language and with emotionalized interpersonal language. A minister is experienced nonverbally by others through his mannerisms; body language of gestures, facial features, agility or clumsiness, and general bearing; and, above all, through his spirit and attitude. Pastors and parishioners are made known to each other through their life-styles of flexibility or rigidity, love or fear, generosity or extractiveness, humor or severity, ego-strength or weakness, integrity or duplicity, and humility or pride. The pastor tells about God and himself through the touch of a hand, the tone of his voice, his participation in worship, work, and play; and through his sensitivity to persons in crises.

The writer once asked a member of a noted church in New York City to contrast her pastor with his distinguished predecessor. "Dr. B.," she said on the spur of the moment, "never seems to be certain that he is accomplishing anything. Whereas, Dr. A. was always so courageous, so strong, and sure." This congregant experienced security with her former pastor's words *and* ways; she sensed weakness in her new minister's uncertainty. This does not imply that the church is a hospital observation ward in which pastors and people eye each other suspiciously. Obviously, however, God has endowed persons with complex communicative equipment—antennae of the soul—with which they feel, resound to, and ex-

---

[17] See Jurgen Ruesch and Weldon Kees, *Nonverbal Communication* (Berkeley, Calif.: University of California Press, 1956).

perience one another. Such two-way experiencing of the "other" is respectful and responsive or it is not true communication. How persons *feel* about each other determines, to a great degree, their effectiveness in mutual Christian care.

Incarnational shepherding centers in depth communication. Harry A. DeWire has written in *The Christian as Communicator* that spiritual renewal occurs within the arena formed by talk, gesture, and attentiveness among Christians. Each church member, therefore, must shoulder the responsibility for maintaining the kind of loving church that was created by Christ Jesus for good works. DeWire affirms that true communication occurs in a loving community.

> Suppose . . . that people are drawn together on the basis of love. Rather than being guarded, our language is free. We do not need to press for our integrity, for we know it is accepted by the other simply because he is Christian. We do not need to protect ourselves from the threats of another because we know that the other is looking upon us in terms of love. In this kind of relationship, it seems almost certain that the consequences will be in an entirely different form of communication. The resistance, the guarded language, the failure to interpret correctly, all give way to the fruits of the spirit, which are joy, patience, long-suffering, kindness, meekness. These in themselves are processes. It may even make a difference in the way we speak. It certainly makes a difference in the things we hear. It makes a difference in the way our eyes fall upon another . . . Though we do not need new equipment to accomplish the change, the processes by which the equipment is set into motion and the dynamics at work in them certainly will be changed.[18]

Viewed thus, pastoral care addresses persons *within* the waywardness, lonely crises, brokenness, and isolation of human existence. *Listening* is crucial in such a process. Some pastors do most of the talking, make the major decisions, and thereby create a conforming church. Being sensitive to and in travail for Christian maturity in persons, however, requires attentive listening (Gal. 4:19). The clergyman's work rhythms require him to speak and to

[18] Harry A. DeWire, *The Christian as Communicator* (Philadelphia: Westminster Press, 1961), pp. 124-25.

listen—a dynamic, *not* a static endeavor! Listening in counseling, for example, is an attentive gesture, a beckoning to begin, an invitation to disclosure, to expression and religious affirmation. To hear a person requires the minister's interest in him *for his own sake,* as well as for the sake of God's kingdom.

Consequently, pastoral care is accomplished in a dynamic communications field, where persons sense and respond to the "other." This suggests that seminarians are to master such skills as how to

1. Initiate genuine conversation,
2. Understand by participant listening,
3. Invite the other person to speak by hearing him, and
4. Demonstrate Christian concern in an impersonal culture.

Communicators who *care* need grace to permit others to be themselves and courage to maintain their own integrity. Note also that the significance assigned to a minister's words is largely determined by his manner of life. Therefore, theological education is concerned first with the student minister's *being*—true selfhood—then with his speaking and doing. Adeptness in depth communication is a learned power, not a charismatic gift. Clinical pastoral education, one of the most significant developments in ministerial training of this century, is directed precisely toward this objective.

3. *Learning from Clinical Experience*

Medical educators have long recognized the value of teaching clinically by (1) treating patients in the presence of a class, (2) performing surgery in an observation theater, and (3) conducting student practice in a clinic under faculty supervision. The crucial test from the clinician's perspective is the doctor-patient encounter in the hospital sickroom. The student's performance in his profession becomes the crucial correlate of reciting principles from medical textbooks. In like manner, theological educators have developed clinical teaching methods which contribute substantially to pastoral effectiveness.

Clinical experience implies a bedside ministry or a counseling ministry by students under skilled pastoral oversight. A clinic may be a general or mental hospital, a church, a counseling or social service center affiliated with a theological school for teaching purposes. Such institutional connections are generally informal. A teaching program in a hospital, for example, is conducted cooperatively with a chaplain supervisor in the department of pastoral care. Through records of interviews and conferences with faculty members and clinical directors, students learn pastoral practice by actual experience.

Clinical pastoral education has been developed as an integral part of theological training for more than a quarter-century in America. Beginning with the pioneering work of Anton T. Boisen, the mental hospital chaplain bent on studying "living human documents" as a source of theological understanding, it has developed rapidly since World War II.[19] While relationships between seminary personnel and clinical teachers have sometimes been tenuous, because of misunderstood objectives and/or a lack of administrative ties and clear communication, clinical training now renders a distinct service in theological education. It has become a resource for the study of human relationships and pastoral functions for hundreds of seminarians each year. If a young minister has a shepherdly love for people, he has a great gift indeed. Clinical pastoral education can sharpen a feeling for persons but it cannot supply it. Such love develops throughout a lifetime.

In essence, clinical pastoral experience embodies (1) opportunities for students to serve as ministers to persons under stress in hospital and other specialized contexts; (2) relationships with trained personnel in related helping fields of medicine, nursing, education, social work, and so on; (3) group interactions and confrontations with fellow students; and (4) careful record-keeping of pastoral work with people, under competent theological supervision. While such clinical supervisors are usually employed by training institutions, they are often considered as adjunct faculty members of theological schools. In some instances, common employment and salary considerations are arranged by a seminary and a

---

[19] A comprehensive history and evaluation of clinical training has been prepared by Edward E. Thornton, "A Critique of Clinical Pastoral Education," unpublished doctoral dissertation, Southern Baptist Theological Seminary, 1961.

clinical agency. These clinical teachers are required to have a theological degree, some years of pastoral experience, and advanced clinical training, as well as meeting certification standards of both the training agency and the theological school.

Some have mistakenly viewed clinical pastoral training as an inexpensive form of personal psychotherapy. Psychiatric treatment for the student is neither its primary design nor its major intention. The student's personal-professional growth, however, is a central concern, and he might be referred for professional therapy if it were needed. While educational methodology is at the forefront of clinical experience, the theoretical content of such training is also significant. When clinicians isolate themselves from a classic theological heritage, they are subject to anarchy and idolatry. Theological education without clinical experience, on the other hand, is subject to pedantry and idealism, stimulating a superficial application of the Christian gospel to man's spiritual needs.

Notes from a clinical supervisor's evaluative report to a theological school dean indicate some of the concerns, blockages, and growth of a student engaged in clinical training during an academic semester.

Student A's beginning interviews revealed a concern on his part in watching for relevant signals in the patient. He revealed a rather flat affect [emotional feeling tone] and did not show too much creativity in making conversation with the patient. Later in the class he began to develop an ability to reveal his concern.

This student is very tenacious and sticks with his goal very closely. One seminar session he demonstrated this in trying to get specific answers for counseling. He first saw counseling as a set of scientific principles which had to be mastered and which would automatically produce results. During the latter half of the course he came to see more clearly the meaning of relationship and the art of handling the relationship towards a therapeutic and helpful goal.

His final exam reflects a great deal of insight in his study of the verbatim interview surveyed in the exam.

The clinical teacher's role in relation to students given to his tutelage is not to foster an unhealthy dependence upon himself, nor to wean the student from his theological roots. Clinical experience and the growth process involved for the student represent a time of idol-breaking and comforting the student in the loss of some of his unworthy concepts and ineffective relationship idols. Poor pastoral vision is corrected with improved clinical eyes. Like much pastoral work, clinical training is a time for affliction of the comfortable and comforting of the afflicted. Rather than training a minister to make a supervisor's remarks after him in unhealthy mimicry, the student is motivated to match his own style with some proven ministerial insights.

Occasionally, the clinical educator experiences massive resistance to personal development or to professional improvement, or both, in a student. This may be expected. Rather than leading to failure, however, the resistance itself may serve as the occasion of new learning. The following excerpt from a supervisor's report reflects this resistance-growth rhythm.

> Student Y was very defensive at first when his interviews were used in the class discussion. He was careful not to put anything before the seminar that would cause him to be criticized or handled too roughly. He soon moved through this feeling, which was displayed in many ways. His fear of rejection by the group would make him hesitant about presenting ideas or material. He would insure his interviews with explanations, which served as buffers.
>
> Y showed a lot of naïveté in calling on patients. He tended to classify all patients in two categories and assumed that all people in these categories were alike. Very slowly he developed some ability to perceive differences clinically.
>
> The mid-term test was on his ability to perceive clinical differences and diagnostic distinctions. . . . I feel that Y responded well to the course and grew considerably throughout the semester.

Learning from clinical pastoral experience involves self-revelation and skill development. Students get an insider's view of the structure, dynamics, and functioning of pastoral care in a training institution. They also gain new insight into themselves and into their interpersonal relationships. Men so trained are subject to the illusion of thinking that they know more than they actually do. Involvement with patients, physicians, God, and themselves can *distort* as well as *correct* a student's vision. He may be puffed with pride as a result of his clinical advantage over nonclinically prepared clergymen. God forbid! Such training may be counted effective *if* it opens new channels of divine grace for human need.

Educators will not read more, or less, into clinical training than reality permits.[20] The perceptive, healthy student usually experiences significant gains as he becomes more authentically a participant in his own education. Resourcefulness and security, consolidated from theological classroom and pastoral clinic, should make his Christian service more effective throughout a lifetime. Some theological schools require one semester or summer quarter of clinical education for the B.D. degree, regardless of the student's vocational goals. Clearly, it benefits those who enter missions or teaching as well as those who enter chaplaincy or serve a local church. New frontiers in pastoral education for all theological students will require the exploration and development of additional clinical resources. As far as possible, such resources should be developed in conjunction with theological schools. This is necessary for correlation with the theological curriculum and for administrative purposes, as well as for the convenience of students and their families.

4. Continuing Education of Ministers

The continuing education of ministers is another recent development with great promise for more effective pastoral work. Theological education can anticipate *some* future experiences for prospective ministers. Yet most seminarians have not borne full ministerial responsibilities: the loneliness of leadership, the pangs of failure, the perils of the prophet's chamber. Students never ask

[20] Theological educators should read the report of the American Association of Theological Schools' Consultation on Clinical Pastoral Education and the Theological Schools, held on April 7-8, 1961, at Evanston, Ill. The report was prepared by Seward Hiltner and Jesse H. Ziegler and published as "Clinical Pastoral Education and the Theological Schools," *Journal of Pastoral Care,* XV (Fall, 1961), 129-43. Reprints of this report are available through the office of the A.A.T.S., Dayton, Ohio.

some of the frustrating questions that occur to pastors, several years after graduation. Reuel Howe has written: "Little do they realize, until . . . after graduation, that their theological learning may have lured them away from an understanding of the people whom they went forth to teach and to serve, and increased the difficulties of communication between them and the world."[21] Paralleling this limitation of education for a pastoral ministry is the lack of adequate feedback from graduates to theological educators. How is a man five years post-B.D. to tell his former theological dean something that will strengthen the curriculum? Some schools are inviting groups of selected ministers to return briefly to their campuses, in order to test the effectiveness of their previous training and to continue their education.

Numerous projects of continuing education for ministers are under way; some experimentally, others well advanced.[22] The concept of *continuing education* includes, yet transcends, traditional lectureships or pastors' conferences, some of which are little more than an alumni relations medium. Administrative, faculty, housing, and financial considerations are involved. When such arrangements are made, small groups of ministers may be invited to the theological school campus during the year for brief periods of seminars, discussions, and library study.

Continuing education was conceived (1) to stimulate pastors and churches to be more effective in their ministries, (2) to explore actual needs of contemporary clergymen, (3) to afford the latest insights of theological study, (4) to provide interpersonal relationship groups oriented toward the pastor's own developing selfhood, and (5) to explore ways for a more effective correlation of theology and pastoral work.

While such programs are structured and content-centered, they

---

[21] Reuel Howe *et al.*, "Theological Education After Ordination," *Making the Ministry Relevant, op. cit.*, pp. 133-69.

[22] In addition to numerous theological school programs, resources of several regional agencies are open to pastors, such as: (1) The Institute of Religion, Texas Medical Center, Houston, Texas; (2) Institute for Advanced Pastoral Studies, Bloomfield Hills, Mich.; (3) The College of Preachers, Mount St. Alban, Washington, D.C.; (4) and centers certified by the Council for Clinical Training and the Institute of Pastoral Care throughout America.

are intended to be informal and person-centered as well. Since continuing education programs are designed primarily for parish ministers, they are usually limited to a one- or two-week period. Specialized groups, such as Christian laymen, campus religious directors, military and institutional chaplains, religious journalists, college teachers of religion, and denominational executives, may be incorporated into a school's continuing education program. In light of the stimulating developments in this area of theological education, denominations should explore methods for the advanced training of their own ministers through their present resources.

If the minister is the growing kind, he will not wait for a formal invitation to continue learning. He sharpens his mind with technical books and journals; enriches his notions of life from drama, poetry, and serious essays; and keeps abreast of his dynamic world on his own. Again, through quiet hours of devotional reading, prayer, and sermon preparation he reaches forth regularly for divine re-kindling of his compassion for broken and enslaved men. And withal, he learns by reflecting upon his family and professional relationships, and upon the successes and failures of his pastoral ministry.

CONCLUSION

The minister's preparation for pastoral care, while reminding him of hidden reefs to be avoided, should magnify personal qual-ities which he is to incarnate in life—strength of character, self-understanding, awareness of persons, and flexible use of time and resources. Such qualities represent ideals which are primarily *pursuits* rather than *achievements*. It is hoped that the pastor will live as a principled man, not merely a technician, as the lines of his ministry unfold under the grace of God.

Fortunately, the good minister of Jesus Christ does not stand nor serve alone. While he experiences certain threats, pursues learning without end, works and prays for the kingdom of God, and anticipates Christ's *parousia* at the end of the Age, he is sup-ported by the friendship of men and the fellowship of God. This sense of a shared ministry should mean for him what Jonathan's friendship was to David. It should "strengthen his hand in God." The concept of the shared ministry of the entire congregation has been revived recently but is actually a biblical concept. As we turn now from principles to the process of pastoral care, the idea of a ministering church will be magnified.

SUGGESTED READING

Bridston, Keith R., and Culver, Dwight W. (eds.). *The Making of Ministers.* Minneapolis: Augsburg Publishing House, 1964. A compendium of some challenging issues in theological education and the pastoral ministry today.

Lee, Robert (ed.). *Cities and Churches: Readings on the Urban Church.* Philadelphia: Westminster Press, 1962. (Chaps. 1-2, 6-9.)

Niebuhr, H. Richard. *The Purpose of the Church and its Ministry.* New York: Harper & Row, 1956. The oft-quoted essay on church and ministry which has appeared in a series of studies, including *The Ministry in Historical Perspectives* (Harper, 1956) and *The Advancement of Theological Education* (Harper, 1957), both co-edited by Niebuhr, the first with Daniel Day Williams and the latter with Williams and James M. Gustafson.

Oates, Wayne E. (ed.). *The Minister's Own Mental Health.* Manhasset, N.Y.: Channel Press, 1961. A symposium of research-reflective essays by a group of theologians and social scientists addressing the thorny problem of the minister's mental health.

Wagoner, Walter D. *Bachelor of Divinity.* New York: Association Press, 1963. A sympathetic appraisal of the minister's vocational dilemma by a minister involved in theological education.

Williams, D. D. *The Minister and the Care of Souls.* See above, p. 33. (Chaps. 2, 5.)

II

The Shape
of the Church's Ministry

CHAPTER 4

☙℃

THE PASTORAL ACTION
OF THE CHURCH

We have now investigated the theological framework and method
of pastoral care. Some attention has also been given to the nature
of man, based upon the insights of theology and psychology, and
certain implications of this synoptic wisdom have been noted for
pastoral care. Educational opportunities were clarified for those
who wish to become more skilled in pastoral ministry. The minister's
own selfhood and relationships were viewed as valuable resources
in his work. To go a step beyond this we need to clarify the shape
of the church's shepherding ministry, including the respective roles
of the pastor and his people.

The servant motif of ministry was established in our thinking
in Chapter 1 as the Bible's most characteristic way of viewing the
people of God. The church, like her Lord, is to be in the world as
one who serves. Every Christian is constantly involved in the
church's pastoral ministry, as either the *channel* or the *object* of
its concern. The consuming goal of such concern is that "Christ be
formed" in persons as they choose to "conform to [his] image"
(Gal. 4:19; Rom. 8:29). A ministering style of life is pictured, for
example, in Christ's metaphor of the vine and the branches (John
15:5) and is implied by the Pauline "in Christ" concept. To this
end, the New Testament proposes that the strong are to bear the

burdens of the weak (Rom. 15:1-3). Christians of every age are summoned to contribute their strength and spiritual gifts "for building up the body of Christ, until we all attain . . . to mature manhood, to the measure of the stature of the fullness of Christ" (Eph. 4:12b-13). A ministering congregation experiences mutuality in caring; there is a reciprocal rhythm of receiving and giving under the Holy Spirit's guidance.

People in the church conceive their relationships and roles from varying perspectives. Some prefer an individualistic religion of the *inner way*, rationalizing: "Am I my brother's keeper?" Such passive folk offer no strategy for life's hardheaded problems and avoid involvement in the institutional church's life. A broad segment of the church population practices religion as a *pious habit*, but it fails to make much difference in such persons' daily lives. Bliss Carmen captured the portrait of persons who merely log hours at church in order to remain respectable.

> They're praising God on Sunday
> They'll be all right on Monday
> It's just a little habit they've acquired.[1]

A third stratum of the religious order represents a more involved life-style, that of *dynamic dialogue* with God and the world. Such persons are convinced that the Christian fellowship has no life in itself. It lives only as it shares the eternal life of God in the celebration of worship and in the common life.

1. THE IDEA OF A MINISTERING CHURCH

The Christian *koinōnia*, by its very nature, implies a shared ministry by the pastor and his people. When the church is gathered for worship, the pastor is the chief minister. Yet when God's people are scattered (dispersed) in the world, each layman is to *be* the church where he lives and works. There he finds that, while religion is everybody's business, God is often left on the borders of human existence. Only when some crisis arises or a catastrophe crushes

[1] Quoted by H. E. Fosdick, *The Three Meanings*, III (New York: Association Press, 1950), p. 11.

a person does he perceive God in the heart of things. Vast multitudes view God as a special lifeguard to pull them out of troubled waters. While pastoral care is not a first-aid, rescue operation, sensitive Christians are to listen for the cry of help. Frequently it is in such a teachable moment that the Christian layman becomes a priest to another.

Being available with a life-giving ministry to members of a spiritually languid society, where one lives and labors, is *being the church* in the world. An oil executive once recounted a shepherding incident involving a member of his staff. A secretary who thought that she had achieved the victory of a desegregated heart returned to the office one afternoon in tears. He listened as her angry words spilled out.

> I was in line, getting a sandwich and things for lunch at Sam's, when this Negro girl came up to me. She had passed five or six in the line, then shoved me out of the way, saying that she was running late and hoped I didn't mind. Oh! Honestly, I thought I had my past feelings about Negroes whipped until today. Now, I don't know.
>
> I don't mind eating with them, or sitting by them, or any of those things . . . but . . it makes me mad when anyone, white or black, pushes me around. That black girl had her nerve! They really want to take over things it seems.

They talked awhile about the need for patience and understanding during this crucial period of social unrest in the nation's history. He accepted her negative feelings, then encouraged understanding and good will during the Negroes' bold march toward freedom. Thus a Christian layman temporarily became a pastor to an office worker who was only formally identified with a church in another city.

Certain obligations emerge from the church's responsibility for a shared ministry, despite the hesitation of some to communicate their concern. First, ministers who have prepared themselves for a pastoral ministry are obligated to educate their people for their mutual task. Many of the key concepts about man's nature, for example, and about pastoral counseling apply generally to all religious counselors. Second, today's agents of reconciliation must shape their service to people's needs where they are. It is easier to stay within the sanctity of the walls of an established fellowship than to reach out to those who are hostile toward the church. Churchmen who live passively, "safe in bondage," are not actually *in* the world rendering responsible pastoral care. For a church staff member to sit in an inquirer's room, waiting for the troubled world to open his door, may imply that he is not available when help is needed. The compassionate Samaritan ministered to a neighbor as he traveled upon the open road.

Authentic pastoral care is possible only when a church establishes contact with those who suffer the traps and temptations of existence in a hostile world. Some adventuresome ministers have established new kinds of ecclesiastical command posts near the front lines of life's conflicts.[2] While we cannot all leave the historic established churches and form bands of committed Christians in embattled communities, we can learn new shepherding possibilities from such imaginative men. Discerning the real from the apparent "demons" where we live and work, and recognizing the Holy Spirit's power over them, remain the twin foci of the pastoral calling. More often it is the discipline of a new alertness and availability that God's people need, not a new location.[3] The church's service is shaped to the dimensions of its loving, not merely to the givens of geography. What then is the mode of mutual ministry in the church?

1. *The Church as a Redemptive Society*

Jesus Christ created his church to be a redemptive society *in* society, not isolated from the world but sanctified to service in the world (John 17:15-25). Before his departure, Christ prayed that his followers would both maintain their inner devotion to him

[2] The East Harlem Protestant Parish, and Judson Memorial Church in Greenwich Village, New York City; the Church of the Saviour, Washington, D.C.; and the Bread and Wine Mission, San Francisco, exemplify new patterns of ministry.

[3] This claim is demonstrated in Joseph McCabe, *The Power of God in a Parish Program* (Philadelphia: Westminster Press, 1959); Robert A. Raines, *New Life in the Church* (New York: Harper & Row, 1961); see also Hans Hofmann (ed.), *Making the Ministry Relevant* (New York: Charles Scribner's Sons, 1960), and Charles E. Mowry, "Significant Efforts in Ministering to Young Adults," *Religion in Life*, XXXI (Summer, 1962), 376-86.

and discharge a missionary task in the world. Christ continues his ministry in and through his chosen instrument, the church, for which he died, which he both loves and empowers for service, and of which he remains the head (Eph. 4:15, 5:25; Acts 1:5).

T. W. Manson was profoundly correct in *The Church's Ministry*, when he noted that each congregation has a dual role to perform in the world—*evangelistic* in relation to those outside and *pastoral* in relation to those within. Churchmen should not try to separate these tasks, for they are two aspects of a single life. Citizens in the pagan world of the first century watched love at work in the life of the Christian community and were won by what they saw and felt. In our day, it is "not enough that men should *hear* the gospel of peace; they must *see* that gospel actually making *peace*."[4] The Holy Spirit turns many to righteousness through the power of compassionate living, as well as by impassioned preaching. Wise churchmen recognize that "evangelism happens when God uses anything we do in order to bring people to Him in Jesus Christ."[5] While churches and their agencies cannot go back to the literal *shape* of the first-century ministry, they can develop continuities with the dynamic *spirit* of Christ and the apostles. Only as Christ establishes its ministry and serves through its members is the church conducting a truly redemptive ministry.

How effective is this ideal in the life of contemporary churches? Sociological studies reveal how readily a church may take upon itself the form of its secular community instead of that of a servant.[6] Beholden to its subtly secularized constituency, such a church becomes what *Time* magazine once called a "chatty spiritual cafeteria" instead of the household of faith. A church can easily become dedicated to perpetuating itself or the American way of life rather

---

[4] H. F. Lovell Cocks, "The Communion of the Holy Spirit," *The Expository Times*, LXVIII (May, 1957), 250.

[5] D. T. Niles, *The Preacher's Calling To Be Servant* (New York: Harper & Row, 1959), p. 28.

[6] See Gibson Winter, *The Suburban Captivity of the Churches* (Garden City, N.Y.: Doubleday & Co., 1961); also, see Robert Spike, *Safe in Bondage* (New York: Friendship Press, 1960); Martin E. Marty, *The New Shape of American Religion* (New York: Harper & Row, 1958); and Peter L. Berger, *The Noise of Solemn Assemblies* (Garden City, N.Y.: Doubleday & Co., 1961), pp. 114-71.

than continuing the ministry of Christ. A church which lives for its own sake alone has ceased to be a true church! There is a story in the Southwest, probably apocryphal, of a church that discovered oil on its property. Immediately the congregants formed a closed corporation, refused new members, and shared their royalties from oil sales joyfully. One may imagine a church under the shadow of an oil derrick rather than of the cross. That *would* reshape its outlook upon the world.

Recent studies such as those of Samuel Blizzard, Roy W. Fairchild, and J. C. Wynn indicate that Americans have largely ceased to think theologically about the ministry.[7] Rather than practicing the priesthood of the whole body of Christ (Heb. 13:13-16; I Pet. 2:9; Rev. 5:10), the vast majority of those interviewed looked upon the church functionally, in terms of what the minister did for the church, and in turn, what the church did for them. One minister, vexed with his self-centered congregation, exclaimed to a small group: "This church wants to *be* served, not to serve!" Fairchild and Wynn reported only a remnant of laymen who view the church as a redemptive society and feel that they have a personal part in its ministry. There are evidences that this remnant is alive and growing, however.

It was the remnant concept in scripture, and the sociological fact that only a remnant of responsible members survive in the Church of England, that led Martin Thornton to formulate a "remnant-type" pastoral theology for Anglo-Catholic communions. Thornton argues that just as Christ ministered to the whole world without moving more than a few miles from his home, and by concentrating on twelve men, so priests can coach their parishioners in prayer and by this vicarious action lead men into Christ's body. "The only positive method of attaining conversions is epitomized in the worshipping Remnant," says Thornton, "that forgets all about trying to convert."[8] Discipline, through "ascetical rule" or prayer

---

[7] Samuel W. Blizzard, "The Minister's Dilemma," *Christian Century*, April 25, 1956; see also Roy W. Fairchild and J. C. Wynn, *Families in the Church: A Protestant Survey* (New York: Association Press, 1961), pp. 174-80.

[8] Martin Thornton, *Pastoral Theology: A Reorientation* (London: S.P.C.K., 1956), p. 69. See also Chaps. 1, 4, 5, and 21. This "reorientation" lacks the

coaching, is viewed as the priest's essential task. Thornton's passion for discipline is akin in some respects to Thurneysen's doctrine of pastoral care, which was influenced considerably by Continental pietism.

Thornton's "reorientation" lacks the comprehensiveness and social relevance of the Reformation principle of the universal priesthood of believers. While retaining a profound sense of the meaning of the pastoral office, Luther, Calvin, Zwingli, and Bucer felt that every Christian should be a minister of the Word of God by virtue of his faith. Involvement in society, living out one's vocation as a Christian, was inevitable and commendable. Wilhelm Pauck has written of the reformers' intentions for ministry in the time of the Protestant Reformation: "[Every believer] must express his faith in loving social action and thereby communicate it to others. All Christians are such ministers; they cannot but bring about a new kind of society—the fellowship of believers."[9] A "remnant-type" pastoral theology tends to be inverted and exclusivistic and is too passive a concept to be applied rigidly in American churches. Were such asceticism to be practiced, the pastoral work of the church would fall into the hands of the *few* rather than the *many*. This seems to me to miss the basic New Testament intent of the corporate responsibility of God's people for each other and the world.

J. A. T. Robinson captures the New Testament pattern of thinking, "All that is said of the ministry in the New Testament is said not of individuals, nor of some apostolic college . . . but of the whole body, whatever the differentation of function within it."[10] The idea of a ministering church, asserting the vocational identity

comprehensiveness of an earlier British study: Henry Balmforth, *et al.*, *An Introduction to Pastoral Theology* (London: Hodder and Stoughton, 1937). A more relevant discussion, in light of contemporary developments in Britain and North America, was published by Paul R. Clifford, *The Pastoral Calling* (London: Carey Kingsgate Press, 1959; and Manhasset, N.Y.: Channel Press, 1961).

[9] Wilhelm Pauck in H. Richard Niebuhr and Daniel Day Williams (eds.), *The Ministry in Historical Perspectives* (New York: Harper & Row, 1956), p. 112.

[10] Kenneth M. Carey (ed.), *The Historic Episcopate*, p. 14, cited in T. F. Torrance, *Royal Priesthood* (*Scottish Journal of Theology* Occasional Paper No. 3, 1955), p. 35.

of every Christian as a servant and defining patterns of participation in pastoral care, is both rooted in scripture and relevant in the contemporary situation.

2. The Interrelatedness of Ministry

The idea of the priesthood of the *whole church* is clear in the New Testament, was enunciated by the Protestant reformers, and is to be understood in *corporate* rather than individualistic terms today. In its practical expressions, the corporate priesthood of pastors and parishioners consists in their interrelatedness of ministry. While this is not the occasion for tracing all the branches of ministry, springing from the high priesthood of Christ through the centuries (Heb. 5-8), some things may be said.

1. The term "pastor" (*poimēn*) in the New Testament originally implied a *function* performed and later was applied to an *office* held in church life. It means "to tend or feed as a shepherd."[11] Pastoral ministries were performed in the early churches by two groups: (a) those *many spontaneous* general ministers who received the charismatic (grace) gifts of the Spirit (I Cor. 12:12-28; Eph. 4:7-12; Rom. 12:5-8), and (b) those *few appointed* as local ministers, elders or bishops, and deacons by the apostles (Acts 20:28; Phil. 1:1; Heb. 13:7, 17, 24; I Tim. 3:8-13, 5:17). Pastoral functions, such as healing, supporting, and teaching, were performed by many unofficial ministers. As churches developed, elders (*presbuteroi*) or bishops (*episkopoi*) were appointed to exercise pastoral oversight over congregations. Deacons (*diakonoi*) were ordained as their associates in such tasks as oversight, preaching, pastoral care, conducting worship, and administering the rites of baptism and the Lord's Supper.

2. A practical strategy, which I shall term the *principle of adaptive ministry*, is evident in New Testament church life. Each group of believers adapted its witness to its environment, without major distinctions being made between pastors and people. All of the

[11] See H. J. Carpenter, "Minister, Ministry," *A Theological Word Book of the Bible*, ed. Alan Richardson (New York: The Macmillan Co., 1960), pp. 146-51. Cf. Frank Stagg, *New Testament Theology* (Nashville, Tenn.: Broadman Press, 1962), pp. 250-76.

early Christians stood on common ground, shared an imperiled existence, and were called (*kletōs*) to serve in the world as the people of God. Theirs was a theology of the catacombs, as well as of the housetops. Before laying hands on a man in ordination, early congregations were to "test the spirits to see whether they are of God: for many false prophets have gone out into the world" (I John 4:1). Churches must still avoid the "spirit of Antichrist" and move cautiously in the ordination of their ministers.

The interrelatedness of ministry recognizes the pastoral services performed by ministers in denominational and interchurch offices, beyond the bounds of a local church. Service and institutional chaplains, missionaries, denominational executives, religious directors on university campuses, and seminary professors—all fulfill pastoral functions in discharging their responsibilities. No distinction should be made between these offices and that of a local pastor. They, too, have been called to a ministry of witnessing and caring, as "workers together with God."

Carrying this principle further, the churches do not exist in isolation; they strengthen each other. "Partisans of the parish are inclined to romanticize its possibilities. We shall have to keep in mind the plentitude of things the local congregation can *not* do."[12] Denominations serve a real purpose in focusing support, channeling ministry in institutions, sending missionaries, creating literature, and challenging the churches in their varied services.

Churches today are wise to follow the spirit and strategy of the New Testament regarding their ministers, rather than certain ecclesiastical developments which are subject to such varied interpretations. While recognizing the biblical principle of the priesthood of all believers, the appointment and work of a formal ministry is clear in the New Testament. There is no limit on the number of ministers and deacons which one church may ask to lead its ministry in a community. The early churches frequently had a multiple ministry. Moreover, there should be opportunities provided for responsible laymen to fulfill *pastoral* functions in churches and in their daily living.

[12] Marty, *op. cit.*, p. 123.

3. *The Layman's Calling to Care*

The renaissance of the church's laity, which Elton Trueblood has called "the greatest new Christian fact of our time," is actually a *new emphasis* upon an ancient biblical truth.[13] Nowhere does the New Testament advocate that a Christian pastor is to monopolize the ministry. His role is to "equip the saints" for their own task of ministering—in family life, in daily work, in the church, and in the world. Hendrik Kraemer's *A Theology of the Laity* has reminded us that "the Church *is* Ministry," and that the services of clergy and laity "are both aspects of the same diakonia, each in their proper sphere and calling."[14] The worlds of the professional clergyman and the responsible layman intersect at the point of what they both really are—the people of God!

The central affirmation of the New Testament is that God calls men from spiritual death into the Christian festival of life. Those cut off from true humanity are summoned to a participant style of Christian living by God's sovereign grace (Matt. 22:3; Rom. 8:30; Gal. 1:6; Rev. 19:9). Such a life is a calling to *identity* (I Pet. 2:9-10), to *community* (I Cor. 1:9), and to *responsibility* (Rom. 12:1-2). The Christian's vocation is to "lead a life worthy of [his] calling" (Eph. 4:1), and to perform the tasks "which the Lord has assigned to him, and in which God has called him" (I Cor. 7:17).

While this book seeks primarily to illuminate the shepherding work of the pastor, one cannot but be deeply conscious of the work of the laity. Some churches have an annual Layman's Day, permitting one or a few men to testify at a worship service. The church thereby recognizes the tasks they have performed and challenges the laity to renewed zeal. Their work, in most cases, is restricted to fiscal management, matters of trusteeship, the upkeep of church properties, committee tasks amounting to "leg work" for the pastor, food preparation for men's night dinners, and church-oriented offices or

[13] Statement by D. Elton Trueblood to a group of ministers, reported in the *Christian Century* for October 31, 1962, p. 1338. See also articles on "The Role of the Christian Layman" in *Review and Expositor*, LX (Jan., 1963).

[14] Hendrik Kraemer, *A Theology of the Laity* (Philadelphia: Westminster Press, 1958), p. 143.

tasks. Some men and women are more devoted to policy-making than to personal service. Others preoccupy themselves with pushing a program rather than with participating in the church as a supportive and accepting fellowship. Many, however, do demonstrate the power of the personal, manifesting genuine love in the relationships of daily life.

Since World War II, challenges have sounded in Europe and North America stirring men and women to participate at deeper levels in the life and witness of the Christian congregation. The lay academy movement, designed for discipline and to strengthen Christian witnessing in family life and in the structures of society, is in some respects a judgment upon the institutionalization of the church.[15] People need more than religious tradition and activism to undergird them in the stresses of life. Yet they *do* need the church at its best.

Dietrich Bonhoeffer, the German minister who sealed his testimony in *The Cost of Discipleship* with his death, has become one of the prophets of this new "springtime of the church." Before he was hanged by the Nazis for his part in the resistance movement, Bonhoeffer foresaw a new day of intense mission by the church. He predicted new forms of ministry, employing the "language of righteousness" in daily life. "The day will come when men will be called again to utter the word of God with such power as will change and renew the world. It will be a new language, which will . . . overwhelm [men] by its power. It will be the language of a new righteousness and truth, a language which proclaims the peace of God with men. . . ."[16] He felt that until that season of renewal Christianity would be a silent and hidden affair, belonging only to those who watch and pray and wait for God's own time.

Reading Bonhoeffer, one feels his concern for the German churches, many of which were forced into silence or compliance

---

[15] See Margaret Frakes' study of the lay academy movement, *Bridges to Understanding* (Philadelphia: Fortress Press, 1960). And cf. Stephen C. Neill and Hans-Ruedi Weber (eds.), *The Layman in Christian History* (Philadelphia: Westminster Press, 1963).

[16] Dietrich Bonhoeffer, *Letters and Papers from Prison*, trans. R. H. Fuller (New York: The Macmillan Co., 1953), published originally as *Prisoner for God*, p. 188.

during the war. His plea to wait upon God's deliverance has been interpreted by some to mean that the religious establishment, as we know it, is doomed to failure. Peter L. Berger, paraphrasing Bonhoeffer, has said that Christianity is not concerned with religion; it is only concerned with Jesus Christ. In *The Noise of Solemn Assemblies,* Berger avows that the church has lost its thrust and relevance and must be "disestablished" as an institution.

While American churchmen are under divine judgment for their failures to relate the "language of righteousness" to daily life, we must be careful *not* to dispense with organized religion! We cannot all retreat to some monastic life in a desert cave and wait for faith to reappear on the earth. What sociologists of Berger's stripe fail to take into account is that "the local church is still the institution which carries the gospel by which it can judge itself to be apostate!"[17] The Word of God judges, cleanses, and reforms Christians, even as they seek to be the people of God in the orders of human society. The note to be sounded here is one of deep gratitude for the layman's renewed interest in both the witnessing *and* shepherding aspects of the Christian life. What is new for our day is the clergy's recognition of the laity and the layman's acceptance of his calling to care.

II. PATTERNS OF PARTICIPATION IN PASTORAL CARE

I have said that *all* Christians are custodians of the answers to human woe—not merely the professional theologians. There is often an unconscious testimony in the lives of humble Christians and of nominal church members as well! For example, a "Christian" physician's lewd vulgarity in a hospital delivery room, at the birth of a child, caused a sensitive Christian nurse to doubt that he cared. Frequently parents mar their children's spiritual development and mental health by their inconsistency of example or discipline. Again, so-called religionists openly advocate and practice social injustice which holds tens of thousands of American citizens in bondage.

[17] John O. Mellin's review of Berger's *The Noise of Solemn Assemblies* in *Religion in Life,* XXXI (Summer, 1962), 466-67.

It could go the other way; one hopes that it often does, as caring occasions arise spontaneously. "The church in your house" is more than a phrase for many parents and children (Philemon 2). A family becomes a foster home for two orphaned girls. A Christian lawyer spends an evening answering the questions of some youths who are considering the legal profession as a career. A hospital administrator admits a charity patient—a child of a Negro family—to his institution's full services and excellent staff. A homosexual employee of an industrial company confers with a Christian sales executive in order to share his plight and request prayerful guidance. This particular sales official, in turn, confers with his minister about a plan of redemptive action in the case.

When defining patterns of participation in pastoral care, the place to begin is not with some idyllic laity movement or a specialized clinical setting, but with the local church and one's own community. Retreats and institutes render a service in theological discovery and spiritual renewal, but they must point beyond themselves to the ministry of God's people in life. The local congregation is strategically poised to serve today "because it is already existing. Whether it plays its role or not . . . the parish is a fact. It is, by right, if not in reality, that tiny cell of Christianity, of the Incarnation. . . . Every community has its own."[18] The church alone, of all institutions, is concerned with the ultimate dimensions of life—its hopes and fears, its joys and sorrows, its achievements and failures. Its ministry is to be directed to the universal needs of the human heart.

1. *Levels of Participation in Church Life*

An untrained eye might view the members of a given congregation as an undifferentiated group at the bottom of a church organizational chart. Names of the paid staff, the diaconate, and members of official boards and committees would appear at the top. Participa-

[18] Quoted from Abbé Michonneau by Tom Allan, *The Face of My Parish* (New York: Harper & Row, n.d.), p. 67. Cf. Elton Trueblood, *The Company of the Committed* (New York: Harper & Row, 1961); Francis O. Ayres, *The Ministry of the Laity* (Philadelphia: Westminster Press, 1962); Georgia Harkness, *The Church and Its Laity* (Nashville, Tenn.: Abingdon Press, 1962); and Franklin M. Segler, *The Christian Layman* (Nashville, Tenn.: Broadman Press, 1964).

tion in church life is more than a matter of offices, however. Pastors frequently misjudge the motives of their most faithful members, as well as the hindrances of marginal members. Those who have a spatial concept of the church as a *place* and a limited concept of ministry as *getting things done* for the pastor tend to overlook the pastoral dimensions of daily life.

A typology of levels of participation in church life constructed by sociologist J. H. Fichter is of interest here: (1) *dormant*—indifferent members, new arrivals, invalids, those with formal ties only; (2) *marginal*—rebels, the withdrawn, the sinful, the rejected, occasional helpers; (3) *modal*—the dependable servants of the church, most frequently present and participating; and (4) *nuclear* —those exemplary Christians who are militant, with an apostolic spirit both in and beyond the church fellowship.[19]

When we examine the motivations of active laymen, it appears that a number of drives inspire their work for the Lord. Some need the pastor's approval and will try to do everything that he asks of them. Beneath this is often a guilt dynamism, prompted by some hidden or open fault. The lay person secretly hopes that his votive sacrifice of himself will atone for his sin. Latent hostility is a concomitant of this life-style, along with an incapacity to receive help from others or to trust God's gracious care.

Some need to be needed; however, they recognize this as a desire to serve where and when they are needed. There is a certain amount of satisfaction which comes in fulfilling one's inner urge toward creativity ("to amount to something"), particularly when this is related to God's work. Others have a deep desire to discharge a duty to God, either out of a great love or a great fear. They usually work without too much external pushing, because of an inner drive to please God in all things. Finally, rewards have their place in a person's investment of himself in church activity. There is the matter of family approval, community status (some choose a "prestige church" because it commands general admiration), and the

[19] J. H. Fichter, *Social Relations in the Urban Parish* (Chicago, 1954), p. 22, cited by Conor K. Ward, *Priests and People: A Study in the Sociology of Religion* (Liverpool: Liverpool University Press, 1961), pp. 1-29 *et passim*.

eschatological consideration of ultimate destiny after death. Empirical findings on this subject are almost nonexistent, indicating the need for social science research into motivations of the laity in church life. Pastoral understanding, not judgment, of his people lies behind his interest in their motives.

We cannot departmentalize life, surmising that what is done in the church building is spiritual and what is done in the world outside is secular. For example, a man is called upon to practice the care of souls in his role as the head of a household, as a citizen of a community, and as an employee of a business firm or other institution. An executive who tyrannizes over his office personnel is not merely a severe boss; he is a malfunctioning Christian. A politician who teaches a Bible class on Sunday and favors special legislative groups on Monday for a "price" is a false prophet. The work of God refuses to be isolated from the world, despite the tendency of some in this direction. While pastors are obligated to enlist their members in formal church offices, they should understand that healing, sustaining, and guiding tasks will also be performed where Christians live and work day by day.

2. The Role of the Protestant Pastor

The pastor's role is paradoxically that of a servant to servants. Ideally, the good shepherd knows his sheep and is known by them. Actually, a minister may know and care for only a fraction of his members in a crisis-type ministry. When one metropolitan minister was interviewed concerning his pastoral work, he lamented the fact that he did not even know hundreds of his parishioners. He found it difficult to particularize his love, though he was much admired as a preacher by his congregation. Another clergyman admitted: "While my people do not *love* me, at least they do *respect* me."

A psychiatrist lecturing at a theological school claimed that he could love only five patients as a case load at any one time, along with his university teaching assignment. He deplored large churches but offered no alternatives to them. While the minister cannot limit the size of his congregation, and is in fact committed to its continual enlargement, he is obligated to know his members as far as is humanly possible. Several ministers may serve as colleagues on a church staff, thereby intensifying relationships with segments of the congregation.[20] The multiple minister principle—a senior minister and associates—in large churches is preferable to the "closed corporation" idea of some who suggest limiting each church to a few hundred members. Some, because of their location or situation, will be small.

What then is the role of the Protestant pastor who gratefully recognizes the corporate nature of the church's ministry? The wise pastor sees shepherding possibilities, not only in personal counseling, but in preaching, group experiences, calling, correspondence, and his other encounters with persons. The modern church overseer need not set up an unwieldy "ministering machine" and spend his time co-ordinating the co-ordinators of pastoral care. This would merely feed his subtle temptation to bolster "distance machinery" between himself and the very persons he should be serving under God.

The pastor's dynamic role should be defined in terms of his congregation's caring concerns, established in Chapter 1, and in light of the following goals:

1. The pastor should seek a *repersonalization of man* through his basic attitudes and actions. Just as he resents being manipulated and dictated to by others, the pastor must recognize that people resent being treated as "things" and tire of being "used up" as expendable inventory in ecclesiastical production. He will avoid duplicity, maintain openness, discipline his emotions, and weigh his words in relationships. He will relate to men as a man, to women as a brother in Christ, and will ventilate his life through conversations with professional colleagues, as well as in prayer. Emphasis upon the worth of the individual is needed in our depersonalized culture, which will avoid superficial optimism about man but truly redeem him from the difficult, often tragic, situations of human existence.

2. The pastor should stimulate a *recovery of reverence* for God

---

[20] See the articles on multiple ministry in *Pastoral Psychology* XIV (Mar., 1963).

and for humanity through the celebration of worship, by his own life-style, and in basic attitudes evoked in others. Modern man suffers from a lost sense of wonder in this scientific age, when all miracles are being explained away and horizons pushed beyond the stars. Worshipers have grown weary of preacher-centered churches, sustained by what someone has called pulpit huckstering. They have turned to modern mystery cults, the performing arts, and nature worship, partly because clergymen have failed to put them in touch with the one true God.

3. The pastor serves as a spiritual catalyst in order to bring about the *realization of community* in church life. The contemporary layman is suspicious of the pastor who constantly demands conforming co-operation and seeks to glue people together by involving everyone in everything all the time. True community, which transcends the terrible loneliness of so many persons of all ages in our world, is a gift—the product of Christian life together. It is the kind of life that survives even under persecution, as the modern journals of Dietrich Bonhoeffer and Ernest Gordon vividly attest.[21] No fellowship of humankind on earth, beyond the ties of family kin, is so strong and sure and inspiring as those of the family of God. Man, who has been "flung into existence" as a contemporary philosopher has said, needs to belong to a local Christian fellowship in order to transcend his fractured humanity.

4. The pastor should magnify the *relevance of faith in life* through his preaching and personal communications with people. A Christian faith which is not workable in life is not a faith at all, but a cruel mockery. The Christian faith summons man to salvation, sustains his daily walk, supports him in trials and suffering, and sees him through the gates of splendor at death. People need a relevant faith in God to grow on, to live by, and to hope with in this age of stress. The pastor who styles his ministry through these objectives is to "make the word of God fully known, the mystery . . . now made manifest to his saints . . . which is Christ in you, the hope of glory"

[21] Dietrich Bonhoeffer, *Life Together,* trans. John W. Doberstein (New York: Harper & Row, 1954); and Ernest Gordon, *Through the Valley of the Kwai* (New York: Harper & Row, 1962).

(Col. 1:25-27). He and his congregation may thus become a redemptive society in society.

3. The "Pastoral" Tasks of Responsible Laymen

How, then, is the laity's role made specific? An American churchman finds it difficult to match his self-image of dynamic, masculine activism with tender shepherding tasks. He reasons that Christ's spirit may work in religious matters but would be ineffective in a tough-minded competitive culture. Thus he partitions off "church affairs" from life's relationships. Such an attitude is typified in a popular magazine account of a World War II nurse in the South Pacific who neglected a wounded serviceman. He had angered her, and her attitude was "Let him die!" Ernest Gordon has written poignantly of prisoner-of-war experiences in the "church without walls" on the bank of the River Kwai in Southeast Asia. There, men literally gave their lives for their friends. It was precisely the removal of "walls of partition" between persons, and between religionists and the world, that concerned Jesus Christ (Eph. 2:13-16). While the church's heart is inclined to God in worship, its eyes must see the suffering world approximately as it is, and its hands must unfold from prayer to service.

I believe that persons can find dignity and meaning in concrete acts of love. So many people are engaged upon a search for meaning in life. The paralyzing pessimism of existentialism, the loss of nerve and breakdown of the self in nihilism, and all types of escapism in world cultures indicate humanity's need for salvation and usefulness. A person's sense of meaning and worth may be found, as Helmut Thielicke has said, in "responsible action, in the *doing* of love, in the engagement. He who would know God and thus break through to the Absolute must first 'do the will of my Father in heaven'."[22] Men must believe that the Christian gospel applies to every concrete issue of life and find joy in its service.

Laymen can perform *pastoral* activities in the church. Opportunities for the care of souls may be found in (1) guiding the mem-

---

[22] Helmut Thielicke, *Nihilism: Its Origin and Nature—with a Christian Answer,* trans. John W. Doberstein (New York: Harper & Row, 1961), p. 162.

bers of a small Bible-study, decision-making, or discussion group; (2) greeting worshipers, receiving newcomers, and supporting visitors in their adjustments to a new place; (3) calling in homes, social welfare centers, and hospitals; (4) corresponding with former members, such as servicemen, college students, those who have moved, and those who are hospitalized in a distant place for an extended period. The prayer ministry of parishioners for their minister, for each other, and for the world reaps immeasurable harvests (John 14:14; Jas. 4:2-3, 5:16).

Some laymen have placed themselves on call for the crises of life in their congregations. One urban church has a Good Samaritan Society composed of men who are pledged to give a helping hand to overburdened persons by day or night. Its members take food into homes where fathers are ill or jobless; furnish transportation to invalids, children, and aging persons who desire to attend church; work with juvenile court officers arranging foster homes for delinquents; visit prisoners; and seek to be serviceable in *preventive* ways through church agencies and community planning. Providing a well-equipped gymnasium, with the services of an athletic director, is at this preventive level of concern.

Retirement may open the door to pastoral activities for numerous men and women. A former civil servant of the government of India confessed: "I had a gentleman's agreement with Jesus Christ, when I met him twenty-eight years ago, that I would serve him in my daily work and give him all of my time upon retirement." One's age influences his or her participation in the church's caring concerns less than such factors as basic temperament, information about needs, time, sensitivity to one's neighbors, and willingness to *do* the truth.

The people of God can also perform pastoral activities in the world. Luther Youngdahl, a Christian statesman, has said: "Lay people in various segments of society are God's messengers for the releasing of grace and power for the healing of human life."[23] Women's gifts for caring are not inferior to those of men, for in

[23] Luther W. Youngdahl, "The Layman's Responsibility in the Mission of the Church," *Religion in Life*, XXXI (Winter, 1961-62), 90.

Christ there is "neither male nor female" but one new humanity, as Paul said. God's people are to reach beyond themselves to others: refugees from war-torn lands, foreign students, displaced families, widows and orphans, service personnel, life's handicapped and retarded citizens, unwed mothers, alcoholics, and those growing old alone.

Sensitive Christians will detect the cries of those who are on the losing side in the struggle for existence. Those who become calloused to humanity's hurt are reminded that God hears man's crying. In Christ "he became their Savior. In all their affliction he was afflicted . . . in his love . . . he redeemed them" (Isa. 63:8-9). Some say that love is an "impossible possibility" in contemporary power-cultures and that justice is love's alternative in the social order. While society requires justice, love is still needed in human life. "We have never yet measured the *justice that is in love*, of which love is the only possible ground, the kind of love that undertakes to win back a lost creation in the only way there is to win it back, the pressure of its own hurt life leaning undefeated against the world."[24] Because God entered vicariously into humanity's hurt, his people are to share the earth's pain, while awaiting the day when there shall be "no more crying."

4. To Be Cared For

There is yet one other aspect of our participation in pastoral care—when we become the object of another's concern. What is it like when life's tide is running out, when things go awry and *we* are the *object* of someone's caring? After all, "patterns of participation" in pastoral care include those tragic moments when we personally need to welcome the healer's hand and to feel the buoyancy of a kinder world. Becoming the object of care—a patient, a jobless man, a bereft person—is not easy, however. Persons who have experienced spurious gifts of friendship, of financial aid, of intimacy, of ideas—whom others have hurt through perverted

[24] Paul Scherer, *For We Have This Treasure* (New York: Harper & Row, 1944), p. 80, emphasis supplied.

generosity—suspect any proffered assistance. They distrust relationships that may hurt them again. Those who have once lived as a patron's pawn or who have suffered the misery of misunderstanding reveal a fatal incapacity to trust a gift. They cannot accept help from well-intentioned men, nor can they trust a gracious Providence.

One angry young man, who had been betrayed by a well-meaning minister, lamented with clenched fists: "I can't trust anyone any more!" Because many generous persons unconsciously obligate the objects of their caring, some persons prefer to suffer alone rather than become beholden to another.

When a man lives at the breaking point, it takes grace on his part to open his wounds and bleed in another's presence. To lay one's soul bare to a minister, a physician, or a friend takes courage. Those who have fought old enemies on familiar battlegrounds so long may actually resent a peacemaker's presence. They are afraid of a new point of view and of becoming involved in deep relationships. While they may long to be understood and accepted for what they are, some prefer old conflicts to new commitments. Yet giving and receiving remain the heart of the Christian gospel. The Incarnation reminds us that acceptance of love from another releases a person from his lonely bondage. "Giving and receiving establishes a community in which there is the acceptance of mutual trust and dependence. Perhaps this is the deeper reason why we are afraid of gifts: to accept a gift from another is to be drawn into a community based not on proving oneself but on mutual forbearance and acceptance in love."[25] The most important things in life are gifts, which we are to trust and to receive.

Robert Frost captured the self-impoverishing style of life in "The Gift Outright." "The land was ours before we were the land's," he wrote of our American heritage. Yet many restrained themselves from receiving the gift.

[25] Charles R. Stinnette, Jr., *Grace and the Searching of Our Heart* (New York: Association Press, 1962), pp. 110-11.

Something we were withholding made us weak
Until we found out that it was ourselves
We were withholding from our land of living
And forthwith found salvation in surrender.[26]

Some feel that a *real* Christian, who has been face to face with
God, need never receive help from any man. Yet, one's God-experi-
ence does not enable him to declare independence from his own
humanity and from the human family. Often shame, cultural snob-
bery, or fear of exposure or reprisal make it difficult for an individual to disclose his spiritual needs to another or to God. But at
least avenues of approach are possible. While every soul has its
mystery, as Dostoevski once wrote, persons do desire strength for
life's pilgrimage. So long as men experience the "peril of hope"
Christian ministers have a starting point, a place to begin.

A white-haired executive, sitting in a handsome office, once
related what it had been like for him to receive help from another.
He had come home from World War I paralyzed, broken in
body and spirit, to die. His elderly mother fed, bathed, and nursed
him for many months. When he was stronger, he went to a government hospital. While there, several miles from the nearest community, a Christian layman who had also been in the war began
visiting him. He told how the man and some young people from
his church came every Sunday afternoon to visit him. They brought
him little gifts and toilet articles. But more important—they gave
him themselves! Through their refreshing moments of worship
and confidential comradeship over the months, he learned to live
again. While his mother and the layman have both been dead
many years, the Christian executive's life has been made rich with
that fragrant memory. In such quiet, noble ways the church cherishes men and offers Christ's healing to them.

III. THE COURAGE TO CARE IN HUMAN RELATIONSHIPS

By now we realize that it takes courage to care, as well as to
share one's suffering with another. *Courage* is that quality which

[26] Robert Frost, *In the Clearing* (New York: Holt, Rinehart & Winston,
1962), p. 31. Used by permission.

keeps one going in the face of danger or discouragement. In pastoral care, courage implies being secure enough to make oneself available to a suffering person in a loving relationship. Our Western culture has exalted the cult of detachment and images of success and happiness, rather than of sacrificial love in human relationships. Persons can protect themselves through indifference or preoccupation, thereby avoiding involvement.

A high-school girl's response to a sermon she heard challenges such detachment. She confessed: "I have found many places in my own life where I keep a secret store of indifference as a sort of self-protection. . . . It takes courage to care. Caring is dangerous; it leaves you open to hurt and to looking a fool; and perhaps it is because they have been hurt so often that people are afraid to care."[27] Caring, which impels a person toward another human being in whom he *may* lose himself, involves a risk. When one loves another person and invests in the relationship, that cherished person can injure him far more than someone whom he does not cherish. Those who are afraid to be hurt do not risk caring, for it is always costly business.

Caring is both *preventive* and *therapeutic,* if trouble comes. Love invests heavily in the welfare of family members, for example—bearing, believing, hoping, and enduring all things (I Cor. 13:7). Many persons have been spared suffering by the preventive power of wise love. On the other hand, love listens with a delicate ear to the often disguised signals which people who want desperately to be heard and understood beam our way. What are those around us really trying to say with their words *and* ways? Bruder has said that "if we maintain our distance, it will only be to perpetuate the shut-up-ness of our deeply troubled people until it must become the demonic spoken of by Kierkegaard and find itself expressed as 'shut-up-ness unfreely revealed.' "[28]

The family is potentially the primary caring community in American culture. The family's strategic role in the spiritual vitality,

[27] Quoted in Elton Trueblood, *The Yoke of Christ* (New York: Harper & Row, 1958), p. 73.

[28] Ernest E. Bruder, "Having the Courage To Talk," *Pastoral Psychology,* XIII (May, 1962), 31.

mental health, and social responsibiilty of individuals is now commonly recognized. Sigmund Freud first brought the *dynamics* of family relations to the world's attention with his psychoanalytic medical practice and research. The primacy of the child's early years of development claimed his chief interest. While Freud's depth psychology was limited by its biological and mechanical models, his theories of dynamic human drives have made an original contribution to Western thought. His dual-drive hypothesis of the life-instinct (in which "sex" became the representative of the life force) and the death-instinct (manifested by aggression and death tendencies) has been incorporated into our synoptic understanding of personality. While churchmen do not agree with all of Freud's claims, they have been informed by some of his clinical observations, notably in family development.

Intrafamily relationships have the paradoxical power of preventing and producing tragic situations in life. Parents who truly love their children will attempt to "train up a child in the way he should go" through positive guidance, with the objective of self-discipline in view. Children learn what they are *to be* and *not to be* first from their own parents, then from their peers, their ministers and teachers, the laws of the community, and life in the "human jungle." The church, like the school, "has its opportunity to influence developing human lives *after* the basic habits, attitudes, and content of conscience have been acquired in the family."[29] Because parents are a child's first "priests," the home is central in personality development, in moral education, and in the socialization process.

It is now accepted generally that a child's earliest images and interpretations of God depend upon the symbolic resources of his parent relationships. John Baillie, Scottish theologian, has testified to God's revelation through parental love in his childhood home. "God's earliest disclosure of His reality to my infant soul was mediated to me by the words and deeds of my Christian parents."[30]

[29] Charles E. Conover, *Moral Education in Family, School, and Church* (Philadelphia: Westminster Press, 1962), p. 129.

[30] John Baillie, *Our Knowledge of God* (New York: Charles Scribner's Sons, 1939), p. 5.

From his earliest memory, Baillie felt the claim of a higher power which had authority over his life. His parents, who lived under this authority, he credited with making God real in his life. Those who know of his life, labor, and influence for Christ's cause will recognize the preventive ministry exercised by those parents.

With every child's need for love, security, consistency, and discipline in mind, let us look into the soul of a boy who at the age of ten was placed in a home for dependent children. The lad's mother had become separated from his alcoholic father when the boy was six years old. The woman was forced to institutionalize her son by court order, following repeated episodes of delinquency. On one occasion, he shared his frustrations and future plans with a Christian "parent substitute" whom we shall call Mr. P.

NED: I have heard several times that if you really want to go to college you can do it. It's a lot harder here because we don't have any encouragement from teachers, dorm parents, or leaders, or anything. Do you think I can go? I really want to go. (Silence.)

MR. P.: Why do you think that it will be harder for you? (Pause.) Will college really be worth the effort?

NED: You see, it's this way. I want to go real bad. I've heard that it takes real good grades. You know that those stupid dorm parents make us get at least a C or they give us licks with that paddle! Some day I'm going to hit them back. I wish I could! . . . You know, I hate this place more than anything. Some of the boys run away from here, but I'm not, because you always get caught. Everyone in this school hates the place. We didn't want to be taken away from our parents; they made us come here. One day I'm going to get out of here and leave for good. I'll never come back. I guess that will be in a few years, because I only have two more years in high school. This is why I'm asking you about college. When you finish high school you have to go to work or go to college. I really want to go to college.

MR. P.: Ned, you say that you want to go to college when you finish high school . . . .

NED: Yes, I want to get through with it as soon as possible. I want to make better grades, but I'm scared to. You see, when you make better grades or make too good grades, the other boys will hate you. The dorm parents let you have more privileges and the other boys begin to hate you . . . I'm scared to make too good grades because they will fight with me. (He told of playing football and of the coach's suggestion of a possible scholarship.)

MR. P.: Ned, you seem to have a real interest in college. This is good, but whether or not you go to college will in large measure be up to you.

NED: I feel that this is what I need, but it'll be real hard for me. I've heard several people who have come out here with their great beliefs and who want to help us poor things. They said that they would help me through college, but I hate them! They think they are so much better than we are. We all hate them. I wish those old snobs would not even come out here! . . . Really, we don't want their pity. We know that we don't come from their old "good homes," but we're just as good as they are . . .

Serious questions arise about Ned's future when we consider the emotional load he carries and his hostility toward life, himself, and all helping hands. A number of instructive things are revealed in this interview.

1. We have a glimpse of what parental failure can do. A child who is denied his own parents finds it difficult to accept the legacy of friendship from his peers, authority figures, or those who clearly are interested in him.

2. When love is lacking in a child's life he is insecure, fears rejection by everyone, and mistrusts himself. Even as we deplore his plight we admire his pluck, his desire to amount to something in life.

3. Ned needed someone with whom he could share his inwardness and way of thinking about persons and problems, someone who would inspire his best in life. An older friend who dared to listen inspired Ned's courage to talk, to transcend his shut-up-ness. While young people need peer friendships and approval desperately, this lad manifested a need for an adult friend. He "talked out" his anxiety with a young adult who would understand his hostile feelings toward "old snobs." While he rejected patronage, Ned longed for an adult guarantor who had a solid and respected

place in society. This is a clue which guides the layman's caring concerns.

4. A love larger than all of life's hostility, fear, aggression, and suspicion is needed to accept this burdened lad and to show him the Christian way of living. God's love, expressed through mature persons and through his Holy Spirit, can illuminate such a darkened life and inspire nobility in his soul.

5. While it takes courage for Christians to care in *words*, more persons are needed who will care wisely in their *ways* of living in the human community. This is something of what is meant by the startling New Testament statement: "Faith by itself, if it has no works, is dead" (Jas. 2:17).

Conclusion

In summary, we have explored the New Testament concept of the church as a redemptive society and the failure of many modern churches to achieve this *caring* ideal. The doctrine of the priesthood of believers was examined carefully and its implications for the *pastoral* roles of clergy and laymen were noted candidly. The performance and perversion of Christian concern were demonstrated clinically at the family level to insure that the principle of corporate ministry might find acceptance not merely in correct doctrine but in the doing of love. In the following chapter we shall consider the pastor's shaping influence upon the entire church's ministry through preaching and worship.

SUGGESTED READING

Bonhoeffer, Dietrich. *The Cost of Discipleship.* Translated by R. H. Fuller. 2d ed. New York: The Macmillan Co., 1959 (paperback). A classic testimony composed during the time of the author's participation in the German resistance movement. Bonhoeffer was executed by the Nazis on April 9, 1945, at the age of thirty-nine.

Gilkey, Langdon. *How the Church Can Minister to the World Without Losing Itself.* New York: Harper & Row, 1964. Answers Bonhoeffer enthusiasts who assume the possibility of a "secular gospel."

Kraemer, Hendrik. *A Theology of the Laity*. Philadelphia: Westminster Press, 1958. An examination of the Protestant concept of the corporate priesthood of believers by a Continental theologian well acquainted with Reformation source materials.

Marty, Martin E. *The New Shape of American Religion*. New York: Harper & Row, 1958. Also *Second Chance for American Protestants*. New York: Harper & Row, 1963. Historical-sociological appraisals of the religious situation in America, with a Christian challenge for Protestants and others.

O'Connor, Elizabeth. *Call to Commitment*. New York: Harper & Row, 1963. The story of the Church of the Saviour and its unusual ministry in Washington, D.C. A caring congregation at work.

Trueblood, D. Elton. *The Company of the Committed*. New York: Harper & Row, 1961. A forceful, popular treatment of disciplined churchmanship addressed primarily to laymen and church leaders.

Webber, George W. *The Congregation in Mission*. Nashville, Tenn.: Abingdon Press, 1964. Pastor Webber reports the exciting work at East Harlem Protestant Parish. Cf. his *God's Colony in Man's World*, ibid., 1960.

CHAPTER 5

🙚❦🙚

PASTORAL ASPECTS OF
PREACHING AND WORSHIP

IN CHAPTER 4 certain implications of the corporate priesthood of believers for the pastoral ministry of the church were explored and illustrated. We noted that the Christian person witnesses to his love of God and neighbor in those areas of life where his time is actually spent, and that the pastor prompts, informs, guides, and supports the layman's life in the world. Accordingly, the pastor of a ministering church cannot betray his role of leadership. Yet he is obligated to develop a comprehensive view of Christian service.

John McNeill has written: "The cure of souls is never merely a *method,* even a method derived from a doctrine, or a task for certain hours in the week, but . . . it involves *both* the faith we live by *and* all our daily activities and contacts."[1] The pastor's ministry sustains the peoples' ministries within the structures of family and church life and the orders of society. While each member shares the church's ministry, the sharing will be unequal. The pastor's leadership is a vocation of necessity, created in the churches under the providence of God. He facilitates the release of each member's talents and energies, both for the individual's fulfillment and for the furtherance of God's kingdom.

---

[1] John McNeill, *A History of the Cure of Souls* (New York: Harper & Row, 1951), p. 87, emphasis supplied.

The purpose of this chapter is to (1) distinguish *how* life is undergirded and Christian service is informed through the pastor's public and private ministries, (2) characterize the pastoral preacher, and (3) focus the shepherding concerns of worship and preaching. The chronology of pastoral care flows from worship to calling, from preaching to counseling, from group work to personal ministry. In turn, the private ministry informs and vitalizes preaching and worship. Frequently a congregant departs from the house of worship with a desire to talk with the preacher about his message. Such a one may say: "You certainly spoke to me today, Pastor; I would like to talk with you about that subject sometime." A supply minister once preached on the theme of the daily providence of God. At the close of the service a woman who had been helped by the sermon said, "I certainly needed that message. Tomorrow we are moving to Colorado. This church and community have meant much to me and my family. We need to feel that we are moving within God's providence." Thus worship leadership and preaching either repel or beckon persons to open their hearts in personal conversation.

I. THE PUBLIC AND PRIVATE MINISTRIES

Christian history clarifies the bipolar dimensions of the care of souls in (1) the preservation of spiritual health (preventive or protective care), and (2) the restoration of health if and when dysfunction comes (therapeutic care).[2] When clergymen turn all their energies to one of these dimensions of pastoral work, they inevitably neglect the other. Both levels of concern are essential. Preventive care is linked primarily (though not exclusively) to the pastor's public ministry and to the people's responsibilities for extending the Christian faith into the structures of society.

The *preventive level* of concern is essential in order to avoid simplistic solutions to life's hazards and crises, many of which are produced by grave social problems. Pastoral care of the individual

---

[2] The classic pastoral functions in Christian history, according to studies by William A. Clebsch and Charles A. Jaekle, include: healing, sustaining, guiding, and reconciling. See Part III of *Pastoral Care in Historical Perspective* (Englewood Cliffs, N.J.: Prentice-Hall, 1964).

person cannot be divorced from Christian strategy for family life and for a truly responsible society.[3] The pastor befriends those talented members of his congregation who are engaged in the helping professions. He supports those who seek the alleviation of social injustices and the prevention of crime and inhumanity. In short, he undergirds persons who seek to live usefully in the world. One of the minister's greatest responsibilities is to encourage the gifted members of his congregation to use their talents and strengths more effectively.

In an essay on education in America, John W. Gardner refers to "the discovery of talent in unexpected places," to releasing "the energies of every human being," and to "toning up the whole society" as individuals are liberated and motivated to turn their talents toward constructive purposes.[4] Pastoral care participates in the drama of "hidden gifts discovered," and in the conservation of human talent for Christ's cause in the earth. Encouraging persons who are potential centers of strength and witness requires as much pastoral imagination and skill as does ministering to persons in special need.

The *therapeutic* or *healing-supporting* level of pastoral care is primarily (though not exclusively) a private ministry with individuals or small groups. Those who serve in Christ's stead extend the Christian *koinōnia* to persons and families who suffer life's tragic failures and often inalterable situations. As a bridge-person between God and man, the minister shares their private worlds in face-to-face meetings, through prayer, and in personal counseling periods. In any case, the lines of his ministry must be extended to include both his public discourses as bearer of the divine-human conversation and his private conversations with individuals. The

[3] A design for responsible family life is illustrated in C. W. Scudder, *The Family in Christian Perspective* (Nashville, Tenn.: Broadman Press, 1962); and for society in Walter G. Muelder, *Foundations of the Responsible Society* (Nashville, Tenn.: Abingdon Press, 1959). Cf. Edgar N. Jackson, *The Pastor and His People* (New York: Channel Press, 1963), pp. 211-13.

[4] John W. Gardner, *Excellence* (New York: Harper & Row, 1961; Colophon paperback edition, 1962), pp. 16-17, 33, 135-44. See Charles F. Kemp, "Some Next Steps in Pastoral Care Literature and Research," *Pastoral Psychology*, XIII (Jan., 1963), 59-60.

minister's spiritual directorship, traced here and in the next chapter, both includes and transcends his therapeutic skill as a counselor, described in Chapter 7.

Admittedly, the pastoral aspects of preaching and worship are of an order different from formal pastoral counseling. Yet both counseling and preaching are concerned with motivating inner change and spiritual growth. Some writers have sought to separate these functions by viewing the preacher as a *prophet* "on God's side" and the pastor as a *priest* "on man's side."[5] Such a false dichotomy cannot be demonstrated from biblical theology. The New Testament bishop or pastor was both prophet and priest as he celebrated the worship of God and interpreted man's life in the light of the Word of God. The testimony of the earliest Christian community in Jerusalem contained both prophetic utterance and "the apostles' teaching and fellowship . . . breaking of bread and the prayers" (Acts 2:14-36, 41-42). The pastoral preacher thus renders a significant service by addressing the personal needs of people from within the categories of the Christian faith.

II. THE SERVANT OF THE WORD

In the memorable phrasing of H. H. Farmer, the Christian pastor is a servant of the Word of God. He is God's gift to the church, responsible for establishing conversations between God and men

[5] Russell Dicks oversimplifies the matter: "Preaching is clergy centered; pastoral work is parishioner centered. It is difficult to bring the two together but it is possible." *Pastoral Work and Personal Counseling* (rev. ed.; New York: The Macmillan Co., 1955), p. 143. Hiltner distinguishes "communicating" as a perspective upon pastoral work of a different order from "shepherding." However, he affirms that the communicating function may be viewed from a shepherding perspective. *Preface to Pastoral Theology* (Nashville, Tenn.: Abingdon Press, 1958), pp. 175-97. In his 1964, revised edition of *The Christian Pastor* (Philadelphia: Westminster Press, 1951), Oates wisely moves from an earlier, restrictive concept of "therapeutic preaching" to Charles F. Kemp's term—"life-situation preaching." Cf. the latter's *Life-Situation Preaching* (St. Louis: Bethany Press, 1956).

My own concept focuses the shepherding perspective upon all types of preaching and is akin to that of Hiltner and Kemp. "It is a point of view we are advocating, not a separate type or kind of preaching. In this sense, a doctrinal sermon, an expository sermon, an evangelistic sermon, or an ethical sermon can also be pastoral" (Charles F. Kemp, *Pastoral Preaching* [St. Louis: Bethany Press, 1963], p. 12).

under the Holy Spirit's guidance. As "bearer of the divine-human conversation," he leads the dialogue of worship and extends the relationships present in worship into "the sacrament of life."[6] The preacher addresses individuals *and* a congregation, each with separate interests and needs, yet with corporate concerns as the body of Christ. He may classify one sermon "doctrinal," another "evangelistic," a third "ethical"; yet he perceives *pastoral* dimensions and implications in every sermon.

Fosdick, the master of life-situation preaching in this century, once described preaching as counseling on a group scale. While preaching is much more than *that*, Fosdick was right when he determined that "every sermon should have for its main business the head-on constructive meeting of some problem which [is] puzzling minds, burdening consciences, [and] distracting lives." Furthermore, he realized that "no sermon which so met a real human difficulty, with light to throw on it and help to win a victory over it, could possibly be futile."[7] The development of Protestant lay centers in America testifies to the remoteness and irrelevance to life-situations of much contemporary pulpit work. There is a widespread feeling that clergymen have lost the capacity to provide help for their members regarding the critical issues they daily confront.

In the research by Fairchild and Wynn to which reference has been made, those surveyed placed "Sermons and Congregational Worship" at the top of a list of the church-related experiences that had most helped them to understand themselves in family relationships. Their reflected opinions in face-to-face discussion, however, minimized preaching and thus qualified their spontaneous selection of preaching and worship on a list of items provided for them.[8] Some interviewees expressed a desire for a prophetic word from God concerning the situations which they were facing in daily life.

---

[6] Douglas Horton, *The Meaning of Worship* (New York: Harper & Row, 1959), p. 72.

[7] Harry E. Fosdick, *The Living of These Days* (New York: Harper & Row, 1956), p. 94.

[8] Roy W. Fairchild and J. C. Wynn, *Families in the Church: A Protestant Survey* (New York: Association Press, 1961), pp. 181-82.

This typifies the need for perceptive pastoral preaching, addressed to man's conscious concerns and unconscious strivings. There has been some discussion in the current theological revival about the "point of contact" in preaching—what in man is being addressed by the sermon. Relevance in preaching cannot be determined by human criteria alone. It is the Spirit of God, using the preacher's wisdom and the divine Word, that makes our preaching effective.

Like the military chaplain speaking to his company on the eve of a strike against the enemy, the preacher must be prepared to share the risks of life on the morrow with his people. Leviathan, their formidable foe, awaits them in the arena of life. Each soldier is ready, yet before the day's battle is done those who remain will bear the burdens of the wounded and weak. Some fighters become shell-shocked in their exposure to the terrors of warfare. Others are overcome by battle fatigue. So it is in life. All do not face the same journey in the week ahead, but each member of the congregation needs assurance for what a day may bring forth.

Some clergymen assume that if preaching is biblical it will be relevant; that if the Word of God is proclaimed it will find its mark in some needy heart. This sounds feasible theoretically, but such reasoning may fail congregants in their search for a better way of life. Alan Richardson's *The Bible in the Age of Science* (S.C.M. Press, 1961), helps us to answer *the bifocal issue* of all relevant interpretation: "What *did* the Bible mean originally?" and "What *does* it mean today?" Despite the preacher's concern, the person for whom a certain message is intended may miss the whole idea, or he may be absent on the day of "his" sermon. In a recent account of a lawyer's suicide the reporter said: "Mr. S. plunged to his death at 11 o'clock, Sunday morning—the exact time he had an appointment with his family to be in church." The sermon intended for that depressed man on that particular day was posthumous, not relevant, preaching. It came too late.

A preacher is addressing his congregation pastorally when he carries the burden of the Lord and of man into the dialogue of the sanctuary. His objective is to drive a shaft of healing light into the cancerous tissues of human existence. He becomes a spiritual mentor of men precisely when burdens are lifted, guilt is relieved, high purposes are forged, and hope in rekindled in the human heart. On a larger scale, he may try to turn the tide in the life of a congregation that has lost its way—become listless or introverted or indifferent about life's great issues. For example, in an effort to stir his church to new devotion one minister delivered a course of doctrinal sermons on the church—its origin, nature, true head, ministry, and message. Under the general theme of "The Fellowship of Confession," his sermons reflected profound pastoral intent.

What then is the content of pastoral preaching to be? Nothing less than the Word of God! It is precisely of thin, superficial sermons that laymen are weary. As they gather in worship to be reminded of that unseen world of the spirit, people need to hear of "a God who does things for us, anticipates us, comes in quest of us, and carries us all the way."[9] Yet the interpreter of the Word has a great responsibility to God and to his people. He must not misrepresent the divine-human situation through superficial utterances or misuse of sacred symbols. Preachers prostitute religion to unworthy purposes who offer God as an antidote to anxiety or as a sure source of strength to obtain personal success in the secular order. God's Word comes as a gift, but also as a claim upon men's lives, requiring obedience.

The servant of the Word is to be a man of the people, a man of the Book, and a man of God. Without God's presence in his life the preacher has nothing of ultimate worth to offer those who hear his words. Jesus reminded the disciples, "Apart from me you can do nothing" (John 15:5). A pastoral preacher who would lead others to sense the presence of God must be at home in the divine presence himself. The burdened prophet prayed of his wife Agnes in Ibsen's tragedy

BRAND:

> Then return, with face aglow
> From His Presence, fair and free.

[9] D. M. Baillie, *Out of Nazareth* (Edinburgh: Saint Andrew Press, 1958), p. 15.

> Bear His glory down to me
> Worn with battle thrust and throe.[10]

When men are struck dumb with grief, baffled by betrayal, crushed in their own clandestineness, stricken with illness, or enslaved by guilt, they need the assurance of a God who knows and cares for them.

Pastoral preaching is an event of dialogue in which the minister speaks for God *and* for his people. He takes into account the audience's doubts, feelings of guilt, and predicaments, and permits persons to speak or to *feel back* in his sermons. Speaking for the congregation enhances the possibility of meeting their real needs with God's good news. The preacher bears responsibility for including his people, not alone in sermon delivery but in sermon preparation as well. Do they really understand the processes of his preaching craft, the quiet struggles of soul that go on in the minister's workshop? Dietrich Ritschl, a Barthian interpreter of preaching, suggests that the sermon is not the sole property of the preacher. It belongs to the congregation as a whole.[11] Imaginative ways of informing his congregation of his sermon preparation procedures may be devised, particularly in casual conversations and in formal teaching periods. The congregation can be trained to study biblical texts along with the pastor and to devise specific applications of divine truth for daily life. Ultimately, the preacher's goal is to be not cleverly contemporary but eternally relevant.

III. PASTORAL CONCERNS IN WORSHIP

The servant of the Word addresses persons in the context of worship. The church that ministers for the world's sake in *mission*, and for its own sake in *nurture and caring*, must also minister for

---

[10] Quoted in Paul R. Clifford, *The Pastoral Calling* (London: Carey Kingsgate Press, 1959), p. 47.

[11] Dietrich Ritschl, *A Theology of Proclamation* (Richmond, Va.: John Knox Press, 1960), p. 155. Gene E. Bartlett offers proposals for including the congregation in sermon preparation in *The Audacity of Preaching* (New York: Harper & Row, 1962). See Charles A. Trentham's treatment of the Colossian letter in relation to the present space age (*The Shepherd of the Stars* [Nashville, Tenn.: Broadman Press, 1962]).

God's sake in *worship*. I have said that a caring congregation, concerned at its best with both God and men, must renew its life and nurture its service in the adoration of God. The pastoral perspective of worship is concerned with the motivation and response of individuals both in church and in life. In Christian worship the believer returns to the upstream region of his life, participates in eternity, sounds the "Te Deum" of the church of the ages, faces the eschatological dimensions of existence, and consecrates himself anew in service.

The constellation of worship locates God at the center of all existence. The orbits of life move about him as planets orbit about the sun. Certain theologians have conceived God in a category "beyond personality," as being an ontological "ultimate reality" concealed in mystery as the "hidden God." Yet in Christian worship we remember that the God and Father of our Lord Jesus Christ has visited his people person-to-person with the gift of eternal life. Christ, while offering individual salvation, created a fellowship of new beings—the church—a community of memory and of hope. The pastor and his people have this "treasure in earthen vessels, to show that the transcendent power belongs to God and not to us." It is not to some mystical, ineffable light that worshipers respond, but to "the light of the knowledge of the glory of God in the face of Christ" (II Cor. 4:6, 7).

1. The Conduct of Worship

The role of the authorized, usually ordained, worship leader has varied in the branches of Christendom from age to age. In liturgical churches the priest celebrates the service as God's representative almost impersonally.[12] While the biblical witness to worship is not liturgical, but rather theological and disciplinary, the celebration of worship and the rites of Christian baptism and the Lord's Supper are taken for granted. In such informal communions as the Society of Friends there is varied shape and action in relative formlessness. Each congregant is a minister and testifies as he or

---

[12] See the significant study, Dom Gregory Dix, *The Shape of the Liturgy* (Naperville, Ill.: Alec R. Allenson, 1960).

she is prompted by the Spirit in an otherwise silent service. And in free, nonliturgical churches the preacher is central as God's spokesman, in some instances almost as a performer before an audience.[13] Worship, however, is more than a performance.

Whatever the particular tradition, the weakness of much Protestant worship lies in its failure to be a truly corporate action, moving toward a single objective. Worship should be, in Dix's words, a "united and uniting action" toward God, a response to his judgment and grace and a stimulus to serviceable living in the world. The portrait of a congregation at worship—the introit, hymns, prayers, offering, and sermon—is not a "still" but a motion picture. "Deep calls unto deep" in the *call* to worship, and each congregant is an active participant in the *service* of worship. He shares the reading of scripture, the pastoral prayer, the ministry of giving, and the message from God's Word. With the benediction ringing in his heart, he departs blessed and determined to be a blessing. The worship leader's specific role will be determined by his particular community of faith, of order, of symbols, of language, of festivals, and of living. Yet each leader is to include all congregants in the service as far as possible.

Some suggestions may be made which have general application regardless of the church's sociocultural situation, size, constituency, and particular communion.

1. The Christian pastor is to *instruct his people concerning their joint roles in the celebration of worship.* One pastor, for example, instructs the congregation periodically concerning the church ordinances. Then, during baptism or the Lord's Supper service the people feel a personal sense of responsibility for true dialogue with God. Informed congregants sense the rich heritage and symbolic significance of these cherished modes of remembrance and hope. Even as Christian persons experience God, not just "something," in such covenantal moments together, they feel that God is experiencing them, too. The ordinance becomes a token of one's gratitude, a mode of remembrance, and a pledge of hope. It is a

---

[13] For background on worship in the free church tradition, see Gaines S. Dobbins, *The Church at Worship* (Nashville, Tenn.: Broadman Press, 1963).

living covenant, ever new, between God and man *and* between man and man. One church, on Race Relations Sunday, used brown, white, and black bread for the Lord's Supper as an added symbol of all persons for whom Christ died. Thus people learn from the practice of worship.

Instruction regarding worship can also be carried on through family education and with children's groups at church. The attitude of reverence, for instance, is *caught* as well as taught and is demonstrated in the acts of life as well as in the house of God. Children learn to love God because he first loved them; thus, they worship him in adoration and awe but not in guilt and fear. Many clergymen design a children's hymn, story, and prayer into the service as a special token of their concern for everyone in worship.

To affirm periodically the manifestation and mystery of God and the sacredness of life refreshes God's people "on their toilsome way." The ground of the sacred is involved with an order of things in which the Christian finds himself in the presence of Someone whom he can know only in part and yet can trust with complete devotion. Christian worship, theologically oriented and psychologically conditioned, calls for a verdict from each worshiper which will be carried into the daily round of life. Accordingly, the pastor will recognize the essential unity of all elements in the service and will prompt each congregant toward a genuine experience of worship.

2. This implies that the pastor will *recognize individual differences within his congregation and remember the participants' concerns in corporate worship.* Such knowledge requires imagination, courage, and sensitivity to persons. People come to worship *from life* with differences in age, sex, social roles, education, inherent capacity, health, motivation, spiritual need, cultural climate, interest, and awareness. They return *to that life* following the worship service either burdened or blessed. At the close of a service, upon one occasion, a woman asked the opportunity to make a public statement. She shocked the minister by confessing that she had been most critical of him to numerous persons in the church. He had had no idea that the conclusion of the service would

go that way, but was grateful for her moment of truth. Of course, each person present bears his own responsibility to worship the Father "in spirit and truth" (John 4:23).

3. The pastor acknowledges that *preaching occurs in a context of worship; it is not an end in itself*. The vision of God, not man, is central in worship! The prayers—personal and corporate—open the people's hearts to the God of their fathers, to the grace of Jesus Christ, and the renewing presence of the Holy Spirit. The hymns, Bible lessons, anthems, offering, and ordinances inspire worshipers' participant attitudes and responsive actions. The centrality of the Word proclaimed in worship affirms God's gracious action in behalf of, and constant claim upon, the worshiper.[14]

Preaching in the biblical tradition was frequently a homily (*homilia*)—a discussion of or conversation upon a religious subject. It had the nature of a discourse by a man of God with men who themselves wished to communicate with God. Yet, as a Lyman Beecher lecturer once said, "The only way in which man can talk to God is with his whole self, the whole living, acting self. Anything less is taking the name of God in vain."[15] It is to this dialectic of church and world, faith and life, that the pastoral preacher and his people must give serious consideration.

4. Pastor and people will attempt, constructively and imaginatively, to *relate their communion with God in worship to their conversations with men in society*. In Book XII of *The City of God*, Augustine wrote that "the two cities (the earthly and the heavenly, to wit) . . . are in this present world commingled, and as it were entangled together." The Christian is a citizen of two worlds, constantly threatened with the loss of the sacred, especially in this technical age. Gabriel Marcel, a contemporary philosopher, has said:

> In a world where technology is given absolute primacy, there inevitably develops a process of desacralization which attacks

---

[14] Donald Macleod, *Word and Sacrament: A Preface to Preaching and Worship* (Englewood Cliffs, N.J.: Prentice-Hall, 1960), discusses preaching within the context of worship, pp. 93-118.

[15] Horton, *op. cit.*, p. 74.

life and all its manifestations, . . . especially the family and everything connected with it.

The only way one can hope to return toward the sacred is by turning away from the world, in order to find once again that simplicity . . . as well as the intimacy which is the privileged ground of the sacred.[16]

Marcel calls such turning from the world "conversion," not in the confessional sense, but in the value-judgment perspective of sensing once again what is vital in life. Indeed, worship points both to Christian conversion as decision and to the Christian life as the vocation of the people of God.

2. The Place of Worship

The second pastoral concern in worship that I shall mention is the *place* of worship, which is of a different order than the foregoing considerations. Modern ministers need to perceive clearly the function of architecture in religious experience. Something of the spirit and soul of a congregation is revealed in the design of its church building: its aspirations, doubts, reverence, symbolic life, and sense of mission. Steel, glass, and stone, shaped into meaningful substance, have the capacity to convey the propriate strivings of man and the steadfast love of God.

Max Weber has said that we live in a disenchanted world, in which matter is only matter and form is only form. Glass is glass, steel is steel, and stone is stone in our utilitarian culture. Modern church building materials seldom appear to point beyond themselves to God at the center of life. Church buildings are intended to be functional, even artistic, but there is a notable lack of unity in contemporary church architecture. Pastors and members of church building committees should remember that "in religious architecture, it is not stone and steel we are trying to reveal . . . but the transcendent, the invisible reality, even God."[17] A congregation's house of worship is a clue to its God-concept and a key to its own identity.

[16] Gabriel Marcel, "The Sacred in a Technological Age," *Theology Today,* XIX (Apr., 1962), 36-37.

[17] Samuel H. Miller, "Sacred Space in Secular Age," *Theology Today* XIX (July, 1962), 216.

Churches in suburbia, housing upper-middle-class congregations, reflect architectural dysfunction as frequently as do inner-city and mission-type churches meeting in former stores, lodge halls, and office buildings. The church is no longer the central architectural shape upon the American landscape; it has been dwarfed by skyscrapers and crowded by shopkeepers. Whether simple or ornate as to cost and style, church architecture should express the reality of divine revelation and human redemption.

A pastor once received a distraught young woman into his study who a few minutes before had contemplated leaping to her death from a bridge. "I looked from the swirling water below up to the tower of your church," she confessed, "and I wondered *what* was beneath that cross." A church's architecture spoke to a potential suicide's despondency and became an avenue of escape from death. The building is more than an impersonal machine. It should mirror man's struggles in existence, his highest longings, and God's gracious help in man's time of need. Some churches have great centers for education and recreation; others are modest halls of worship only. Architecture need not be ornate in order to communicate a church's character and theological conviction or to facilitate the varieties of its functional life.

I myself stand within the Free Church tradition, in which the central focus of worship is upon the Word proclaimed and upon the ordinances celebrated. I am sympathetic with Samuel Miller's suggestion that architecture dramatizes the dynamic action of God and man in worship and should not detract from this ministry. "As a Protestant . . . I should like to ask for a church in which space symbolizes an active sanctity, reveals the moving power of grace, surprises us with its singular beauty embracing a rich content of meaning. . . . It should speak with a profound simplicity of order . . . for in simplicity there is rest and joy. It should permit the natural exercise of whatever liturgy the Church uses."[18] The church building, designed for worship, will also facilitate the educational, administrative, and small group life of the church.

[18] *Ibid.*, p. 223. Cf. Karl Barth, "Protestantism and Architecture," *ibid.*, p. 272. See also Frank Stagg, *New Testament Theology* (Nashville, Tenn.: Broadman Press, 1962), pp. 204-49, 266-68, 293-96.

From a pastoral perspective, the place of a church's meeting and the symbols of its sacred life should bring order to man's chaotic existence. The elevated ceiling of its sanctuary should symbolize the majesty of God and man's highest aspirations of faith. The materials—glass, wood, tapestry, and stone—should convey the tenderness of God, reassure man of his presence, and inspire each worshiper to reach beyond his own narrow limits. A church's doors should extend an abiding invitation to passers-by to move from life's chill routine into a house of wondrous miracles. From its sturdy steps departing worshipers should go to persons in need of God in the world, who are to be ministered unto even at great cost.

IV. THE PASTORAL FOCUS IN PREACHING

Christian preaching remains the most nearly normative activity of all Protestantism. Proclamation has a unique place in the world. While the "word of the cross" has always been "folly" to some, Christian ministers are under orders to herald the message of God in contemporary society (I Cor. 1:18-21, 9:16; II Tim. 4:2). Many preachers, influenced by C. H. Dodd's *The Apostolic Preaching and Its Developments,* have concentrated upon *kerygma* (proclamation of the central gospel events) and *paraclesis* (exhortation) and have thereby neglected *homilia* (discussion of some theological subject) and *didache* (teaching). To the extent that this is true Dodd has rendered us a disservice, for persons need all levels of Christian discourse. And proclamation has pastoral implications, for it focuses truth upon individual persons.

A contemporary interpreter, Roy Pearson, has proposed a four-fold purpose of preaching which parallels Dodd's scheme: "To celebrate the wonderful works of God; to contend for the faith delivered to the saints; to fill the hungry with good things; and to speak unto the children of Israel, that they go forward."[19] Pearson suggests that ideally every sermon ought to be a proclamation of

[19] Roy Pearson, *The Preacher: His Purpose and Practice* (Philadelphia: Westminster Press, 1963), of which one chapter appears as "The Purpose of Preaching," *Religion in Life,* XXXII (Spring, 1963), cf. p. 278. See also pp. 267-78.

the total gospel. Yet he confesses wisely that the gospel is too vast to be encompassed by a thousand sermons. Pastoral preaching, directed toward filling "the hungry with good things" and encouraging "the children of Israel," must be informed by "the wonderful works of God." Whatever the focus in a particular sermon might be, that "God was in Christ reconciling the world unto himself" is determinative for all preaching for all time.

The Christian preacher's *pastoral* concern is to interpret man's life in the light of God's Word. Human existence is viewed in the context of salvation history and life's great realities. He is concerned not merely to mirror the demonic depths of life destitute of hope, but to illuminate human darkness and despair with the light of life. The two poles of his preaching are the Word of God and the hearers before him, eternal truth and man's fragile life-in-history. Herein lies the validity and wisdom of life-situation preaching.

On one occasion I was in the congregation of Riverside Church in New York City when the pastor, Robert J. McCracken, preached on "The Quest for Religious Certainty." The biblical text involved the experience of the woman of Sychar who addressed her doubt to Jesus Christ at Jacob's well one noonday: "I know that Messiah is coming (he who is called Christ); when he comes, he will show us all things" (John 4:25). In the background was a recent air disaster in Colorado, caused by a bomb explosion. A boy had sabotaged the airship, killing all persons aboard, in order to murder his own mother and collect some insurance. All Americans had been shocked by the affair. The members of that great congregation needed certainty themselves! Pastor McCracken told of the necessity and universality of man's religious quest, its paradox in that Christ did not show us *all* things, and the certainty springing from a faith-love relationship with the living God. An expository sermon with a pastoral intent countered human fear, tragedy, and sin and offered certitude in Christ.

Or consider the message, "The Discipline of Disillusionment," preached by Wayne E. Oates to a national radio audience. He interpreted the "shaken world and unshaken kingdom" passage in Hebrews 12:26-29, as the need to have human illusions and doubts shaken to the foundations in order that "what cannot be shaken may remain." This was illustrated variously—illusions of marriage that must *go* before an "unshakeable covenant that rests in God" can be forged; disillusionments in the business world, in friendship, politics, and in love that must be disciplined. He concluded thus: "The unshakeableness of [God's] Kingdom is made more apparent than ever in the presence of the fragility of our own little schemes. The brightness of his hope is made more luminous in the darkness of our despair. The end result of our submission to the discipline of disillusionment is that we can give thanks for a Kingdom that cannot be shaken and offer to God acceptable worship with reverence and awe."[20] Such pastoral interpreters fill "the hungry with good things," so that they are nourished with the Word of God and the desire is stirred to live again.

Each Lord's Day the preacher addresses persons who are experiencing hazards and decisions, joys and sorrows, physical pain and mental anguish, conflicts of conscience and epochs of growth. In every congregation there are those who feel that their lives do not amount to much. Some have proof of their personal failure; others suspect that in quiet ways life is slipping unchallenged through their fingers. Men of all seasons are there who know the secret sadness of sin and long for escape from some blind alley of existence. Some persons in the pews before him face uncertain futures. Most of them will go from church to bear great responsibilities in family, educational, vocational, and civic tasks. The sensitive minister will not be content to discourse upon some popular topic as a lecturer. Rather, he will address persons-in-situations from within the categories of biblical faith with pastoral intent.

Since all preaching is in one way or another concerned with human existence, what factors characterize the pastoral focus in preaching?

1. Christian preaching which is skillfully diagnostic and spiritually therapeutic reflects pastoral intent. Gaston Foote once

[20] Wayne E. Oates, "The Discipline of Disillusionment," *The Beam* (July, 1963), 46.

interpreted the feeding of five thousand people, through Christ's miracle with a lad's loaves and fish (John 6:9), in personal terms. Rather than discoursing upon the problem of miracles, he viewed man's little and God's much. The problem addressed was the human tendency to live "on one's own," without reliance upon God. Said he: "This is more than a miracle. Jesus was doing something more than feeding five thousand people. He was explaining to his disciples and to us how we can take man's little and God's much, put them together and meet the problems of our day."[21] Such a sermon offers God's gracious Word afresh for healing and inspiration *from within.*

2. Pastoral preaching reveals God to man, man to himself, and prompts faith for the redemption and integration of personality. The preacher's own faith and love are herein revealed. Augustine once said: "What I live by, I impart." In this light "it might be well at times to subject our preaching to . . . critical self-analysis to determine how much of it is a projection of [the preacher's] own inner needs."[22] The preacher occasionally projects his own anxieties and aggressions upon others, thereby engaging in a monologue rather than in authentic preaching. Words can wound, even as they have power to heal!

3. The pastoral interpreter illuminates human experience in each of the developmental epochs of life with Christian truth. Thus, he shares the primary moments of life—birth, conversion, vocational choice, marriage, death—and supports individuals when crises come.

4. Rather than moralizing upon particular subjects, the pastor's goal for his hearers is the development of insight, character strength, and personal responsibility. He is concerned with the *doing* of truth.

In the Preface to this volume I acknowledge a personal debt to Lewis J. Sherrill's profound wisdom in *The Struggle of the Soul.*

[21] Gaston Foote, "Man's Little and God's Much," sermon preached at First Methodist Church, Fort Worth, and printed for private circulation among members of that congregation.
[22] Carl J. Schindler, *The Pastor as a Personal Counselor* (Philadelphia: Fortress Press, 1942), p. 136. Cf. Jackson, *op. cit.*, p. 199.

Reading that book inspired me to address sermons to the great rhythms of life—to what Robert J. Havighurst calls the "developmental tasks" which arise from infancy to death. One course of sermons, carved from biblical texts, included these subjects and goals:

1. *Children of Desire*—centered upon the central problem of childhood—becoming an individual—and upon the family's readiness to receive a new infant and to participate in his or her personal growth.

2. *Striving for Maturity*—focused the chief characteristics, claims upon, and choices of youth.

3. *Living Under Tension*—addressed young adults' responsibilities, stresses, and resources for growth.

4. *A Faith for Maturity*—pointed those in the middle years toward a mature view of life, a Christian philosophy of history.

5. *Unto the Perfect Day*—recognized the prospect of aging, changes including the need for simplification, and the church's role with its aging members.

6. *If I Should Die*—discussed the biblical view of death and resurrection, permitting each listener to face the prospect of his own death. Also, grief work was viewed in Christian perspective.

The response of a congregation to a pastor who cares enough to undergird their living *here* and *now* is heartening indeed. The awesome epochs of our existence cannot be reenforced by slick phrases and pious words, however. The Christian faith is "not just a mood or a spirit of a climate or an atmosphere. . . . It is a faith in someone and something!"[23] Preaching with pastoral intent requires substance, depth of conviction, and frank admission that man's redemption draws nigh, not by his self-sufficiency, but in reliant faith upon a reliable God.

One sermon may not fit every need. Fortunately, the flock gathers with some degree of regularity week by week, and within the Christian year the preacher will have addressed the majority of his members several times. His twofold objective is the renewal of spiritual health in those who are relatively whole and the recovery of spiritual health in those who are sick (Mark 2:17). In either

[23] Martin E. Marty, *The New Shape of American Religion* (New York: Harper & Row, 1958), p. 146.

case, he will say some things which are neither popular nor easy for certain individuals to receive. The true pastor does not shrink from *confronting* man with God's judgment-grace, even at the risk of suffering agony in the process himself. And he rejoices in *comforting* man with God's love and mercy when a gracious word is needed to put him on his feet again. His goal is useful living within the kingdom of God.

CONCLUSION

To summarize, the public and private ministries should be synthesized rather than separated in pastoral work. The prophet and the priest are not two different persons, for these roles converge in the personality of the servant of the Word. The shape of a church's liturgy and the role of the worship leaders remain flexible, with the suggestion that they be appropriate to one's tradition and cultural setting. Pastoral considerations in church architecture and worship leadership were stated as general principles rather than as categorical methods. The pastoral focus in preaching was viewed within a comprehensive context of four great concerns in Christian preaching. Each aspect or purpose is valid as the preacher addresses the life of man with the Word of God.

Finally, persons who traditionally view the church program as the *end* of their existence must rediscover the church's instrumental nature. Accordingly, worship is not the "end that crowns all" but the dynamic means to a larger purpose—life spent as a "living sacrifice" unto God. Thus, people go to church not to hear a grand finale at the week's close but to sound anew the grand melody of Christian faith upon the Lord's Day. Beginning life anew, they pledge to carry that faith into the rhythms of life during the week. Theirs is a fellowship of forgiveness and of hope for eternal life.

SUGGESTED READING

Baillie, D. M. *Out of Nazareth.* Edinburgh: Saint Andrew Press, 1958. Sermons of pastoral intent having excellent theological content.

Casteel, John. "Homiletical Method for Pastoral Preaching," *Pastoral Psychology,* VI (Nov., 1955), 11-15; (Dec., 1955), 27-34. A suggested pattern for sermons aimed at life-response.

Fosdick, Harry E. *The Living of These Days.* New York: Harper & Row, 1956. Autobiographical study by a master of life-situation preaching.

Howe, Reuel L. *The Miracle of Dialogue.* New York: Seabury Press, 1963. Discusses barriers to communication and examines dialogue, not as a *method* but as the *principle* of communication.

Jackson, Edgar N. *A Psychology for Preaching.* Manhasset, N.Y.: Channel Press, 1961. Sensible, popular treatment of preaching and worship based on synoptic wisdom from theology and man-sciences.

Kemp, Charles (ed.). *Pastoral Preaching.* St. Louis: Bethany Press, 1963. Sermons from person-minded preachers in varied settings.

MacLeod, Donald. *Word and Sacrament: A Preface to Preaching and Worship.* Englewood Cliffs, N.J.: Prentice-Hall, 1960. Discusses preaching within the context of worship.

CHAPTER 6

❧❧

DIMENSIONS OF THE
PASTOR'S CARING

I HAVE SAID that a joint obligation rests upon the Christian pastor
and his congregation to be a truly ministering church in the world.
While a formal order of ministry is reflected in the New Testament,
all Christians are involved mutually and reciprocally in both the
evangelistic and the pastoral dimension of church life (II Cor. 1).
The shape of a particular church's ministry will be determined
largely by the spirit and example of its official leadership. The
pastor is thus obligated to pace the shepherding ministry of his
congregation. The question to be answered now becomes: What
are the dimensions of the pastor's caring in the church and community?

In Chapter 5 we noted that the pastor has a unique opportunity
to extend life, health, joy, and power to his people through preaching and leading worship. Yet there are further elements of his
pastoral office to be considered. *The process of pastoral care is conceived here as a continuum in time and in depth.* Through the week
the minister encounters numerous persons in superficial contacts:
in the church offices, before or following worship services, on city
or village streets. He crosses trails with some church members
several times each week: in committee meetings, in hospital calling,
or in private counseling. His public ministry with the *many* is ex-

tended in time and depth with the few in administration, teaching, visitation, correspondence, community contacts, and most intensely in counseling.

Here, we are considering the spectrum of pastoral relationships and resources that lies between his contacts with the *many* in worship and his conversations with the *one* in counseling. This includes (1) administrative and group contacts, (2) calling and correspondence, (3) the pastoral uses of Christian literature, and (4) the pastor's role within the larger community of concern. Principles of pastoral counseling and case studies of clinical relationships comprise the remaining chapters.

1. LEADERSHIP THAT LIBERATES LIFE

Whether a clergyman functions in a church setting, as a chaplain, as a teacher, journalist, or church executive, his days are enmeshed in administrative processes. However idealized his conception of the ministry was at the outset, he finds that to change settings or responsibilities will not cancel his role of administration. A teacher, for example, must continue to read, revise lectures, meet classes, confer with faculty committees, counsel with students, evaluate their papers, entertain visitors, conduct research, write for journals, correspond with others, and maintain time for his family and a limited number of special engagements—all within the limited amount of time at his disposal. For the minister, whatever his particular function, some order must be brought out of the chaos of his existence. Goals must be pursued and satisfactions built into life by himself and his people.

To administer religious affairs is to make the services of oneself and one's people truly possible. The pastoral director has been vested with the responsibility and authority to nourish and motivate the leadership potential within his own congregation. Some groups, such as the Churches of Christ, view the minister as a stated preacher, minimize his leadership role, and charge a board of elders with church management. Some denominations under congregational polity leave local church affairs strictly in the hands of the pastor and his people. Presbyterial and episcopal forms of church government look to sessions, assemblies, and synods at a level beyond the local congregation for ultimate decisions and authority.

Whatever a clergyman's particular ecclesiastical identities and boundaries may be, he is often viewed as an authoritarian person in administrative affairs. This public image greatly influences his pulpit work, his priestly functions, and his private ministries. In addition, his leadership style evokes certain community reactions which influence his wife's feelings and his children's relationships. Perhaps the criticism most frequently leveled at clergymen today is that they are rigid and authoritarian. Pinning the label is much easier than healing the malady, however. "He's a Mr. Great-heart in big things," observed someone about a religious leader, "but in administrative details he is a miserable failure." As the minister searches his heart in this matter, he should strive to transcend the need to dominate decisions and control church affairs. He may equally expect his people to be democratic rather than autocratic, to share decisions rather than dictate policies, and to work together under the Spirit of God.

Interestingly, the minister's cherished attributes of "warmth, sympathy, and understanding are assets for success and control over his parish."[1] The fact that he represents spiritual power and is a potential source of strength for satisfying human longings increases his potential for controlling lives. Because he exerts an instructive and inspirational influence upon people, he is sometimes unconsciously tempted to keep them in his debt, to lord it over them. Like the Apostle Paul, the very thing the minister would prefer to avoid he occasionally finds himself doing.

Effective pastoral administration liberates the talents and strength of others through consultative direction, democratic deliberations, and group decisions and action. Becoming a leader in a Christian fellowship through whom the Holy Spirit can liberate each member to give his best is a learning process. The minister and each member

[1] Edward Bennett, *The Search for Emotional Security* (New York: Ronald Press, 1959), pp. 53-54. Cf. pp. 46-61.

of the church staff need to have healthy interpersonal relations if they, in turn, expect church members to follow their leadership. Investing educational workers and committee members with responsibility and praising their well-done tasks is essential in this approach. Sharing the limelight of success and the pain of failure with the entire congregation is also necessary. The true pastoral leader takes neither full credit nor full blame for church affairs. Again, the minister's spirit is magnified since he provides a model for teachers and leaders in all church activities. This ideal becomes specific as we consider the role of the church group leader.

II. THE ROLE OF THE SMALL GROUP LEADER

One area of church life in which a Christian leader's enslaving or liberating powers appear frequently is in small groups. Thus, the pastor should familiarize himself with the varieties of small groups in modern churches, educate capable volunteer group leaders, and discharge a pastoral ministry to them. Here it is instructive to study the relation of Jesus and the Twelve in the Gospels. While the following principles of group life and leadership are addressed primarily to ministers, they also apply to all persons who participate responsibly in church groups.

1. Small Groups in the Church

The church serves a useful purpose through the numerous relationships which its varied forms of group life make possible. Persons enter small groups in the church from small groups in society. The man-sciences have demonstrated that a person's identity and emotional needs are linked very closely to the primary groups of his existence. His identification with family members, close friends, and members of educational, religious, social, and vocational groups serves as a significant shaping influence upon his personality.

One of the reasons why people attend a particular church is that they need to belong to a congenial group in which they (1) experience acceptance for what they are; (2) can mature through spiritual comradeship; (3) develop altruism; and (4) participate responsibly in the church's life and work. *Belonging* is more essential than merely *attending*, both for the individual and for the common life of the entire church. In the light of its significance as a resource for character enrichment, as well as for furthering church causes, the group should be appreciated and fostered as a medium for pastoral care.

The term *group* designates any number of persons who are in dynamic relationship with one another, have some significant commonality, and assume some responsibility for one another.[2] According to this definition, not every meeting of a few persons at church constitutes a true group. *Dynamic relationship* recognizes the flow of energy, feelings, and levels of communication occurring simultaneously between members in any effective group climate. The *common bond* may be age, sex, subject matter, goal, task, belief, interest, and so on. The tie may be very strong for some, moderate or weak in others. *Assuming responsibility* for the other person implies the development of an altruistic "we-feeling" by group members. Such responsible participation is not the equivalent of "togetherness," which may be artificially arranged or imposed by an authority person.

Kurt Lewin, a pioneer researcher in group dynamics, once said: "Relinquishing of a certain amount of freedom is a condition of membership in any group."[3] Life in church groups obligates participants to unity within diversity. To belong to a group implies that there will be a relative loss of freedom. One's individuality will be limited. The capacity to identify with and to share responsibility with others, however, contributes to the individual's own sense of esteem, spiritual growth, and inner freedom. A group member's self-discipline and sensitivity to others presupposes his sense of

[2] At this point the author is indebted particularly to discussions by Michael S. Olmsted, *The Small Group* (New York: Random House, 1959); Rudolph M. Wittenberg, *The Art of Group Discipline: A Mental Hygiene Approach to Leadership* (New York: Association Press, 1951); L. K. Frank, *How To Be a Modern Leader* (New York: Association Press, 1954); and Malcolm S. and Hulda F. Knowles, *Introduction to Group Dynamics* (New York: Association Press, 1959); all of whom write from the perspective of the social sciences.

[3] Kurt Lewin in G. W. Lewin (ed.), *Resolving Social Conflicts* (New York: Harper & Row, 1948), p. 102.

belonging to and commonality within the group. Rudolph Wittenberg's studies led him to assert that self-control for the sake of the
group actually liberates the individual and releases his energies
for the good of the whole group.[4]

*What kinds of small groups develop within the larger church
structure?* Churches maintain or recognize groups (1) for planning
and service, with a task orientation; (2) for Christian education
and guidance, with a teaching orientation; (3) for interpersonal
discussion and problem-solving, with a therapeutic orientation; (4)
for renewal and discipline, with a prayer and worship orientation;
and (5) for fellowship and leisure time, with a play orientation.
Groups may arise out of common problems, by ages, or interests,
such as: a service group, a teen group, couples preparing for
marriage, new church members, older persons, and the like.

Some ministers have wondered about the practice of group
counseling in a church setting. Perhaps they have read of this
process in medical practice, beginning with the pioneering work
of Joseph H. Pratt and Jacob L. Moreno, both M.D.'s. Role-
playing, psychodrama, and group therapy are practiced widely in
mental hospital settings, having begun during wartime as an
economy measure. Sociometric research in the structure and emotional responsiveness of group members reveals some things of
significance for the church.[5] Because the shared life of small groups
is therapeutically significant, new interest in the powers of the
small group has developed in recent years. It is particularly important to perceive the implications of church group activities upon
personality development.

It may be argued effectively that "group therapy" is a medical
term, implying professional treatment in a hospital setting. How-

[4] Wittenberg, *op. cit.*, p. x.
[5] See Jacob L. Moreno, *Who Shall Survive? Foundations of Sociometry,
Group Psychotherapy and Sociodrama* (Boston: Beacon Press, 1953). Cf.
Helen I. Driver (ed.), *Counseling and Learning Through Small-Group Discus-
sion* (Madison, Wis.: Monona Publications, 1958), and Alan F. Klein, *Role
Playing in Leadership Training and Group Problem Solving* (New York:
Association Press, 1956). Perhaps the most notable effort to correlate these
findings and to illustrate their validity in church life is the study by Paul F.
Douglass, *The Group Workshop Way in the Church* (New York: Association
Press, 1956).

ever, Robert Leslie has indicated that "when the focus of attention is directed to what is happening to the members as a result of their participation in the life of a group . . . then 'therapy' is involved whether it is so designated or not."[6] Personal growth may occur in church groups which begin as Christian discipline, theological inquiry, role-playing, literary discussion, problems of living, or service fellowships, which develop therapeutic overtones as group life progresses.

This implies that church groups may be viewed from two perspectives: (1) the external or organizational view of the-church-as-groups, and (2) the internal or psychological view of groups-as-the-church. Viewed externally, such bodies may be designated as *primary* intimate groups of family members and close friends; or as *secondary* formal interest, age-graded, or task groups. Another way of viewing church groups externally is to see them as *informal* and *formal.* Persons are related informally in families, peer groups, talent or interest groupings, and the like. Whereas persons in designated church offices, such as the deaconate or committees and organizations such as the Sunday school, are related in more formal fashion.

When the internal perspective is assumed, however, we turn from a substantival question about the group's nature or purpose to a dynamic process appraisal of essential group relationships.[7]

[6] Robert Leslie, "The Minister and Group Therapy," *Pastoral Psychology,* XI (Nov., 1960), 51. Cf. also articles in *Pastoral Psychology,* VI (Apr., 1955) devoted to the theme "Group Work in the Church."

[7] Michael Olmstead catalogues three general theories that have been developed in this country for analyzing the social structure of the small group, *op. cit.,* pp. 105-32. These include: (1) The *Homans* technique, developed by George Homans, *The Human Group* (New York: Harcourt, Brace & World, 1950), and (2) *group dynamics,* the most widespread theory, developed initially by Kurt Lewin, a German emigrant whose perspective was *Gestalt* psychology. This approach is also called "field theory" because it attempts to study both the *cohesiveness* (total forces) and *locomotion* (movement toward an objective) operating in a group. Lewin's follower's have continued his investigations, notably through the Research Center for Group Dynamics at the University of Michigan. Cf. Dorwin Cartwright and Alvin Zander (eds.), *Group Dynamics: Research and Theory* (Evanston, Ill.: Row, Peterson, 1953). (3) The method developed by Robert F. Bales of the Harvard Laboratory of Social Relations has been described in *Interaction Process Analysis* (Cambridge, Mass.: Addison-Wesley Press, 1950). Inspired by pragmatic philosophy, Bales sees all group activity as problem-solving or task-oriented behavior.

Here the question becomes, not "What kind of group is this?" but "What is happening in this group? Will it have bearing in other relationships?" The leader's concern is with the participants as well as with group morale, teamwork, and achievement. The simple question about the group's goals in the light of the church's program is reconstructed into the not so simple question of what is happening to persons who participate in church groups. The pastor's concern is that group members cannot be treated as *means* but must be seen as *ends* of infinite worth, who are potential instruments in God's hands. He desires that the individual develop and that the church's mission be pursued faithfully.

2. The Leader's Role in the Group Process

Some groups are the "givens" of religious fellowships, indigenous to church administration, religious education, family life, and Christian mission. Other groups arise spontaneously out of internally felt needs.[8] In either case, the pastor or some leader will be recognized by each group, for a group will be led by someone or ones! Its leadership is a reflection upon the needs of its members at a given time and may change periodically. It is to be hoped that the group can use its experiences to point beyond itself to spiritual growth on the part of each participant. In this process the leader's role is vital.

While he is not an official member of every group in the church's life, the pastor finds himself meeting frequently with task units and small fellowships. As an authority figure in any group, his views may be sought out with due respect, though he may not be the most knowledgeable member of the particular body. His role of worship leadership and general administration tempts the clergyman to throttle the talents of group members and assume the posture of an authoritarian personality. Interpersonal relations in groups are significant because they influence the climate, spirit, and health, not just of that group but of the entire church. While it is not easy for a Christian leader to be democratic in groups, it

[8] See John L. Casteel (ed.), *Spiritual Renewal Through Personal Groups* (New York: Association Press, 1957), for an introduction to varieties of spontaneous groups which have arisen in churches in recent years.

is necessary. Being sensitive to others in delicate human relationships is not to be equated with laissez-faire passivity and irresponsibility, however.

Pastoral care is as operative in group processes as it is in personal contacts and private counseling. Wayne Oates has suggested quite correctly that "pastoral counseling may be eased in its weight or increased in its difficulty in direct proportion to the pastor's insight, commitment, and ability as an administrator."[9] The pastoral leader is concerned with the spiritual meaning and emotional content of group behavior, as well as with maintaining units for work, play, teaching, and renewal in church life. *From a pastoral perspective, group behavior is purposeful*: (1) when a climate of relative democracy facilitates personal initiative and participation, (2) when the participants discipline themselves for the group's welfare, and (3) when the small unit discharges its responsibility in the light of the entire church's mission and welfare.

Leading a small group in the church requires a measure of professional competence and skill. The term *professional* is used here to indicate the leader's disciplined objectivity, which cherishes the group's interests and goals above his own moods and feelings. Frequently a group recognizes a *natural* leader from its own membership, a best-liked person of particular strength, whom the *formal* leader must also recognize in administering the group. "The natural leader," states Wittenberg, "gives us a clue as to what the group is like because he represents . . . certain things to the group that many of them want."[10] He serves as something of a group *ego*, an index to the body's identity, feelings, and needs. Group morale is linked to the formal leader's capacity for recognizing the natural leader and each member through group processes.

Some persons have group leadership roles thrust upon them spontaneously out of a situation; others are selected deliberately. In any case, leaders need to perceive basic concepts of group responsibility, morale, discipline, handling controversy, revising

[9] Wayne E. Oates, *Protestant Pastoral Counseling* (Philadelphia: Westminster Press, 1962), p. 124.
[10] Wittenberg, *op. cit.*, p. 82.

plans, and so on. The following principles are suggestive for leading a group in the church.

1. *The designated leader should understand the varied functions
of group leadership.* While he may be in charge of a group, his
thoughts, feelings, and words are commingled with those of his
fellows. They are his comrades-in-Christ, not under his command
as members of a military platoon. The leader must learn to gauge
the group's capacity for self-direction and the degree of leadership
pressure needed at a given time. Some leaders function more as
convenors and consultants, others as arbiters and aids to action.
When aggression or antagonism develop in group interaction, he
must function as a conciliator, interpreter, and peacemaker.

The leader may be the group's friend or enemy, the object of
their hero worship or a scapegoat, receiving the blame for all their
problems. He may be temporarily disregarded in group action or
discussion. Thus to maintain objectivity is essential, so that the
leader will not use the group to work out his own anxieties or
hostilities.

2. *The leader should perceive clearly the purpose of the group.*
He will help the small unit to formulate an idea of its identity,
purpose, and goal. While such "housekeeping details" may appear
mundane, defining realistic goals and structuring methods of action
assist the group members to experience purposeful behavior. Once
their functional roles are clarified, the members' energies are released and directed toward the group's goal. As individuals accept
the we-feeling of the group, they work more effectively to achieve
their objective. Maturity comes with added responsibility.

3. *The leader should understand the group process and assist
each member to perceive the nature of group experience.* Each
member retains his own individuality, ideas, beliefs, expectations,
and ways of thinking and feeling. Yet the welfare of the group takes
precedence over the welfare of the individual, so that each member
experiences new relationships, certain limitations, and a new way
of feeling and acting. Some individual notions must be bypassed
and feelings sublimated for the benefit of the whole body. A communication pattern develops in time and the group's skill for life

together matures gradually. In this process the Christian group has a clear advantage in that its communications do not depend upon raw competition or aggresive action but are grounded in love.[11] The pastor's chief concern is that healthy emotions be engendered and expressed in group experience, that self-interest be transcended, and that Christian selfhood mature through group relationships.

4. *The designated leader should know the group members and recognize the natural leader cherished by the group.* The leader's strategy is not to manipulate the group but to release the creative forces in it, so that its true purpose can be achieved. This process is aided or impeded by its *natural* leader—usually one of the group's own age or interest, best-liked or respected at a given time. In the light of what has already been said about the significance of such a person, the pastor will rely upon him or her to build morale, relieve tension, and keep the group moving toward its goal. Such a natural leader is rejected by the designated leader at great risk. A crucial problem arises, however, when the natural leader brings out the destructiveness of a group. A subsequent case study will demonstrate how a pastor handled this problem in creative fashion. As the leader places limits upon group behavior or emotions, he perceives that the members will not forego satisfactions unless they are replaced by other equally desirable satisfactions. Such knowledge is essential in group discipline.

5. *The pastoral leader should discharge the role of a spiritual catalyst,* releasing the leadership qualities and talents of each member of the group. As the group develops strength, the leader's role changes from "boss" (expert, chairman, authority) to "belonger" (member, participant, discussant). "The leader is dependent upon his group for his own encouragement and development as a leader," L. K. Frank has said.[12] The group's positive response to him strengthens his capacity as the leader; or it may go the other way. The group may turn upon him or reject him. He functions at

[11] Edgar N. Jackson, *The Pastor and His People* (Manhasset, N.Y.: Channel Press, 1963), p. 165; cf. pp. 159-70.

[12] Frank, *op. cit.,* p. 34. Experiences in interpersonal relations groups in clinical pastoral education settings have demonstrated the validity of the catalyst concept of leadership.

his best when members of the small unit alter their customary patterns of thinking and relationships to include others. Together, the Christian leader and group members share themselves, find approval, feel security, and perform their desired ministry in a relationship of Christian faith, hope, and love. The pastor thus grows along with the group in knowledge, consecration, and maturity.

3. The Shared Life of the Small Group

The pastor will cherish his participation in small fellowships once he perceives them to be the primary arena of personal decision and spiritual development in church life. Also, he will lead his parishioners to appreciate the confidentional comradeship of Christian groups and to develop a high degree of concern for each other in group processes. The participants should be

> sensitive to each other's needs and feelings, not because of any superficial notion about the "dignity and sanctity of human personality" but out of knowledge of the tragedy of human life, recognizing their common need for love, understanding, and for forgiveness of sins. [Their] sense of belonging . . . is not based simply on similarity of interests or background.
>
> In groups of Christians . . . the members and leaders alike will realize that they live in a community of guilt and acceptance. They are able to love and accept each other because they have known the love and forgiveness of God.[13]

Here then is the distinctive quality of Christian groups. The other person is one for whom Christ died; thus he will not be dominated nor rejected but cherished in Christian love.

Christian life develops from infancy to maturity in small group experiences in the church. Small homogeneous groups are indispensable in Christian education. They make varied approaches to religious training and experience possible. With adults, for example, Bible study may be approached through identification with life-situations and personalities. Or, position papers through which

---

[13] Margaret E. Kuhn, *You Can't Be Human Alone: Handbook on Group Procedures for the Local Church* (New York: National Council of Churches in the USA, 1956), pp. 3-4.

each member teaches the others by his or her responses to a scriptural text may be assigned to supplement the lecture method of instruction. And with children, role-playing of Bible characters, scenes, or incidents stimulates learning through improvisions, dialogue, actions, and participant understanding. Such group responsibility in teaching and learning aids members in carrying religious instruction from the church classroom into life's decisions and tasks. Persons who are shy, retiring, or lonely may be strengthened through participation with others. Those suffering the stigma of divorce, alcoholism, homosexuality, a previous mental illness, and certain handicaps may come to life again and flourish through sharing experiences with others in an environment of Christian love.

What findings are available from clinical experience that can inform the pastor's participation in the small group life of the church? The following summary was prepared by a pastor who felt a particular concern for four teen-age girls who were members of a larger adolescent group in his church. The pastor and young people were associated during a vacation church school in which a thirty-minute discussion period followed the Bible lesson in the day's schedule. The pastoral leader introduced some pamphlets on controversial issues at the opening of school which catalyzed discussion, sharpened differences, and eventually led certain members to change.

He described the four members for whom he was particularly concerned as follows:

A is 14 years of age, the older of two children. Her parents are inactive church members. She is obese, unattractive, and rather talkative. She is rebellious against all types of authority and showed much hostility toward her parents, especially her mother. She resented any kind of religious service. A is the leader of the group of girls.

B is 14, the middle child of three. She is tall and physically mature. She appears to be 17 years of age. She is not as open with her hostility toward her parents as A, but she does resent the church.

C is 14, nice-looking, about normal size for a 14-year-old. She is the youngest of five children. Her father is an inactive Methodist and her mother is a leader in Plainview Church. She is openly hostile toward her mother and religion.

D is 14, the youngest child in her family. She is tall and large for her age, plain-looking and not very neat. She is hostile but not talkative. Her father is not a Christian and her mother is a member of the Pilgrim church but attends the Methodist church.

Observe that he detected the natural leader of the group and knew details of family life, religious background, and some under-surface feelings in each of the girls.

The pastor taught the Bible lesson each day and functioned as designated leader of the "gripe (therapy) session" which followed. Selections taken from his daily log of feelings and responses in the group appear here.

First Day:
(He described the seating arrangement around a table.) The first day was spent by the boys and girls testing me and trying to get me to give them authoritative answers to their questions. Much hostility was expressed toward me in one form or another. (According to our definition, this preliminary meeting was not a "group" in the true sense.)

Second Day:
The seating arrangement changed (he described this). A started the session with a bang, discussing subjects from parents to dancing. The discussion always found its way back to parents. About halfway through the session D, who had been quiet most of the time, agreed with the others that she could not talk with her mother any more. Tears came to her eyes; she coughed and bowed her head. While her head was down she wiped the tears from her eyes.

During the next three days, B and C were not as verbal. D was quiet and pleasant. In all the school activities these three girls were more friendly and cheerful.

Fifth Day:
The seating arrangement changed today. (A moved closest to the pastor.) We had been discussing obscene literature the day before and A had brought a pulp magazine to prove her point. The magazine was the object of discussion the first part of the session. She did not get the support she wanted from the group, so A dropped the subject. The rest of this session was spent in dis-

cussing the effect of this kind of literature upon dating and marriage.

The second week the seating stabilized; feelings were more positive. While A tried to dominate the group, the boys and girls did not let her. Leadership shifted more into the whole group's hands. During a spiritual commitment service at the close of school, B and D made public professions of personal faith in Christ. In the final two sessions, the spirit of the group turned into rejoicing. A and C tended to be quiet and thoughtful. Later A volunteered to serve as pianist for a Sunday school department on a regular basis. The pastor observed that her hair-style had been changed and that her appearance generally had improved following the vacation school. He followed up each of the other three girls with special needs, noting experiences at home, with their age group at church, and in community life.

In sharing the life of a small church group, this pastor refused the role of an authoritarian personality in an effort to serve as a spiritual catalyst, eliciting the group's strength. This role was felt by the pastor to be permissive but not passive. His introduction of literature in order to stimulate thought, discussion, and growth indicates that he rejected a laissez-faire role of avoiding all responsibility. When he was rejected the first day as an authority figure, he recognized this as a natural response of feelings carried over from certain family and social relations patterns. Rather than reacting judgmentally, he accepted their hostile feelings with Christian love.

His concern for the group made him sensitive to the expressions of each member, including the "problem" personalities. He recognized a significant turning point when the group moved from the natural leadership of A to a more democratic assumption of responsibility. Each member gained strength for living in this process, including two who professed their Christian faith publicly and four others who rededicated themselves during the commitment service. This pastor recognized the redemptive-therapeutic possibilities of the shared life of small church groups. Such insight in leadership is instructive for others who lead small groups in the church.

III. PASTORAL CALLING AND COMMUNICATION

Changes in contemporary pastoral work like that illustrated with church groups have also been reflected in clerical calling. The charge is heard occasionally in churches of different social settings that laymen no longer see their ministers visiting private homes. Clergymen appear to order their days so that there is very little time for visitation of the nature enjoyed by pastors and people in the past. The situation is usually more complex than a pastor's personal preference, however.

Before the urbanized, pluralistic situation developed in American society, getting around systematically to most of the homes in the average community was both feasible and essential. The minister in rural settings often traveled a circuit (as is still done in mission fields), staying in the homes of hospitable hosts as he traveled. Calls were often spontaneous, social in nature, yet might last for hours. The agrarian economy geared its schedule to crops, cattle, and seasons, rather than to clocks and commuter trains. Church programs were informal. Time was a universally available commodity.

1. *New Occasions and New Duties*

In one generation, many ministers have made the transition with their people from rural to urban or suburban areas and into a new economic order. Their church calendars are geared to industrial production schedules and to increased denominational activities. They have found themselves separated from their church members by time, space, social roles, and focal concerns. Conceivably, a metropolitan clergyman could have parishioners as patients in five or more widely separated hospitals simultaneously in a single city. Church programs have become more complex, requiring the pastor's presence in numerous evening meetings when he might otherwise be free for calling. Visiting during the day, without appointments, may yield a few contacts with housewives, who usually are unprepared and therefore embarassed by an unannounced visit from the minister. To see the family together demands that calling be done in the evenings when father and children are at home. The tempo of school activities, sports contests, and civic affairs also militates against making time for calling.

Furthermore, some pastors, unwilling to undertake an apparently pedestrian task, rationalize that they have no time to waste in purposeless visitation. They find the plan of Richard Baxter, the seventeenth-century Puritan pastor who called systematically upon each church family annually, inconceivable in modern life. The prevailing attitude toward apartment and house-to-house calling is generally negative. Except for hospital calling, membership enlistment, and emergencies, the modern minister prefers to be in his study, in a committee meeting, or enjoying some relaxation. He also hopes to spend some time with his own family, for they have covenants to keep in order to preserve their social identity and integrity in modern life.

A number of remedies have been prescribed for this apparent failure to live up to one's pastoral heritage of systematic, though often superficial, calling. Some ministers employ radio and television facilities for communicating with members and for carrying worship into listeners' homes. Others organize the laity for calling, yet abstain themselves, indicating that they are available only in emergencies or difficult cases. Others set up a priority of calls—critical, essential, and so on—down to routine visits, which they tend to minimize;[14] whereas some still call upon their people with pastoral intent and with some degree of regularity. Personal and group counseling have supplanted the need for calling in many homes. Further proposals are offered in the design for calling that follows.

Admittedly, contemporary clergymen must conserve their time, talents, and energies for those things that are most needful. As "stewards of the mysteries of God," their time must be well accounted for to God and men. However, honesty should be encouraged in examining some reasons given and rationalizations

[14] Such a priority system or "hierarchy of calling" where the pressure is greatest is advocated by Wayne Oates in *The Christian Pastor* (Philadelphia: Westminster Press, 1951), p. 14; and by Jackson, *op. cit.*, pp. 190-94.

used to explain why ministers avoid calling today. It would be a great mistake to assume from what has been said here that all or even most pastoral visitation is purposeless. It need not be. I feel both from theological conviction and from clinical observation that *pastoral contacts with persons are essential to an effective Christian ministry in our time.*

2. Design for Pastoral Calling

The term *pastoral calling* has been employed to denote that vital aspect of ministry in which the clergyman's concern is communicated in a personal way to his people. Some writers have designated it as "precounseling interviews," with the result that many clergymen disregard the essential worth of such contacts. It is quite likely that visits will prompt deeper-level counseling relationships with *some* persons. However, not every pastoral call will be devoted to the discussion of personal problems. There is much to be said, for example, for a friendly visit by the pastor and his wife to new residents of a community, who have left familiar faces and surroundings and may be overwhelmed with adjustments to the new environment.

The minister's loving interest in and concern for people form *the basic motivation* underlying his calling. There may or may not be some severe problem or major crisis. At any rate, the pastor should examine his motives, which may lie more in the direction of compulsiveness, meeting community expectations, or keeping up with a previous pastor than that of true compassion.

All pastoral calling in a modern church need not be done by the senior minister. When a congregation's size and demands indicate a multiple ministry, colleagues should be sought who will share his responsibilities. Staff members assigned one area of work—education, administration, or youth—may assume pastoral responsibilities for their volunteer workers, for example, as well as for some members. Large churches often designate some staff members as "church visitors"; or a retired minister of visitation may be retained. A division of labor among staff members can be agreed upon at the time of employment and worked out in staff meetings.

Members of the diaconate and church membership committee should be instructed in the conduct of pastoral, as well as other kinds of calls. They may accompany the minister or a staff member until they feel secure enough to establish depth relationships in visiting individually.

There are three major types of pastoral calls: (1) *routine* calls, in which the church's message and fellowship are carried regularly to some persons and families; (2) *crucial* calling, in which Christian resources are offered to those experiencing crises or distress; and (3) *casual contacts*, in which the minister encounters persons in unstructured settings yet seeks to make such contacts vital. His calling may be accomplished by telephone, by visits in homes, hospitals, business houses, or wherever people are encountered in wayside contacts with a pastoral intent. Home visits should be purposeful, well planned, and faithfully conducted in order to give the pastor a feeling of security as he calls and of achievement upon their completion.

Planning includes a wise employment of the appointment system in city churches, so that maximum use of time is made by both the minister and church members. This may be achieved by asking a family if they will be at home on a certain evening, for example. Once the commitment is made to call, the pastor should follow through or cancel the engagement. Rural people generally prefer the informality of spontaneous calls and would probably resent setting a specific time.

It would be erroneous to refer to *routine* visitation as "nonspecific," for each call should perform some service. Calls in this category include: newcomers, the handicapped, the aged, the indifferent, and those who have become isolated by choice or injured in relationships. The pastor also makes regular administrative, teaching, and occasional social calls, which mirror God's care of the strong and faithful as well as of weak and indifferent members. The skilled caller makes himself available to be used as people need to share the significant concerns in their lives. Such a visit may provide an opportunity for a parishioner to talk to the preacher (for a change) and to tell him how he or she feels about some church matter. Even as he ministers to others, such visitation usually strengthens the pastor's hand in God.

Obviously, regular pastoral calling is not to be depreciated in the estimate of pastor or people. On the other hand, there is little reason for methodically visiting every church home and apartment in a given period. The pastor's concern is *depth* of relationship, not speed nor the multiplication of superficial contacts. One call may require fifteen minutes; another three-quarters of an hour. At home, a person generally dares to be himself, though some do keep up a façade. The pastor will certainly be alert to what is being said and felt during his visits. Schindler suggests that "little unintentional gestures and remarks are indicative of existing conditions in a home."[15] While routine calling is not conducted for the purpose of increasing one's counseling load, some contacts will lead into private conferences or follow-up calls at another time. Much of what is said in the next chapter on the "dynamics of the pastoral conversation" should guide the pastor's face-to-face visits with his people.

In some areas of the country it is customary to share a meal, a practice that is conducive to friendship and true intimacy between church families and the pastoral family.[16] Christ is often represented in the Gospels as partaking of a meal with old or new friends. Invisible bonds of devotion may be formed among the participants in such modern "love feasts," who dare to company in the secret places of each other's presence. Mealtime visits can seal friendships, overcome barriers of distance, transcend temporary estrangements, and restore unity once it has been disrupted. Some routine visits are failures because of the great spiritual, social, or emotional "distance between the office-bearers and the members of the church, a distance which is unjustifiable both from the point of view of love

---

[15] Carl J. Schindler, *The Pastor as a Personal Counselor* (Philadelphia: Fortress Press, 1942), p. 5.
[16] See Wallace Denton, *The Role of the Minister's Wife* (Philadelphia: Westminster Press, 1962), pp. 43-54, 101-16 *et passim*, for family attitude toward participation in pastoral work.

and from that of the communion of the saints."[17] Such contacts should be as human, sincere, and open as possible.

Crucial calling in response to acute needs and crises cannot be scheduled in advance. Yet the pastor can make himself available to his people in times of sickness, prior to surgery, in family conflicts, at the birth of children, at moments of death, and in grief work. The church members should be encouraged to notify the pastor of such distresses and crises. Like the family physician, the Christian pastor is as close to his people as their telephone by day or night.

While clergymen will not be able to please everyone by conducting social-level calls every week in many homes, they are to be available for comfort and support, confession and counsel, when these deeper-level ministries are indicated. Frequently the pastor is afforded a crucial depth ministry with some person or family precisely because he took the initiative on some previous occasion in getting acquainted with them. Because of the magnitude and significance of such aspects of ministry, Chapters 8 and 9 are devoted to case-examinations of pastoral care in life's primary moments and crucial situations.

Many people who need the church the most in this troubled era are at times unconscious of that fact. They will never come to a church building or to a pastor's home to discuss their problems. The Christian faith and fellowship must be taken to them. Contemporary pastors should note that the brilliant preaching of men like Harry Emerson Fosdick, George W. Truett, and Henry Sloane Coffin of a generation past was linked vitally to pastoral wisdom and work. The careful preparation of sermons should be coupled with a wise pastoral understanding of one's congregation. Coffin, who as pastor of New York's Madison Avenue Presbyterian Church made approximately a hundred personal calls each month, once said: "As ministers of Christ we deem personal evangelism our primary duty. . . . In order to accomplish this we feel that we

[17] G. Brillenburg Wurth, *Christian Counseling in the Light of Modern Psychology*, trans. H. de Jongste (Grand Rapids, Mich.: Baker Book House, 1962), p. 135.

must be free to meet [persons] on their own ground, to understand their outlook upon life, to face with them their perplexities,
to feel the force of their intellectual difficulties . . . that they may
submit themselves unhampered to the easy yoke . . . of Jesus himself."[18]

While the Christian pastor's ministry grows more complex and
demanding with the passing years, his personal contacts should
never become perfunctory. Above all, his visits should strengthen
an individual's or a family's link with God.

3. *Communicating Pastoral Concern*

In Chapter 4 we noted that Christian compassion penetrates
human need at the level of daily life. The pastor's personal concern may be communicated through his friendship with persons
of all ages, his preaching and prayers, his spirit and availability
to people; and by his concrete overtures of love. Along with seeking
social justice which might prevent many crises from developing in
his community, the clergyman has certain tools for establishing
points of contact between himself and those who need the church's
ministry. Using radio and televsion facilities for worship or dramatic
presentations may be worked out in consultation with local station
personnel. Other religious programs are prepared by church groups
for national presentation. Some clergymen have employed a news-
paper feature column regularly to demonstrate their perception of
the battles people win or lose week by week and to undergird life
with Christian assurance. A number of other instruments—correspondence, drama, and the congregation itself—also communicate
either concern or indifference in modern churches.

1. *Pastoral correspondence* renders a specific ministry of friendship and encouragement and points beyond itself to conferences
or counseling, if they become necessary. When moving to a new
church, for example, the minister should write a personal letter
to each household in the congregation, voicing his gratitude for the
privilege of being their new minister and making himself available

---

[18] Morgan P. Noyes *et al., This Ministry: The Contribution of Henry Sloane
Coffin* (New York: Charles Scribner's Sons, 1946), p. 11.

to them in life's common ventures and crises. He will also write notes of appreciation to those who extend courtesies, hospitality, or give gifts to him or his family members. Occasions such as birthdays, anniversaries, and commencements offer opportunities for him to express a salutary interest in his people. Personal notes may be written in his own hand, correlated with a calendar through the church office. This is the "power of the personal" in action. The birth of a child and crises such as illness, character failure, or death should be supported through correspondence as well as by visitation. All new members of the congregation should receive a welcome letter from their minister, extending the full ministry of the church personally to them.

I would caution the busy clergyman who may be tempted to care for such "burdensome details" with form cards or printed letters. While such materials are accepted, their arrival in any mailbox is usually marked with mild or little enthusiasm. They are considered promotional matter by the recipients, rather than words of pastoral interest. Frequently new residents of a community select the church that demonstrates concern for them as *persons* rather than as potential "grist for the mill." Thus the personal element, even in greetings to church visitors, is vital.

2. Pastoral care on a group scale may be accomplished occasionally by the *discriminating use of audio-visual materials* in the church. Problems of doubt, decision, vocational choice, Christian biography, mental health themes, matters of dating and preparation for marriage, family worship, and Christian stewardship are subjects which may be faced creatively through films.[19] They may be followed by a discussion period. Also, role-playing through *religious drama* is of great value in picturing moments of decision, faith in conflict, family situations, and Christian responsibility in human relations. Nora Sterling's *Family Life Plays*, which may be produced under church auspices, have been designed to heal a wound,

---

[19] Catalogues of films and rental fees are available through the Broadcasting and Film Commission, National Council of Churches USA, 475 Riverside Dr., New York, N.Y.; through offices of major denominations in the U.S.; and through state and local mental health associations, state departments of health, and university film rental libraries.

ease an ache, or start a new train of thought. In a preface to that volume, Margaret Mead wrote: "These plays provide occasional strength for occasional needs" rather than daily strength for daily needs.[20] They are addressed to life's hidden struggles and quiet crises, as well as to open conflicts, delinquencies, doubts, and decisions.

3. Wise clergymen learn to establish ties with trusted parishioners who function as *communications centers* within the congregation. These are *natural* leaders, commonly held in high regard by the congregation, but not to be confused with officers or authoritarian personalities in the church. In some instances, soon after the minister is established in a new situation certain church members may create pressure upon him in an effort to gain his favor or control his influence. They may be wealthy patrons or influential figures in the community power structure who seek to control the clergy through favors and friendship. While he need not suspect the rich, nor be intolerant of those with whom he disagrees, the wise pastor will not let his relationships become distorted for cultural or financial reasons.

Of necessity, however, he must establish a relationship of trust with those reliable men and women who have demonstrated their worth as leaders of the church through the years. The lines of their existence will cross frequently in personal ties and in professional relationships. Both as perceptive administrator and loving pastor, he will rely upon these natural communications centers for reliable information about people's needs and church conditions, for interpretation of his own feelings or actions to others, and for comradeship in their joint Christian ministry.

IV. STRENGTHENING FAITH WITH LITERATURE

It has been suggested that the church's ministry is to inform and strengthen the faith of Christians who face life's great responsibilities and decisions as well as its hazards and crises. Some parish-

[20] Nora Sterling, *Family Life Plays* (New York: Association Press, 1961), p. viii.

ioners, however, are beyond the pastor's immediate reach in preaching, calling, and small group experiences. Some of the church's young people are away in college and university centers. Others are working in great cities, training in technical schools, or traveling abroad in military service. There is need for a Presence in such lives, a reminder not merely of home and friends but of life's great realities, of divine grace, and of resources for survival. The religious affections of such persons may be kept aflame with carefully chosen books.

There are scientists, teachers, homemakers, statesmen, professional persons, craftsmen, and tradesmen who desire to fortify their devotion with information. Perhaps the Christian's greatest danger in this technological age is not a bookish faith but an illiterate one. Literature should nourish the mind and lift faith to new horizons, not merely prompt pious sentimentality.

Some persons who are considering the Christian faith may profit from reading Dietrich Bonhoeffer, *The Cost of Discipleship* (The Macmillan Co., 1959); or Ernest Gordon, *Through the Valley of the Kwai* (Harper & Row, 1962). Those troubled by conflicts they find between religion and science should read Alan Richardson's *The Bible in the Age of Science* (S. C. M., 1962). Some persons may need literature for a home study group or to prepare themselves for Christian responsibility, such as Robert McAfee Brown's *The Bible Speaks to You* (Westminster Press, 1955), or Suzanne de Dietrich's *God's Unfolding Purpose* (Westminster Press, 1960). Young persons choosing vocations, facing ethical decisions, caught in traps of guilt or mild depression need sources of insight and spiritual strength, like Seward Hiltner's *Self-Understanding* (Abingdon Press, Apex, 1962); Waldo Beach's *Conscience on Campus* (Association Press, 1958); or Curtis Jones's *Youth Deserves To Know* (The Macmillan Co., 1958). A "pastoral aid" book may become a pointer to pastoral counseling, to the church's fellowship, or to community resources for help.

The home-bound—ill, handicapped, aged, invalids—often appreciate devotional literature, such as: Paul Scherer, *Love Is a Spendthrift* (Harper & Row, 1961); Carolyn Rhea, *Such Is My*

Confidence (Grosset & Dunlap, 1961); John Baillie, *A Diary of Readings* (Charles Scribner's Sons, 1955); and Nels F. S. Ferré, *Making Religion Real* (Harper & Row, 1955). A lay retreat may focus its worship and discussion by concentrating upon one theme or book, such as D. Elton Trueblood, *The Company of the Committed* (Harper & Row, 1961); Benjamin E. Mays, *Seeking To Be Christian in Race Relations* (Friendship Press, 1957); or Charles Stinnette, *Grace and the Searching of Our Heart* (Association Press, 1962).

Members of therapeutic groups in churches, hospitals, prisons, and the like may supplement therapy sessions with literature of diagnostic value and redemptive intent, such as H. E. Fosdick's *On Being a Real Person*. It should be noted, however, that reading is *not* a substitute for psychotherapy, if such treatment has been suggested by one's physician. Families of hospitalized patients will find help in Edith Stern's *Mental Illness: A Guide for the Family* (rev. ed.; Harper & Row, 1957). And an alcoholic or his family should profit from a careful reading of G. Aiken Taylor, *A Sober Faith* (The Macmillan Co., 1954)—a discussion of religion and Alcoholics Anonymous. Such books may be loaned personally from a "pastoral loan shelf" or through a church library. Others may be sold inexpensively through arrangement with publishers or bookstores.[21]

Specific occasions may arise for giving books as presents, through prearranged church budget provisions. For example, gift books may be presented to couples whom the pastor is assisting in marriage preparation, to the grief-stricken, lonely, and discouraged. Adoptive parents, divorcees, and persons adjusting to community life after an extended period of institutionalization need insights which transcend the past and lift vision to new heights. Robert Frost once spoke of an incident which had given his heart a change of *mood*. Certain books have the capacity to break a deadlock in relationship, to offer a new vantage point, to stir the imagination,

[21] Reflection Books, designed for this purpose and moderately priced, may be ordered from the Association Press, 291 Broadway, New York, N.Y., or through the Pastoral Psychology Book Club, Manhasset, New York.

kindle compassion, make the reader see life from another's point of view. A writer can say it for us—putting feelings into concrete expression and ideas into words.

What criteria shall guide the minister's selection of loan and gift books? (1) The pastor should recommend books with which he is well acquainted, sources that have spoken to his own concerns. He should not refer persons to reading sources indiscriminately. (2) The book should have a religious orientation or should assist the puzzled person to interpret his situation in the light of the Christian faith. The literary criticism of Roland M. Frye in *Perspective on Man: Literature and the Christian Tradition* (Westminster Press, 1961), provides a reliable guide to writings from varied perspectives. (3) Problem-focused literature, such as psychiatric case studies, may injure an emotionally disturbed person. Particularly when a person is in therapy, a consultation with his physician should precede the recommendation of literature. (4) The book should be gauged to the person's capacity, intellectual and spiritual, as well as to his or her need. If a book is too technical or abstract it may distort, not interpret, experience. (5) The book should have the capacity to stir the person's reflective ability.[22] It should help him make sense out of life's tangled threads, perhaps through resurrecting certain levels of consciousness from their dormant condition.

Beyond the Bible itself, writings from the church fathers like Augustine's *Confessions*, devotional literature from the Middle Ages, Luther's letters, Shakespeare's dramas, Pascal's *Pensées*, and more recent works such as Kierkegaard's *Either/Or* and Martin Buber's *I and Thou*—all have this quality. Such literature may call a reader to praise or to prayer, to confession or renewal, to agony or to greater responsibility. When life is blinded by tears or sheer stupidity, when guilt hangs about a person's neck like a stone, the understanding of a writer may drive a shaft of light into his awareness and stir him to joyous activity again.

[22] I am indebted to Samuel H. Miller for ideas from an address presented at the 100th Anniversary of the founding of the General Theological Library, Boston, Mass., reprinted from their *Bulletin*, LIII, No. 3, in *Protestant Church Buildings and Equipment* (Nov., 1961), pp. 17, 42-43, 51-52.

v. The Larger Fellowship of Concern

Persons take all kinds of concerns to ministers—spiritual, legal, medical, financial, educational—often *prior* to consulting some other professional person. Clergymen, charged with many complex tasks, sooner or later sense their human limitations. They are dependent upon resource persons within their own churches and in the community who can share their pastoral labors. In early centuries, both in primitive tribes and in advanced civilizations, priests assumed responsibilities not only in religious matters but also in medical and other affairs. They were "all things to all men," largely because there were few other sources of help available. In recent centuries, however, entire orders of professions have developed in various cultures, and in the present century excellent vocational training has become requisite for physicians, educators, nurses, and social workers, as well as for ministers.

Because of both the complexities of modern life and the partialness of persons who now specialize in one area, those in the helping professions have become dependent upon each other's wisdom and aid. Specialization within the professions has created the necessity for group consultation, referral, and therapy. While lines of demarcation are not always distinct between helpers in churches and communities, pastoral consultation and co-operation with others is essential today.

1. *Resource Persons*

One of the chief advantages of functioning within a church setting is the larger fellowship of concern comprised by the pastor and his people. Some skilled resource persons are available within his own church membership. Others are employed on the staff of a sister church or serve professionally in the community. A volunteer church school teacher may have a greater redemptive influence upon his or her group than can the pastor—through the gentle pressure of personal interest, availability, understanding, kinship of sex, age, or cultural background. Like a vector in science, one personality exerts force of greater magnitude upon a certain church member than does another. When troubled, facing a decision, or in crisis, an individual turns for help to that trusted person whom he cherishes, who understands, listens, prays with him, and truly cares.

A division of labor has been necessitated not only among church staff members and volunteers, but also between clergymen and available persons in the helping professions. Interprofessional co-operation in ministering to persons has to be made effective between local practitioners at the community level. There have been misunderstandings and malpractices in the past. Ministers resent the tendency of certain medical specialists to cut a person's church ties, once he has been referred temporarily to them. Again, clergymen and physicians frequently fail to correlate their professional interests and to communicate even in a joint clinical ministry to the same individual or family.

This mutual exclusiveness has usually been broken down when representatives of the varied professions discuss their mutual concerns and problems. Action research in interprofessional co-operation, such as the Kokomo Project conducted by Granger Westberg, indicates clearly that ministers and doctors *can* meet, share their wisdom, and unite in support of health and improved family life.[23] The "priesthood of believers" must operate in community service, or this great Christian principle remains only an ideal instead of a reality.

Certain principles guide the clergyman's relationships with community resource persons. First, interprofessional co-operation must be a two-way or dialogic affair, founded upon ties of trust between practitioners. This implies that social workers, educators, physicians, and ministers are to determine how each group perceives its task and must develop respect for what is distinctive in others. Getting to know the other person's perspective is disarming and usually leads to mutual confidence. Ministers cannot expect to have the esteem of others unless they give mutual respect to them.

Second, community health team members can admit their partial-

---

[23] Granger E. Westberg, *Minister and Doctor Meet* (New York: Harper & Row, 1961), pp. 163-76.

ness as specialists and call upon one another's resources when referral is clearly indicated. In a recent national survey on mental health, a majority of the interviewees indicated that they had experienced some type of emotional problem. Forty-three per cent of those who sought help reported that they sought it first from a minister. Thirty-five per cent went first to their physician.[24] Yet the report further indicated that ministers are slow to refer disturbed persons on to medical resources. Referral need not be viewed as a pastoral failure. Rather, it is an opportunity to help people focus their needs and obtain help appropriate to them.

Third, there are occasions which call for particular resources or skills, and therefore for pastoral care by referral. This calls for community information as well as for pastoral introductions to other persons or agencies. This leads to the pastor's question, "To whom shall we refer?" In his index, *The Pastor and Community Resources* (Bethany Press, 1960), Charles Kemp has listed the civic, medical, governmental, educational, and social welfare agencies of the average city. He provides space for writing in the addresses of the local Family Service agencies, Travelers' Aid Society, mental health unit, Red Cross, Salvation Army, day schools, employment agencies, hospitals, and public welfare personnel. This index, plus the publications of local church councils and Community Councils, provide essential sources of information for referral.

"Why should I refer my people away from God and the church, their best sources of spiritual help?" asks the minister. To which we reply: a pastor does not refer people *away from* God and the church. He simply puts them in touch with a skilled helper; he does not deny them the help they need. The pastor cannot expect a psychiatrist or social worker, for example, to be a lay evangelist, but he is free to ask the resource person directly about his attitude toward the religion of his clients. It is just as erroneous for a psychiatrist to deny his patient a clergyman's counsel in some religious matter. A pastoral counselor is not to be perceived as a "psychotherapist"; he is to be relied upon as a Christian min-

[24] Gerald Gurin *et al.*, *Americans View Their Mental Health* (New York: Basic Books, 1960), pp. 314-17.

ister. Neither is the church to be viewed as merely another "service agency" in the community. The church majors in man's spiritual welfare before God. Thus referral is a mutual rather than a one-sided affair. The pastor helps as he can and depends upon the aid of others when it is clearly necessary.

2. *Referral Procedure*

Suppose that a teen-age girl who is an expectant mother out of wedlock turns to the church for guidance. She needs emotional support in her mixed feelings of regret, of being trapped, of hostility, and shame. She may feel that she does not want the child, that she has jeopardized her future and deeply injured her parents. There is the question of marriage, abortion, running away, staying at home, or entering a home for unwed mothers. Legal, medical, and financial considerations are involved, plus large blocs of time for her counsel and care. Shall the pastor consent to arrange medical care and a private (and probably illegal) adoption for her unwanted baby? If a deformed child is born, who will provide for him or her, the young mother, *and* the minister who has assumed such great risks?

Several of these matters fall clearly into the specialized areas of other professional persons. More time, medical care, money, and legal aid will be required than the minister alone can muster. Clearly, he will not want to injure the girl further. Neither will a minister do for a person what someone else in the community or adjacent city can do more effectively. He can hear her confession, inspire her hope, stand with her and her stricken family, help them to clarify the future and call upon the resources that are most needful. Also, there is a ministry to the young man involved, and to his family.

The minister calls upon community resources, not in order to pass the buck, but because he wishes the best for all persons concerned. He may say to the girl: "Your situation calls for medical assistance, some legal work, and child care. Would you like for us to talk together with your family about getting this necessary assistance? You have come to me in confidence and I have no intention of betraying your trust. Yet matters will become more complex unless you decide soon upon a course of action." Once such a course of action is begun, the parties are free to move one step at a time. The parents are consulted. The pastor is free to contact professional persons, the young man's family, and to keep in touch with the girl and her family. In this way she will not feel that he has tried to "get rid" of her, or is too busy, judgmental, or embarrassed to see her.

When a person has been a patient in a home for unwed mothers, a resident in a mental hospital, a prisoner, or has received therapy for alcoholism or drug addiction, he or she does not need to be treated as a "case" upon returning home. An individual may be in consultative aftercare with a professional person for months or even years. He or she may have great difficulty communicating with persons at home, in the church, and community. Yet the pastor need not suspect such folk, alter his relation to them, or keep them locked out of church life. Such persons need the strengthening love and spiritual comradeship of Christian people, an opportunity to pick up life's roles, risks, and responsibilities again.

The minister's commitment to seek the finest help available for his people and to function in those roles which he best fills *as a minister* prompt his participation in a larger fellowship of concern. When going to a new community, he should meet persons in the helping professions, interpret his pastoral interests to them, and establish lines of communication and co-operation with them. In this way, he is fulfilling the law of Christ and extending the gospel into the world.

SUGGESTED READING

Casteel, John L. (ed.). *Spiritual Renewal Through Personal Groups.* New York: Association Press, 1957. Various ministers describe the spontaneous groups that have arisen in their churches in recent years.

Knowles, Malcolm S. and Hulda F. *Introduction to Group Dynamics.* New York: Association Press, 1959. A brief survey of the group dynamics process, including terminology and literature. Helpful for laymen.

Oates, Wayne E. *Where To Go for Help.* Philadelphia: Westminster Press, 1957. A reliable guide to community health services, with a discussion of principles for interprofessional co-operation.

Olmsted, Michael S. *The Small Group.* New York: Random House, 1959 (paperback). A carefully constructed sociological appraisal of small-group processes and recent research. A comprehensive guide.

Wittenberg, Rudolph M. *The Art of Group Discipline: A Mental Hygiene Approach to Leadership.* New York: Association Press, 1951. Written from a psychiatric perspective, for social workers and others who work with young people in groups.

III

Procedures and Problems

in Pastoral Care

CHAPTER 7

❦

DYNAMICS OF THE
PASTORAL CONVERSATION

THROUGHOUT this volume, the church's shepherding ministry to the flock of God has been interpreted as the corporate responsibility of pastor and people alike. We have noted that the pastor's distinctive tasks focus upon informing, guiding, and sustaining the church's ministry. The discussion of certain technical considerations in pastoral care and counseling in this and the remaining chapters applies generally to the people of God. In order to keep the focus clear, however, the discussion is addressed primarily to the Protestant minister who serves in a church, educational, or institutional context. As his own situation permits, the spiritual leader is obligated to interpret his ministry to his people and to enlist them in a joint ministry under God.

Clarifying certain concepts and terms seems pertinent at the outset. Since informal calling in homes, hospitals, and so on, as well as more formal multiple-interview counseling sessions, partake of the nature of spiritual conversation, the designation *dynamics of the pastoral conversation* is being used in both an inclusive and an intensive sense. "Pastoral conversation" describes the contextual nature of the minister-person nexus, though the formal tie may be that of pastor-parishioner, chaplain-patient, teacher-student, or layman-neighbor. "Conversation" suggests the give and take of interpersonal dialogue, yet includes such nonverbal factors as the way of life of the participants in the encounter and their changing impressions of each other. "Dynamics" suggests (1) the dimension of depth in human development, (2) the energetic forces at work in interpersonal relationships, as well as (3) the process of personal change through pastoral counseling. All pastoral contacts are not "counseling," when viewed in terms of time and intensity, but may partake of its nature in principle.

God's Word reminds us that his conversations with men are as old as the human story. As God's minister moves along the continuum of caring, from experiences with the *many* in worship to conversations with the *few* or *one* in counseling, he recognizes that God himself continues his conversations with men. In the listening-responding dialogue of counseling, the pastor functions as a facilitator of the divine-human conversation and as a loving personal catalyst, accelerating a counselee's spiritual change and growth. Both the dialogue of the sanctuary and of the pastoral interview are essentially transactions with God.

The particular character of the pastoral conversation, as partaking of the God-man dialogue of existence, is illustrated in an Old Testament paradigm (Gen. 32:24-32). Jacob's wrestling with God's messenger at Jabbok typifies the process of spiritual growth through struggle and encounter. Jacob's history of deceit (he had outwitted Esau, Isaac, and Laban), strange dreams (such as the Bethel vision), and dread of meeting his brother are part of the background. When the news reached him that his alienated brother Esau was approaching, Jacob divided his flocks and family and sent them ahead. Like T. S. Eliot's "hollow man," Jacob remained alone at the camp, facing soul-size problems of old animosities and guilt feelings. At Bethel he had dreamed of God's nearness. Now, alone by the brook, he experienced the divine reality in an awful way. Before Jacob could face his brother he had to give an account of himself to his Creator. As the story proceeds, an anonymous protagonist engaged Jacob in a mortal struggle that night. Rather than avoiding the encounter, Jacob grappled with God's messenger through the night and pled for a blessing. Jacob the deceiver's life was seen to be out of joint; yet he held onto the man until a blessing was given. While this experience is set in antiquity, the pattern of the God-man encounter is clear and provides clues to the process of spiritual change through counseling today.

This brief but significant episode is an integral part of the spiritual biography of a man who was plagued by his past and who worked through his God-man relations with pain and profit. Note the process. (1) A man with a record of failure in relationships was trapped in a crisis with his brother. (2) His wrestling with the dreadful mystery of existence was in reality a reckoning with God. In the process he discovered certain previously hidden truths about himself. (3) Jacob was highly motivated to hold on, to stay with God's messenger until he had worked through the crisis. In its original meaning *crisis* implies a turning point, a dangerous opportunity. Spiritually, it implies an experience of judgment and grace. (4) God's new covenant wth Jacob attested his blessings upon the man's spiritual insight, maturing wisdom, and responsible obedience. (5) Jacob lived thereafter with a new sense of identity, a new name (Israel), new clarity of judgment, and a spirit of venturesomeness springing from his healthy relationship with God.

Aware of divine forgiveness, guidance, and provision, Jacob possessed a new determination to set things right with his brother. Their reconciliation was an application of or generalization upon the new modes of relationship which Jacob had achieved through his encounter with God's messenger. As we consider the nature of contemporary pastoral counseling it is possible to read too little or too much into this and other such conversations in the Bible. While the ancients held a more concrete view of personality than do present-day interpreters, their working through and assimilating past experiences with pain and profit to some degree parallels the counseling process today.

1. Types of Pastoral Conversations

The foregoing paradigm pictures the religious counselor's frame of reference and chief concerns: the perplexed person, the minister, and their interactive relationship before God. With his limited sources of accurate information, a minister cannot know *all* about those who turn to him for help. Concerned about counseling *relationships*, ministers generally do not hold rigidly to one counseling system or therapeutic technique. However, this does not free the pastoral counselor from the responsibility of insight into himself, of learning from experience, or of improving as a facilitator of the divine-human conversation.[1] He can improve in basic attitudes, in understanding relationships, and in the counseling process.

From the outset it has been acknowledged that the minister and his people have both prophetic and pastoral tasks to perform in the world. While winning persons to a saving relationship to God in Christ is crucial, a church's evangelistic function does not exhaust its mission nor fulfill its pastoral obligations to persons (II Tim. 4:1-5). One of these ministries does not seek an imperialism over the other, for the minister is both herald and pastor of God's good news. *Evangelistic* conversations, while primal in church life, are not discussed here but may be explored elsewhere.[2] The loving spirit and personal concern of *pastoral* conversations should inform a church's soul-winning efforts and be carried into the full spectrum of human relationships. Like the evangelist, the counselor is concerned about the "grandeur and misery" of man and about God's gift of eternal life. Shrinking from the peace of shallow minds, he labors so that persons who are weary of cures which do not cure may experience life at its best.

Men turn to Christian guides for help from the pressures of life, even as they turn initially from life in sin to Jesus Christ for salvation. Conversations of a pastoral nature and intent are thus seen to be crucial for relating the implications of the gospel to life. Yet all pastoral conversations are not identical. In *Pastoral Counseling*, Seward Hiltner distinguished *counseling* interviews from

[1] While reading counseling interviews with comments, as in Seward Hiltner's *The Counselor in Counseling* (Nashville, Tenn.: Abingdon Press, 1950; Apex paperback ed., 1962), increases pastoral information, supervised training in a clinical setting is a surer resource for learning pastoral skills.

[2] Samuel Southard, *Pastoral Evangelism* (Nashville, Tenn.: Broadman Press, 1962); Simon Doniger (ed.), *Evangelism and Pastoral Psychology* (Great Neck, N.Y.: Pastoral Psychology Press, 1956); and George E. Sweazey, *Effective Evangelism* (New York: Harper & Row, 1953).

other pastoral contacts which are *precounseling* in nature. Subsequent works on Protestant pastoral counseling have maintained these distinctions, for they indicate a valid qualitative difference in relationships.[3] This distinction involves the amount of time spent with one individual, the degree of intensty of the relationship, as well as the intent of those engaged in the interviews. The concept of the pastor's *continuum of caring*, from the many to the few or one, expresses this distinction without minimizing those conversations which are not of counseling depth. All pastoral conversations—whether counseling or not—in which the human condition is laid bare are significant.

Precounseling conversations may be distinguished from the pastor's perspective by (1) their relatively short duration, (2) the initiative and responsibility which the minister must take in many such interviews, (3) the varied settings in which they may occur, and (4) the fact that they consist chiefly of acute or *cross-sectional* concerns in the immediate life-situation rather than *longitudinal* problems which have developed over an extended number of years. Concerns expressed in such conversations have arisen usually within the "givens" of an immediate choice, crisis, opportunity, and so on rather than out of long-term intrapsychic conflicts or interpersonal tensions. Ministers will note, however, that the individual's need for ordering his existence, for spiritual strength, and for clarification of direction may be as urgent in a single-interview contact as in multiple-interview counseling. He will not minimize such conversations, for from the person's perspective they are usually most significant.

Conversations with persons which precede counseling in time

[3] See Seward Hiltner, *Pastoral Counseling* (Nashville, Tenn.: Abingdon Press, 1949), pp. 125-48; Carroll A. Wise, *Pastoral Counseling: Its Theory and Practice* (New York: Harper & Row, 1951); Paul E. Johnson, *Psychology of Pastoral Care* (Nashville, Tenn.: Abingdon Press, 1953), and Wayne E. Oates (ed.), *An Introduction to Pastoral Counseling* (Nashville, Tenn.: Broadman Press, 1959). The trend for pastoral counseling to determine its own fundamental theory and distinctive practice, with appreciation for advances in other disciplines, is demonstrated by comparing the above with earlier works, such as Richard C. Cabot and Russell L. Dicks, *The Art of Ministering to the Sick* (New York: The Macmillan Co., 1936), and John S. Bonnell, *Psychology for Pastor and People* (New York: Harper & Row, 1948; rev. 1960).

and depth include: (1) social contacts in the community, church, hospital, and elsewhere; (2) supportive calls, often accompanied by prayer, in the hospital or home; (3) teaching interviews, frequently initiated by the pastor in order to prepare persons for church membership or for marriage, interviews for the purpose of interpreting some ecclesiastical or doctrinal matter, or conversations which are disciplinary in intent; (4) confessional interviews in which the person reveals feelings of guilt, hostility, anxiety, and so on in a single conversation; and (5) consultative conversations with staff members, fellow ministers, or other professional persons in behalf of some person or family.

A more formal counseling relationship is recognized when the pastor and an individual who has turned to him for help appraise their past conversations and define a more intensive, longer-term counseling situation. This shift in relationship should be clarified by both participants in the spiritual conversations. Following a reconnaissance or exploratory interview, usually not more than one hour in length, a more formal counseling relationship may be agreed upon. The relationship is structured so that the counselee has major responsibility for continuing the interviews, for terminating them, or for reopening them at any time. While the idea of structuring the interview situation came initially from psychotherapists, defining the counseling relationship and procedure is a requisite for any professional counselor.[4] Structuring the counseling situation involves scheduling *time* periods which are needed to work through the counselee's concerns; agreeing upon a *place* of discreet privacy for the interviews, such as the minister's church office; *clarification* of the counselee's expectations, initiative, and responsibility in the interviews and of the minister's role as counselor.

Conversations with a parishioner, scheduled over a period of some weeks, may enable him or her to work through major concerns with the help of God and clarification of insight. Even as they collaborate in an effort for the counselee to gain a new vantage point, to

[4] Harry S. Sullivan, *The Psychiatric Interview*, ed. Helen S. Perry and Mary L. Gawel (New York: W. W. Norton & Co., 1954), pp. 9-38, and Carl R. Rogers *et al.*, *Client-Centered Therapy* (Boston: Houghton Mifflin Co., 1951), pp. 66-71.

drain guilt feelings or old hatreds, to break a deadlock or turn his life's course in a new direction, others are involved. The person's family may turn to the pastor for help. Appointments may need to be scheduled with both husband and wife, for example. Such social involvement may require additional time and place additional strains upon the counseling relationship, but may be essential for true progress. In pastoral conversations the possibility of professional collaboration and referral should be held open, if such specialized consultation is indicated. With these distinctions in mind, we shall now consider pastoral counseling's function, perspective, and process. In Chapters 8 and 9, ways in which pastoral conversations enable persons to move from an impasse to spiritual pilgrimage again will be demonstrated through case notes of counseling interviews.

II. The Nature of Pastoral Counseling

According to the report cited in Chapter 6, four in ten Americans with deep personal problems turn first to clergymen for help. While encountering such persons is only one aspect of pastoral work and may require only a few hours each week, counseling entails technical understanding which is crucial if these relationships are to be effective. Rather than being a new idolatry or secularized movement, as some clergymen fear, counseling is linked indissolubly with other aspects of pastoral work.

Viewed in its classical theological setting, spiritual conversation is not a novelty but is very ancient indeed. However, counseling is being refined in pastoral work today. Perhaps the *new* aspect of pastoral counseling is the synthesis of interdisciplinary wisdom, discussed in Chapter 2, which has been made available to clergymen. This clearer understanding of the dynamic formation and function of personality is a great resource in pastoral care. Pastoral counseling is commonly recognized today as a skilled means of communicating the implications of the Christian faith in life *with precision*.

While pastoral counseling has received considerable attention in revised theological school curriculums and in varied literature, some clergymen still view conversations with their congregants indifferently. One such minister, a capable Bible expositor, said that he employed "sanctified horse sense" in guiding puzzled parishioners. Such men take a dim view of the necessity for clinical experience as an essential aspect of theological education. A contemporary survey reveals that about one in ten American clergymen has received some kind of supervised clinical experience. According to educational trends, however, this percentage should increase considerably in decades ahead. Many ministers, pushed by the plaguing problems of perplexed persons in their churches and pulled by the numerous opportunities for continuing education today, will sharpen their pastoral skills through competent clinical education.

1. *Distinctive Elements of Pastoral Counseling*

What distinguishes *pastoral* counseling from other kinds of counseling today? First, the pastoral conversation presupposes the God-man dialogue of existence, though theological subjects per se may not be discussed by the counselee. Any human concern in any area of life is the accepted topic of pastoral counseling. When one's life is laid bare before a representative of the Christian faith, the two may rely upon God's presence in their midst (Matt. 18:20). It is unnecessary for the participants to *do* or to *say* something "religious," for the entire relationship partakes inherently of religious experience. Such counseling has been called a means of implementing the expectancy inherent in the Christian life. To a degree, Christian counseling may be viewed as a form of prayer— a conversation with God in the presence of another.

Second, pastoral counseling may be distinguished from other kinds of counseling (educational, psychological, medical, and so forth) on the contextual grounds of a Christian setting and unique resources.[5] While employing principles which are common to other professional counselors, ministers generally engage in interviews

---

[5] An empirical study of the significance of context in counseling has been reported by Seward Hiltner and Lowell G. Colston, *The Context of Pastoral Counseling* (Nashville, Tenn.: Abingdon Press, 1961); see also Wayne E. Oates, *Protestant Pastoral Counseling* (Philadelphia: Westminster Press, 1962), pp. 117-62.

which are church-related in context and pastoral in character. Whether he intends it or not, some persons endow the pastor's counseling with special authority and unique expectations. The Protestant pastor may disavow a father-figure role in preference for a brother-man relationship. However, he cannot control the varied ways in which congregants use him; some will relate to him as a spiritual father. While initiative and responsibility in counseling rest primarily with the counselee, the pastor may have to assist the person in clarifying his or her specific expectations and employment of the counseling process.

For example, a man who had been operating a small contracting business declared bankruptcy. Because his family had been accustomed to a substantial income, they continued personal expenditures as usual. When ready cash had been exhausted and the maximum had been borrowed, the family lost its mortgaged house and some furnishings. Almost desperately, the man turned to his pastor in a period of depression, feeling not only financial impoverishment but a sense of personal failure. After two or three brief conversations, it became clear that the man was trying to use the minister as a financial guarantor to gain refinancing for some future business venture. Progress was made in their relationship with the passing of brief time periods between interviews and with the clarification of the pastor's supportive role. The man was directed to resource persons in the community who might help him to regain financial solvency. Meanwhile, the pastor supported the man's sagging self-esteem, which was slowly recovered as he experienced his own worth before God.

Third, pastoral counseling may be distinguished by the kind of ministry it attempts to perform in relation to what is distinctive among other professional counselors.[6] Fundamentally, *pastoral counseling may be viewed as the process of conversations between a responsible minister and a concerned individual or intimate group, with the intent of enabling such persons to work through their con-*

[6] See the report of a recent conference in which representatives of varied counseling professions, including the ministry, clarified their presuppositions and procedures, *Counseling and Psychotherapy* (New York: New York Academy of Sciences, 1955).

cerns to a constructive course of action. Such a process view of pastoral counseling magnifies the relationship itself rather than a technique per se. Pastoral counselors are eclectic in that they find clues in varied approaches to personality theory and to therapeutic methods. Rather than approaching counselees *either* directively *or* nondirectively, skilled pastoral counselors prefer to share an empathic relationship of mutual trust and responsibility with counselees. Carl R. Rogers and others have determined through extensive research that once a person is able to express his feelings to a responsible listener, who sincerely seeks to perceive his situation, the healing process begins.[7] Such researchers have helped ministers to clarify their own unique counseling methods and goals.

While listening acceptingly to the counselee's feelings, the pastor's mediatorial function is to reflect the mind of Christ as well as the person's own feelings back to him in the interviews. His goal is that the one being counseled develop insight into his feelings and experiences *and* into Christian resources and approaches to life. In this respect, pastoral counseling must move beyond a purely non-directive posture, with confidence in its unique goals and tasks.

In order to perceive the spirit and approach of responsible pastoral couseling, let us contrast brief excerpts from two interviews. The first pastor attempts to control the conversation and to manipulate the counselee, whereas the second is more accepting and responsive to the person's feelings. Though these illustrations overstate the case, the point should be clear.

1. *A directive approach* (the minister's office was the setting for this conversation):

MRS. P: For sometime now things haven't been going very well at home (Mrs. P begins to weep softly).

PASTOR: Come now, Mrs. P, I am sure that things aren't as bad as they seem and I feel sure we can find help in God's Word.

MRS. P: Pastor, you just don't know how bad it is.

[7] See Carl R. Rogers, *Counseling and Psychotherapy* (Boston: Houghton Mifflin Co., 1942); Carl R. Rogers and Rosalind F. Dymond (eds.), *Psychotherapy and Personality Change* (Chicago: University of Chicago Press, 1954); and Rogers, *On Becoming a Person* (Boston: Houghton Mifflin Co., 1961). Also, cf. Johnson, *op. cit.*, pp. 96-102; and Charles W. Stewart, "Relationship Counseling," *Journal of Pastoral Care* (Winter, 1959), pp. 209-19.

PASTOR: I certainly think you have done the right thing, coming to your pastor, I mean. Let's talk about it honestly and openly. Why don't you just start at the beginning and tell me everything.

MRS. P: I just had to talk to someone . . .

Here, the counselor's rigidity and need to control the interview is obvious despite his effort to appear nonchalant. He unconsciously belittles Mrs. P's feelings, reassures her prematurely, and suggests that she tell "everything" in one interview. Rather than conveying acceptance he appears insensitive to her suffering. To his credit, he is willing to listen to her story, though on a fact-gathering basis. A manipulative counselor may help, but obviously may also injure counselees with such superficial relationships.

2. *An accepting-responsive approach* (the following conversation transpired in a general hospital setting):

MR. B: It's like this truck hitting me. Man, it knocked all the evil inside me out of me and I feel clean inside. When we suffer the evil goes out of us. (He described how badly his leg was injured in a truck accident.) When they asked me if my leg was broken, I said, "Broke, broke, broke," and it was. I told 'em to turn it back up toward heaven.

MINISTER: You feel that your suffering is for a purpose then?

MR. B: . . . I really have caught a hard time in life. I don't know why my wife would leave me like this, just when I need her so much . . . alone . . . with nobody to care. She don't love me; she just loves herself. She thinks I'm nuts.

MINISTER: Why do you suppose she thinks that?

MR. B: Because I was in a mental hospital . . . that's before we got married. (He continued his explanation at some length.)

Here there is a clear effort by the minister to "get with" and stay with the patient's feelings. The man expresses several things, but rejection and dependency are paramount. Until Mr. B confronts himself through their visits, however, his talking will provide primarily a release of strong emotions rather than true perception of his feelings. He may gain *support* rather than *insight*. Fortunately, the minister will permit him to use their times together in an accepting fashion and to grow, *if* he is the growing kind.

As far as time, the person's condition, and circumstances permit, the pastoral counselor will hear him patiently, respond reflectively, and comment carefully, all so that the counselee may clarify his own feelings and assume responsibility for his own decisions and life tasks. Pastoral counseling is prudently permissive *and* persuasive, accepting *and* confronting, rather than being what one thoughtful commentator has termed an adventure in passivity. The uniqueness of pastoral counseling lies in the use which the participants make of the self-confrontation occurring at any moment in the relationship, and of the illumination—human and divine—given in their face-to-face meetings in a Christian context.

Pastoral counseling focuses upon distinctive resources and objectives, keeping in mind the counselee's God-relationship, contemporary calling among persons, and ultimate destiny. The minister's appraisal of the counselee's potential for growth (gaining *ego-strength*) through pastoral counseling is strategic to the whole process.[8] He needs to distinguish supportive and growth processes, which will be clarified in later discussion. While paralleling some specialized therapeutic procedures, pastoral counseling claims unique contextual grounds and qualifies the kinds of ministry it seeks to render.

2. *Pastoral Counseling and Psychotherapy*

A counselor's perspective determines the resources upon which he may rely and the goals he keeps in mind. The minister sees a person in a religious setting who is facing some decision, problem, or loss and who is shaping a better strategy for life. Whereas the psychiatrist, in a medical setting, sees a client or patient whose illness has become a strategic retreat from the pressures of life. He or she turns to therapy in order to regroup resources and regain some degree of health and composure for life's demands. On the illness-health continuum, pastors assist counselees who are relatively free from immobilizing symptoms. Psychiatrists, on the other hand, diagnose and treat those who are enslaved by some emotional stress or disorder.

[8] See Howard J. Clinebell, "Ego Psychology and Pastoral Counseling," *Pastoral Psychology*, XIV (Feb., 1963), 26-36.

While psychotherapists look primarily to the "healing forces of life" within their patients for recovery, pastoral counselors depend upon the power of God present in the midst of life for constructive changes in counselees. All healing forces are God-given initially. In Luke 17:21, Jesus implies that *sensitivity* to the revelation of God "within you" is the clue to his coming for anyone. Christian redemption includes both a point of decision and a process of spiritual development. The primary *goals* of pastoral counseling are (1) to facilitate growth in the counselee who desires spiritual wisdom and strength for constructive character change, and (2) to support an individual who seeks to mobilize resources for life during some crisis.

Growth or insight counseling is *longitudinal* in nature in that the childhood roots of adult behavior are revealed in the counselee's self-history. A counselee may reveal certain patterns of mental dynamisms in various areas of life adjustment, such as his childhood family, school, social, religious, marital, and vocational situations.[9] Psychiatrists are trained to cope with such patterns and drives in psychotherapy more effectively than are ministers in counseling. It is to be hoped that insights gained in the growth counseling process will be generalized in the person's present and future life relationships. Some problem-solving counseling, on the other hand, is *cross-sectional* in nature, in that immediate concerns or conflicts are explored in a series of relatively short-term interviews. Here the need may be for reassurance, wisdom in some decision, family harmony, forgiveness, support during grief work, or the recovery of hope.

These goals for pastoral counseling are predicated upon a relatively enduring relationship of trust between the minister and his people. His evaluation of the counselee's situation, spiritual re-

[9] The term *mental dynamisms* or *defense mechanisms* is clarified in *A Psychiatric Glossary* as: "Specific intrapsychic defensive processes, operating unconsciously, which are employed to seek resolution of emotional conflict and freedom from anxiety. Conscious efforts are frequently made for the same reasons, but true mental mechanisms are out of awareness (unconscious)." *The Glossary*, prepared by the Committee on Public Information, American Psychiatric Assn., 1957, may be obtained from Mental Health Materials Center, 1790 Broadway, New York, N.Y., or from local mental health centers.

sources, regressions, plateaus, and growth is most significant. Generally, the pastor faces many time demands and will limit his counseling with one individual to a maximum of eight to ten interviews. As in other pastoral conversations, the minister must decide whether he will continue as counselor or refer the person to someone else for help. The clinically trained pastor *may* extend counseling periods beyond this limit but should do so in consultation with a psychiatrist.

With such criteria in mind, it is clear that some disturbed persons are inaccessible to pastoral counseling. Rather than talking out their problems, they "act out" conflicts through antisocial, dangerous, or otherwise *sick* behavior. While they do not need *labels*, persons whose destructive or compulsive behavior usually invites social disapproval or rejection actually need help. If an individual's behavior is appraised by family, friends, or his minister to be highly inappropriate or bizarre, a medical referral is in order.[10] The man who hates the world, the woman who dresses eccentrically, or the hostile young person may simply want attention or affection. The *degree* of social or emotional disorder is the clue to seeking medical advice. A person in a prolonged period of depression, the delusional individual who feels himself to be constantly persecuted, the person who withdraws from all social contact and sits staring at the walls of one room, or the person who becomes religiously "out of character" through obsessive Bible reading, compulsive praying, crying, and so on—each of these is beyond the limits of time and skill of pastoral practice. Referral for medical consultation, in co-operation with the person's family, is appropriate in such instances.

How then does counseling by responsible clergymen differ from the psychotherapeutic relationship between a troubled person and a psychiatrist? *First,* while the pastoral conversation may and should

[10] Guides for recognizing serious mental illness, as well as for rehabilitation of the formerly ill, may be obtained from the National Assn. for Mental Health, 13 East 37th St., New York, N. Y.; local mental health offices; the National Institute of Mental Health, Bethesda, Md.; the National Academy of Religion and Mental Health, 2 East 103rd St., New York, N. Y., and the center mentioned in n. 9, above.

be therapeutic (healing) in the redemptive sense, a minister's work is not to be viewed as "therapy" in a medical sense. *Second*, while he is aware of unconscious drives in counselees, the minister is trained to relate to persons primarily at conscious levels of experience and conflict, whereas a psychiatrist is trained to cope with unconscious dimensions of experience. Such a therapist is free to explore deeper levels of intrapsychic development and to employ such mechanisms as identification, projection, transference, and countertransference with his patients. Hypnosis, drugs, and various forms of shock therapy may also be employed in a hospital setting. Meanwhile, research remains to be made into the lower levels of prayer, the effect of faith on "dated emotions," the influence of forgiveness upon unconsciously motivated regressive behavior, and the power of Christian love.

Third, while Christian counseling and psychotherapy are both social, collaborative, and growth-oriented, the former is directed to persons who are relatively free to carry out their constructive strivings whereas the psychiatrist is trained to treat those whose defenses are so shattered that they are temporarily immobilized by illness. *Fourth*, while the home and church setting is relatively free and unprotected, an institutional setting provides controls and protection for the person who may be dangerous either to himself or to others.[11] *Fifth*, the psychiatrist has several years of clinical preparation for his task, plus the resources of medical diagnosis, team treatment, and varied forms of therapy at hand.[12]

While he is not an alien to his patient's religious orientation, the medical therapist's task is to help the patient understand the nature of his bondage and to acquire a reasonable mastery of life. He labors in order that the patient's illness may become a gateway to health. The pastoral counselor, on the other hand, facilitates the individual's relationship with God and men, depending upon

[11] See Edith Stern, *Mental Illness: A Guide for the Family* (New York: Harper & Row, 1957); paperback copies are available from offices indicated in footnote 10, above.

[12] The medically trained psychiatrist (an M.D.) should be distinguished from the psychoanalyst who may not have a medical background. The latter functions as a professional therapist in long-term psychoanalysis, often without the careful diagnostic services of a psychiatric consultation.

the help of the Holy Spirit. He holds the Christian faith to be the
integrating center of life. Both clergymen and Christian psychiatrists
are concerned with the preservation of spiritual-mental health in
our society, and with the diminution of the incidence of emotional
illness. They are interested in the recovery of health but are concerned, too, with family living and social programs which will reduce stress and prevent much illness and suffering. The preservation
of health is an area for collaborative concern, mutual understanding
of perspectives, and responsible action by representatives of all the
helping professions.

3. *What Can Talking Do?*

We noted in Chapter 3 that the church is always in the process
of being born and reborn within the arena formed by talk and
attentiveness among Christians. Counseling, wherein hearts are examined in an environment of love and trust, has become a vital concern of all who live at the center of religious communications.
Yet talking is as old as the human race. God created man in his
own image for companionship, for communion; thus, to talk is to
be both human and Godlike. The words of persons struggling for the
moment of healing have long been disclosed in the prayers, solilo-
quies, and dialogues of the Bible and great literature. Psalm 42
discloses the conversation between the stronger and weaker selves
within *one* psalmist: "Why are you cast down, O my soul, and why
are you disquieted within me?" (42:5). The stronger self responds:
"Hope in God; for I shall again praise him, my help and my God."
The act of talking to oneself is a solitary experience, reserved in
our thinking for the lonely person, the remote mystic, the tender
child, and the puzzled citizen of earth.

Talking with another breaks the lonely monologue of existence.
The discourse of one troubled or overwhelmed, previously conducted within himself, breaks into dialogue with someone who desires to understand. The depths of the overburdened one meet the
depths of one who listens with perceptive, liberating love. As in
prayer, so in counseling God grants the sufferer his steadfast love
and provides a way for him to live again. Spiritual self-discovery

and affirmation come not in "mere talk" alone but in meeting God in another's presence. In this respect, ministers dare not view their conversations with others indifferently. It is precisely in the pastoral conversation that pastoral care focuses most intently upon the individual and his needs.

Talking to oneself can do little more than confirm one's need to truly communicate, to be heard. Talking to a responsible pastoral listener opens the person to the possibility of community, of love, and understanding. Language is a vital part of being human and of experiencing others as persons. For some, *small talk* is enough. Language is a convenient façade for holding the other person at a distance. The superficially humorous person, the shy or withdrawn person, the dictatorial talker, and the flighty conversationalist are each basically insecure individuals. Thus they dare not exchange the coin of conversation in depth for fear of losing control, of being discovered in their weakness. Others, with tremendous feelings of guilt or hostility, fear that the truth will come out if they talk to another. Some persons, however, long to share their lives with someone who will listen, who will hear them express their true feelings, help them to ventilate their souls and affirm their real selfhood.

The following excerpt from a conversation between a non-Christian businessman and one of his Protestant employees reflects the need to clarify feelings, to be understood and accepted. The employer, Mr. Streckman, middle-aged and divorced, had been dating a married woman, a friend of his employee, Mr. Doty, with whom he asked to speak one day. Doty perceived his boss as an insecure man, dominating every situation in which he found himself. He also knew of Mr. S's illicit love affair with another employee, Mrs. W. One day Mr. Streckman called Doty in for a conference.

MR. s: Doty, I asked you in here because I wanted to talk with you about a personal matter. I would count it a privilege for you to give me some advice.

DOTY: Of course, if I can. I'd be glad to try.

MR. s: Mrs. W has been gone now for about one month. Isn't that right?

DOTY: Yes, about four weeks, I guess.

MR. S: Tell me, truthfully, what did you think about us?

DOTY: In what way did you mean?

MR. S: I mean, what did you think about us together?

DOTY: Actually, it was none of my business; but, as a Christian, I certainly couldn't condone your relationship. Aside from that, I'm disappointed in both of you.

MR. S: Why?

DOTY: Well, after all, Mrs. W is married.

MR. S: So . . . ? She doesn't love her husband.

DOTY: What makes you feel so sure that she doesn't love her husband?

MR. S: Because she loves me. However, I don't understand why she went back to Chicago with him.

DOTY: Could it be that you have been wrong about her?

MR. S: No, but I guess she just had to be sure. I never really have understood. Do you know?

DOTY: Did you know that she and I talked about this several times before she left?

MR. S: I knew you had talked, but I didn't know what about.

DOTY: She was concerned about the situation you two were in and just wanted someone to talk to.

MR. S: What did she tell you?

DOTY: We talked about several things . . . she is confused. She thinks she loves you both. She just couldn't make up her mind what to do.

MR. S: Yes, she told me that. (Pause.) She must have told you quite a lot.

DOTY: We did talk quite a while.

My purpose in citing this sequence is not to demonstrate the *how* of pastoral conversation but to call attention to the desire of some anxious persons to talk to someone. In this instance, a Christian employee exchanged words in rather direct fashion with his narcissistic boss. Their subsequent conversations were primarily intellectual exchanges about religion, with Mr. S remaining adamantly opposed to the Christian faith and ethic. He did not clarify his ambiguous feelings during this interview, for he wanted primarily (1) to have Mrs. W back and (2) to have Doty's approval of their relationship, if possible. This account also bears out the fact that life itself is the larger arena of *pastoral* conversations, as church members relate daily with others in the world. Conversing with persons with redemptive intent, while not pastoral counseling, is a true form of spiritual conversation.

Pastoral counselors perceive that merely getting people to talk is not sufficient. In fact, prolonged talking may be dangerous if the person is deeply depressed; he *could* talk himself into suicide! Again, it has been long recognized that the "presenting" problem—the thing or things that the counselee speaks about in the beginning —may be only the preface to his deepest concerns. Persons tend to send up "trial balloons" in order to test the minister's acceptance and good faith. Participants in pastoral conversations will recognize that the moment of truth has come when the counselee's willingness to encounter himself in another's presence is made explicit. Until that time, he may use the relationship to gain sympathy in a situation, to gain control of some person, or to use the minister in ways other than as a counselor. Insight in *growth* counseling and support in *crisis* counseling begin when self-discovery begins. When the counselee experiences himself with the counselor as the kind of person he really is, self-disclosure moves toward self-perception, self-acceptance, and self-affirmation within the community of faith.

Wayne Oates' *Protestant Pastoral Counseling* suggests that the pastor's interviews with a counselee form a series of covenants—of confrontation, confession, forgiveness, restitution, and concern—under the guidance of the Holy Spirit. Normally, the person moves from preoccupation with himself to tender concern for others in such a process of growth. Oates has written of counseling in a Christian context:

> Pastoral counseling is not *just* talking with people, [nor] . . . just listening to people. Pastoral counseling is not *just* focusing on specific "problems" that must be "solved." Pastoral counseling includes all of these, but it is not *just* any one of them. Pastoral counseling . . . takes place either implicitly or explicitly within the commonwealth of eternal life as we know it in Jesus Christ. The way of life we have known in times past, the decisive turnings in our way of life called for in the living present, and the consideration of the end of our existence, our destiny—all these

come to focus in the spiritual conversation known as pastoral counseling.[13]

Talking things over with a minister may *not* help. Some ministers' files record numerous instances when counseling has failed to help a distraught or struggling soul.[14] Memories of failures haunt some clergymen—the counselee who went from a pastoral interview into a psychotic episode, or to prison for some act, or deeper into alcoholism, on to the divorce court, or to take a life—his own or that of another. Few failures of pastoral counseling have ever been published, partly because ministers are reticent about revealing their mistakes. Some common hazards and examples of unskillful counseling appear in a *Casebook in Pastoral Counseling*. The editors present many helpful cases with comment and conclude the work with a few cases in which pastoral mismanagement of the relationship is obvious.[15] While humbling, a minister's failures may teach him more than constant success.

Thus far, several principles have been implied which should guide the minister's conversations with others. Believing in the integrity of counseling, he is to (1) approach this aspect of pastoral care, not with a hit-or-miss attitude, but with clinical skill and redemptive intent; (2) cherish every individual as one created in God's image for whom Christ died; (3) rely upon the counselee's capacity for decision-making and responsible action as far as the person's condition permits; (4) when a person turns to him for help, structure the counseling relationship with the individual so that their times and places of meeting and his helping role in the conversations will be clear; and (5) commit himself to counselees with due recognition of his own limitations of training, time, and skill, and due respect for the best interest of his people. Rather than moving beyond his depth professionally, risking further injury to a suffering person, he may refer certain counselees into the skilled hands of trusted colleagues. The cardinal principle that *all pastoral con-*

[13] Oates, *Protestant Pastoral Counseling*, pp. 164-65, 183-88.

[14] To their credit, Hiltner and Colston, *op. cit.*, record instances when counseling apparently failed to help, pp. 147-68. Pastoral counseling is not conceived as a universal panacea for human woe even by its most ardent advocates.

[15] Newman S. Cryer, Jr. and John M. Vayhinger (eds.), *Casebook in Pastoral Counseling* (Nashville, Tenn.: Abingdon Press, 1962), pp. 289-309.

versations partake of religious experience both heightens and intensifies the counseling relationship.

III. COUNSELING AS RELATIONSHIP AND PROCESS

With the foregoing principles in mind, how does the Christian pastor become a *counselor* to persons? I have suggested that a minister cannot force a counseling relationship upon an unwilling object of his pastoral art. While he is at liberty to take the initiative in most clerical functions, when the focus is upon counseling the minister is invited as guest into an ongoing personal or family situation. When a burdened person needs to use his clergyman as a counselor, he should be cherished and sustained more intensively during the difficult period of his pilgrimage. A counselee's need for intensive care is thus viewed as temporary, until he is able to assume full responsibility in life again.

It is difficult for some troubled persons to ask for help. How does the minister get his people to come to him with their concerns? Primarily, through experiences of pastoral sharing *prior* to counseling—such as preaching, worship, letters, visitation, and his spirit—people discover whether or not they can turn to their pastor in confidence. They will *not* turn (1) to a perfectionist who leaves the impression that "real" Christians have no problems; nor (2) to a rigid authoritarian person who sees only one side to every story; nor (3) to the cocky debunker who likes to impress people rather than minister to them; nor yet (4) to the preoccupied administrator who "uses" people in order to achieve successful church operations. The true pastor's spirit, skills, and readiness to act in another's behalf will be sensed by his people. When overpowering problems arise they will feel free and welcome to arrange a meeting with him in order to discuss their concerns.

Once the counseling process has been initiated by an inquirer, how shall the participants use their relationship, determine progress, and finally terminate the counseling interviews? Theoretically, the stages in their relationship, when viewed in linear fashion, will include: (1) experiences of pastoral sharing prior to counseling, (2) entering the counselee's private world in a more formal interview relationship, (3) appraisal of the person's situation, (4) sharing the person's plight in Christian perspective, and (5) termination of counseling and resumption of a less formal relationship again.[16] Since we have previously explored varied dimensions of the pastor's caring, appraisal, and referral, we shall be discussing chiefly the counseling process itself. Unlike psychotherapy, pastoral counseling is both preceded and succeeded by a relatively enduring pastor-person relationship within the Christian community.

1. *Pastoral Sharing Prior to Counseling*

A counseling relationship may arise voluntarily as the pastor shares some crisis or difficulty with persons in the church. At two o'clock one morning, for example, a minister received a telephone message from the sister of Mrs. James, a member of his congregation. Calling from a midtown hospital, the sister reported that Mrs. James had just come from the delivery room and had been told that her baby was dead at birth. "Would it help if I came on to the hospital immediately?" the minister inquired. She said that it would, so he made a brief hospital call in order to reassure the young couple by standing with them in their loss and sorrow.

From that experience a counseling relationship was born between the young couple and their minister. Following the child's burial and the mother's return home from the hospital, the pastor had several counseling conversations with Mr. and Mrs. James. They told of their childhood religious backgrounds, of their indifference to God as young adults, and of their interpretation of the child's death as a religious experience. In time, the participants in these interviews grew closer to God and to each other as they sought to interpret both the child's death and their own Christian responsibility in life. Also, the young husband and wife were drawn into the larger stream of the church's fellowship and ministry. Rather than rejecting God, through the counseling periods they affirmed his presence in their lives and their desire to serve him more adequately through the church.

[16] Cf. Sullivan *et al.*, *The Psychiatric Interview, op. cit.*, pp. 59-137. Personal contacts with Seward Hiltner and Wayne E. Oates have helped me to refine my concept of the stages of the pastoral counseling process.

An individual's reaching out to the minister may come quietly as someone speaks to him after worship services, or during a home visit, or in a casual moment: "I've been wanting to discuss a little matter with you for some while now." If it is not convenient to talk at that time, the minister may suggest that a time and place be made for their meeting. Then the person will be free to express himself without fear of exposure or feeling that he is imposing on the minister's time. Upon other occasions, the cry for help may come instantly, almost violently. The minister may learn that a person is threatening suicide or that a crushed wife is leaving her alcoholic husband. A young person in his church may have been apprehended in a crime, with family dreams for their son shattered by one delinquent episode. Such forces push people to their minister for help.

2. *Entering the Counselee's Private World*

At some stage of personal conflict or family disruption persons often turn to the church for help. They may wait until they are quite desperate, feeling that the Christian pastor is their last resort. The formal inception of counseling begins in an exploratory interview initiated usually by a person who is seeking help on life's journey. When a minister is permitted access into a person's inner world, he may be assured that the sufferer seeks resources beyond himself in his difficulty. In their meetings the minister will be alert to the person's view of his life-situation, reasons for turning to the counselor, varied forces working as "hidden agenda" in their relationship, and the person's own expectations in relation to him. Troubled persons turn to a clergyman because of his availability and because he represents certain resources or kinds of help in the counselee's thinking.

Pastoral counseling's effectiveness is influenced considerably by the *motivation* of the person who seeks a pastoral conference. Occasionally a friend, marriage partner, parent, church staff member, or some professional person in the community will suggest that an individual consult a Christian minister. Such a person may feel that he or she has to talk to a minister in order to comply with a

demand or to satisfy someone who is significant to him. He may
not be motivated from within to get help for himself. Ministers
know that spiritual insight cannot be forced down unwilling throats.
With human will and freedom in mind, we know that persons must
want help before they can actually profit from counseling.

When a congregant turns to a minister for counsel, certain *unspoken influences* are at work in their interviews. The counselee's
"hidden agenda" requires skillful management throughout their
relationship. For one thing, a person likes to put his or her best
foot forward in the presence of a man of God. He had a need to
be respectable or to feel worthy in the presence of someone whom
he respects. Thus, the surface materials in their early interviews
may be only a mask, a façade, a smoke screen. The counselee may
struggle painfully to keep up appearances even as he suffers and
longs for release from his bondage. Some predicament has driven
him into a counselor's office; yet, he may repress or project his unworthy feelings in an effort to avoid their reality. When such a
person is confronted with his self-avoidance or mask-wearing, he
may deny it and regress, may rest on his old plateau of respect-
ability—or push on to new wisdom and responsibility.

Along with this childlike need to be nice in a minister's presence is the fear of talking too much, of becoming too well known
by another. A person may say, for example, "Some people talk too
much, like I've been doing here. I'm sorry for bursting out like
that. I hope you'll forgive me." Fear of reprisal or exposure may
persist subterraneanly. A person may avoid the real issue through
the pretense of sharing. When a counselee feels that he or she has
divulged too much and fears rejection, exposure, or punishment,
the pastor should reassure him of their confidential relationship
and of God's acceptance of his thoughts and feelings. At the point
of professional ethics, the minister must be certain that he does
not divulge such *privileged communication* nor use personal information in a hurtful manner.

Another unspoken influence upon the process is the counselee's
capacity to relate to and reveal himself in depth to another person. Pastors recognize that "people vary widely . . . in the tempo

with which they become close to and involved with others."[17] Withdrawn or depressed individuals may have been betrayed previously by parents or other persons (including other ministers) who have run roughshod over them. Reticent counselees may speak slowly and quietly but will resent being pushed for information by an impatient counselor. Others experience stricture of though or speech processes when the conversation turns to such matters as sex, money, and feelings of hostility toward parents, guilt toward one's children or mate, or sin against God. Still other persons demonstrate a parading posture, a need to be dramatic and to impress their minister with their unique situation or peculiar history.

I have said that beneath-the-surface forces such as needing to be nice, fear of self-disclosure, and one's tempo of relatedness operate as hidden agenda in counseling relationships. Another such factor is that of the *private meanings* which different persons assign to religious symbols and theological concepts. Closely related are their quaint cultural taboos, superstitions, powerful prejudices, and resistance to growth or change. What meaning, for example, does the counselee assign to such remarks as "I feel that my daughter has become my *cross* because of the way I treated her years ago," or "I can't *trust* anyone any more," or "My *prayers* don't seem to get out of this room." "I think that I have committed the *unpardonable sin*." I don't have anything left to *live* for since daddy *died*." "The *devil* has really gotten into me lately." "Why does *God punish* us like this?" or "My *faith* is all I've got"——? Communication in depth is impossible until such words are assigned meaning by the participants in the interviews. Semantic problems are more complex for ministers who serve in foreign lands, for chaplains who work with retarded and emotionally disturbed patients, and others in specialized settings. Acquaintance with the counselee's cultural subgroup, religious tradition, intelligence level, and personal idioms of thought will help the minister to perceive a person's private world with greater clarity.

Another nonverbal force at work in the relationship is the kind of hopes or *expectations* the burdened person holds in relation to

[17] Oates, *Protestant Pastoral Counseling,* p. 209.

the minister. Some expect the minister to "patch up" everything from academic failure and premarital pregnancy to general nervousness and amnesia. Yet he is not a miracle-worker. Some may try to push him into the role of family peacemaker or ecclesiastical policeman. The pastor's ministry of family reconciliation is valuable. Yet he is not to become an errand boy for whimsical church members, nor make pawns of estranged marriage partners. Helping a person to clarify his hopes and to redefine life directions is a valid part of the counseling process.

While the relationship is still in its early stages, if the person's condition, *upon appraisal,* merits specialized medical or other attention, the loving pastor will rely upon the best possible sources of help for his church member. His ministry may be that of interpretation, assisting the individual to focus his needs and clarify the best source of aid available to him. On the other hand, as the counselor develops sensitivity to the situation of the other person, enters his world and walks around "in his skin," the healing process has already begun. Together, he and the counselee must transcend the pretense of sharing and move into the real areas of suffering. Their shared conversations and the healing presence of God in the intervals between their interviews form significant links in the process of spiritual healing.

3. *Sharing the Person's Plight and Pilgrimage*

Longer-term pastoral counseling is essentially an interpersonal process in which a Christian minister shares an individual's plight intensively and temporarily until the person works through his concern and resumes his pilgrimage once more. The counselor's effectiveness will be determined in large degree by his employment of *resources available within the counseling relationship itself.*

Whether he engages in long-term growth counseling, shares the primary moments of life, or supports persons in crises, the minister's objective is to *meet* his people in order to facilitate their spiritual development, not to *use* some method *on* them. Were his people to feel that he prefabricates their conversations, threads stock phrases into interviews, or uses schemes to manipulate their decisions to his side, they would avoid close encounters with him. At times, the man of God will not know what to say in response to some confession or plea for help. Rather than utter some superficial prayer or meaningless remark, he and the person concerned will both rely upon God's Spirit for guidance and strength for life.

While the relationship itself is crucial for the counselee's support or growth, what specific resources are open to participants in counseling conversations? Pastoral counseling consists chiefly of listening and responding to *words* and *feelings* being expressed, of asking questions for clarification, and of making comments of a responsive nature. Occasional questions may be asked by the counselor (1) in order to clarify information, (2) to enable the counselee to clarify his thoughts or feelings, (3) to facilitate transitions in thought, and (4) to confront the counselee in order that he or she may perceive the consequences of their feelings or course of action.

In order to become aware of another's life-situation, *listening* is the primary resource available to counselors. The pastor listens not to get the facts but to perceive the person's world and enable him to view his plight from a Christian perspective. Neither does he listen in order to provide superficial palliatives for obvious problems. The minister has more to offer that mere patent medicines for the grievous wounds in men's souls. As a physician refrains from covering cancerous tissue with a bandage until the tumor has been excised, so the minister does not urge "peace of mind" upon persons who are practicing an inadequate way of life. Counselees resent being pushed from clergymen's offices with oversimplified solutions to their overpowering concerns. Some solutions *are* simple, but the person needs to experience restoration *from within*. He must recover spiritual health for himself! In discussing counseling skills, Dean Johnson wisely suggested that any statement from the counselor should be offered tentatively rather than with an attitude of finality.[18] His comment was directed to marriage counselors but applies to pastoral counselors as well. If the helper "takes things

[18] Dean Johnson, *Marriage Counseling: Theory and Practice* (Englewood Cliffs, N. J.: Prentice-Hall, 1961), pp. 128-51.

over" for the counselee, a situation of unhealthy dependency or resentment may be created.

The dialogue in pastoral counseling is dynamic and responsive rather than static or passive, as the two meet in God's presence. When the counselor comments, his words should be chosen with deliberate care, with one of a variety of purposes in mind. His comments may (1) express *empathy* as he seeks to identify with the counselee; (2) *invite* the person's self-disclosure; (3) *reflect* the counselee's feelings back to him for thought or clarification; (4) *affirm* what has been said; (5) help to *effect transitions* from one pattern of thought to another; and occasionally (6) *confront* the person with Christian truth or with possible consequences of his feelings or plan of action. Also, the counselor is free to (7) *summarize* what has been said so that a plateau may be achieved in the conversation. Comments in order (8) *to reassure* or offer support may be made when in keeping with the reality situation. Some counselors err in reassuring sufferers prematurely, prior to the dawning of an inner pathway of light. Comments along the lines indicated above will be noted in conversations recorded in subsequent chapters.

As the clergyman shares a person's plight he cherishes both his counselee and his Christian faith. Once their relationship is secure, the person comes to feel that his pastor truly desires to understand him. When he senses that he is being understood, he interprets the pastor's statements as attempts, not to control, but to facilitate his growth. The counselor is viewed as an enabling rather than a threatening person. Through participant listening and responding the minister serves as an instrument of spiritual healing in which interpersonal blocks are removed, hostilities drained off, guilt feelings turned over to God, and constructive forces released for living.

Beyond listening, the minister's resources include (1) his identity as a man of God as he shares a person's plight; (2) his representing a community of Christian faith, love, and hope; (3) his personal interest in and affectionate bond with the counselee, manifested in his sensitivity to the person's deepest thoughts, emotions, values, and strivings; (4) his therapeutic employment of prayer and the Word of God in relation to the person's concerns; (5) his abiding faith in God and in help which God makes available to his people; and (6) his devotion to the eternal kingdom of God beyond the tragic struggles of men. His entire ministry is oriented toward illuminating those values and relationships which shall endure for eternity (Heb. 11:27, 12:1-2, 13:14).

Throughout, both counselor and counselee are related to one another and to the church's healing fellowship through their common devotion to God, the source of all healing. Whatever progress is made, as the counselee moves from plight to pilgrimage again, may be attributed not to themselves alone but to the love of God, the grace of our Lord Jesus Christ, and the abiding fellowship of the Holy Spirit. This triune orientation of person, God, and minister is the crucial difference between pastoral counseling and other therapies. Paul Johnson was profoundly correct in noting that "the honest pastor knows that true growth is not his creation or the person's but the work of the creator God."[19] Through counseling new channels are opened to creative God-man relationships. Beyond counseling, the minister continues to support the person through prayer and personal interest after formal interviews end.

4. Termination of the Counseling Relationship

Leave-taking is quite significant in pastoral counseling, for the minister and the individual continue their associations in a larger framework of church and community life. Ministers are less free than other counselors to terminate counseling relationships. Neither do they have a fee-taking basis for assisting the person to value their times together and to assume responsibility in life. Some interviews are discontinued when a person fails to appear for an appointment and does not mention counseling again. Ideally, the participants terminate their relationship in good faith when their agreed-upon mission has been accomplished. As the person gains wisdom or strength for living he or she "drops" the pastor *as counselor*. Their relationship shifts once again to pastor-parishioner contacts in the church and community setting.

[19] Paul E. Johnson, *Psychology of Pastoral Care*, p. 101.

While I have not discussed the matter of *special feelings* (dependency, transference, and so on) which may arise in pastoral counseling and which are treated in full-length works on this subject, reference should be made to one matter. When a person's life has been laid bare before a minister, he or she will tend to feel either quite close to him or quite defensive toward him in the future. A grateful counselee may invite the pastor into his home, give him a personal gift, or find other appropriate ways for expressing gratitude. The minister can aid the person's adjustment back into church life (1) by receiving a gift, if offered, with appreciation; (2) by directing the individual's feelings of affection or hostility Godward, and (3) by providing specific occasions and ways for the growing person to serve God within the church. In this way the minister transfers the person's deepest feelings, whatever they may be, toward God and his gracious purpose for the individual's life.

IV. ULTIMATE CONCERNS

Two dynamic aspects of pastoral conversations which are of paramount significance to ministers will be mentioned here in conclusion. One has to do with *acceptance* in counseling. The other deals with the *unique contribution of counseling* in modern church life. We noted earlier that Jesus Christ embodied the "living of forgiveness" in all his relationships as well as in his redemptive death on the cross (II Cor. 5:18-19). Those entrusted with the ministry of reconciliation today are to incarnate Christ's spirit of love and forgiveness in their manner of living, witnessing, and conversations with men. Christian love does not abrogate the intention of God for men. Rather, love characterizes those who are "joint heirs of the grace of life" (I Peter 3:7).

Acceptance in pastoral conversations in no way cancels the ethical ideals and obligations of those who are citizens of the kingdom of God. His true children are both expected and empowered to live with spiritual excellence in the world (John 1:12-13). Christians are provided a new vantage point and rich resources for life's pilgrimage. Yet their relationships in this sinful world are not free from conflict and inner agony (Rom. 7:4—8:38). While Jesus Christ intercedes "in the presence of God on our behalf," those who minister in his stead are obligated to undergird and guide God's people in the transactions of life (Heb. 9:24).

There is a bipolar tension in the minister's life between (1) the need to be an authority figure, a convincer, persuading men to his own position; and (2) the necessity to be a flexible person, a co-worker with God and persons, permitting each individual to grow at his own pace and affirm his own faith under God. In pastoral work, God's *claim* (judgment) and *gift* (grace) go together. His wrath is the other side of his love; one is not experienced without at least sensing the other. A pastor's accepting love implies, not ethical indifference, but discriminating awareness of human sin, divine judgment, and mankind's need for the mercy, grace, and love of God.

Ministers communicate acceptance or rejection both verbally and nonverbally in their attitudes and encounters.[20] The feeling-tone of an interview will be influenced by the warmth of the pastor's greeting, by his facial expressions of approval or disapproval, his kindness or sternness, his sincerity or superficiality, and his perceptivity or dullness regarding a person's situation. A counselee who feels the minister's rejection will have great difficulty expressing himself or herself in a way that will prove to be redemptive. His life is already *under judgment;* that is one of the reasons he has turned to God's representative for help.

Acceptance implies, not necessarily approval, but that the minister will try to understand without projecting his judgments prematurely into the person's frame of reference. The counselee who experiences acceptance can utter his feeling of helplessness, ex-

---

[20] Thurneysen suggests (I think mistakenly): "If we join the counselee—perhaps only tentatively and experimentally—on the ground from which he first comes, we base our pastoral care not on the Word but on a secular understanding of man and on a corresponding 'natural theology.' . . . Fundamentally, our efforts will be lost" (Eduard Thurneysen, *A Theology of Pastoral Care,* trans. Jack A. Worthington and Thomas Wieser [Richmond, Va.: John Knox Press, 1962], p. 92). *Acceptance* refers not to a counselor's theological position but to his willingness to understand the person's plight as *he* conceives it and to help him from *within* his own perspective.

press his anxiety or hostility, confess his sin, offer his prayer for divine wisdom, knowing all the while that he is not alone in his struggle. Acceptance is not something to be turned on and off like a faucet in counseling, but is conveyed in every area of a minister's life.

Going back to the question of ultimate concerns, our second is for an answer to the question: *What is achieved in counseling that cannot be achieved elsewhere in church life?* Is it not enough for a person to share in the life of a healing fellowship of love, worship, and work without expecting to talk occasionally to his minister? Are not all Christians obligated to build up the church in spite of their personal struggles, ethical conflicts, and religious strivings?

Building up the church, when viewed from an *administrative* perspective, includes enlarging the budget, improving the physical plant, and increasing the membership. Each of these efforts is essential in modern church life, but they are not everything! In viewing the building up of the church from a *pastoral* perspective, ministers are obligated to cherish the faithful pilgrims *and* the tortured people who comprise the congregation. Carroll Wise has said, "When the pastor helps one person he is helping many others. . . . Indeed, one of the functions of pastoral counseling is helping to remove barriers to fellowship, and thus in a real way creating a sense of Christian community."[21] As barriers to belief, to love, and to labor are removed in pastoral conversations, persons are liberated to live and to labor more effectively for God in the church.

While pursuing his caring ministry preventively in every dimension of life, the skilled pastor will cherish those therapeutic opportunities when burdened persons turn to him to be made whole. Remembering God's conversations with men from of old, he will not shrink from those opportunities which could move a person from an impasse to spiritual pilgrimage once more. A single conversation might pave the way for numerous changes in many lives. A person's life may cluster thereafter around a new allegiance to God and to persons. A little revolution may come in another's soul. A

[21] Carroll A. Wise, *Psychiatry and the Bible* (New York: Harper & Row, 1956), pp. 131-32.

new strategy, a bit of self-esteem, growing self-control, a deeper faith, renewed strength for family tasks—all may denote a great achievement for a person previously blocked in life or humiliated in relationships. The emergence of new feelings—of understanding, of love, gratitude, sensitivity to others, and responsibility to God —can come from counseling.

When the minister recalls the personal interviews of Jesus, the time the Lord took for one man or one woman in trouble, crisis, or decision, he will cherish personal conversations afresh in his own ministry. In counseling, as in all other aspects of his calling, the Christian pastor labors and lives in anticipation of the life everlasting. His lively hope is well-expressed by Mr. Stand-fast in Bunyan's *Pilgrim's Progress:* "I have formerly lived by hear-say and faith, but now I go where I shall live by sight, and shall be with Him in whose company I delight myself."[22] This hope is the Christian pastor's confidence.

SUGGESTED READING

Hiltner, Seward. *The Counselor in Counseling.* Nashville, Tenn.: Abingdon Press, 1950; Apex paperback edition, 1962. Focuses the counselor's role clearly through case-examination. Written in popular style for ministers.

Oates, Wayne E. *Protestant Pastoral Counseling.* Philadelphia: Westminster Press, 1962. Views pastoral counseling in a theological context.

Rogers, Carl R. *On Becoming a Person.* Boston: Houghton Mifflin Co., 1961. Nontechnical essays reflecting Rogers' anthropological outlook and recent therapeutic philosophy.

Sullivan, Harry Stack. *The Psychiatric Interview,* ed. Helen S. Perry and Mary L. Gawel. New York: W. W. Norton & Co., 1954. An empirical study of the *method* of interviewing from the perspective of an interpersonal therapist, although his views of treatment do not reflect recent advances in the field of psychiatry.

Wise, Carroll A. *Pastoral Counseling: Its Theory and Practice.* New York: Harper & Row, 1951. A standard introduction by a pioneer in the field of pastoral care and counseling.

[22] John Bunyan, *Pilgrim's Progress,* ed. J. B. Wharey (Oxford: Clarendon Press, 1929), p. 326.

CHAPTER 8

SHARING THE PRIMARY MOMENTS OF LIFE

THE Christian minister shares what Lewis Sherrill once called "the career of the human self . . . as it passes through certain major stages, or types of experience," from its inception in infancy to the discovery of death.[1] A Christian couple, for example, looks to the church for support during those years when children are being added to the family circle. The birth of a child, so intrinsic to family experience, remains one of life's primary moments in which persons are open to pastoral care. In like fashion the minister shares life's spiritual renewal, youth's choice of a vocation, the commitments of adulthood, and the process of aging with his people. As he incarnates ways in which God "makes [man's] steps secure" the minister serves as one with whom persons may identify imaginatively and participate meaningfully in the Christian pilgrimage (Ps. 40:2; I Tim. 4:12).

Ministers often possess only a peephole perspective on their congregants' lives. They see people one or two hours a week in formal worship periods where faces look much alike. Yet these persons come to church from a social matrix of relationships representing varied values, with educational and class differences, each bearing a sense of personal frustration or fulfillment in life. Furthermore,

[1] Lewis J. Sherrill, *The Struggle of the Soul* (New York: The Macmillan Co., 1952), p. 3.

man must be viewed in a "cosmic context" if his problems and possibilities are to be perceived correctly.[2]

Once the man of God becomes alert to what Kierkegaard called the stages along life's way he will address his pastoral care to the unique concerns of his people. Some stages of human development —preadolescence, the middle years, and old age, for example—are not discussed here. For reasons of space, I have selected for discussion five primary moments of life. The pastoral conversations appearing in Chapters 8 and 9 do not in every case convey an ideal approach, but they do illustrate Christian concern in selected crises.

Life's primary moments, from birth to death, do not always arrange themselves in a balanced cycle according to the expectations of those who wish to help others. For example, a minister in a rural setting may find that his congregation is composed dominantly of older people. His major pastoral assignments may come at the "discovery of death" end of the life-spectrum. A neighborhood church with a flexible and dynamic ministry may attract children and youth in large numbers but fail to attract their middle-aged parents. While a minister is available to everyone in his church and community, some persons suffering adversity may avoid him and share their concerns with a friend or a stranger. One church family may resent a minister's presence in a set of circumstances in which another household is greatly dependent on his care. Again, what one individual experiences reverently in spiritual terms another may look upon lightly with irreligious eyes. Such factors influence the pastor's ministry.

The Christian pastor and his people are enmeshed in life's relationships, decisions, and pressures day by day. Young and old church members alike feel that their minister either accepts and prizes them in their daily struggles or rejects them and remains aloof from life's tough realities. At best, they will experience him as one possessing a discriminating understanding of the human situation, one who can clarify the central issues of life, and who can chart the pathways between God and the human soul. In each

[2] Gordon W. Allport, *Pattern and Growth in Personality* (New York: Holt, Rinehart & Winston, 1961), p. 567.

great moment of life the pastor and his people share a common conviction that they may "receive mercy and find grace to help in time of need" (Heb. 4:15-16). With this faith the skilled shepherd participates meaningfully in the moving dramas of the life of the soul.

1. THE BEGINNING OF LIFE

The birth of a child is a very ancient yet significant event in family life. The process of becoming parents is freighted with questions and complexities for most persons according to their emotional maturity, economic condition, and state of health. Childbirth is *akin* to religious experience whether or not the parents *assign* religious significance to the event. A Protestant chaplain's survey of maternity patients in a metropolitan hospital revealed that about one-half of the interviewees interpreted their childbirth experiences spiritually. In biblical thought the birth of a child was viewed as a divine blessing and as an occasion for a festival of joy and dedication. Naming the child and inaugurating certain "rites of passage" in the family have had religious significance from ancient times (cf. Gen. 33:5; Ps. 127:3; Luke 2:21-52). God's representative, usually a priest, presided at the dedicatory services and strengthened the parents for their new child-rearing responsibilities. The event of parenthood is thus one of life's great ventures in which the Christian pastor's role may be activated from age to age.

Pastoral care of children and young people properly begins with the minister's concern for their parents even before the children are born. Because children reflect the kind of social-spiritual milieu in which they grow up, the home and church share a joint responsibility in preparing persons for parenthood. Parents and others who work with children in the church must be genuine persons "in a genuine milieu" themselves in order "to develop a child with a healthy personality."[3] Spiritually immature or emotionally deprived adults frequently fail to nourish their offspring with loving disci-

[3] Erik H. Erikson, *Identity and the Life Cycle* (New York: International Universities Press, 1959), p. 99.

pline, whereas homes in which durable relationships of love and trust abound provide a creative atmosphere for proper personality development. Delinquent or irresponsible children develop most often in homes or institutions that are inadequate or delinquent in some way. For example, when lightening strikes in husband-wife conflicts, it often strikes *through* the children in that home. Thus churches should contact potential parents prior to the birth of children and seek to prepare them for their new family tasks.

A young married couple's preparation for parenthood should be undertaken with the same honesty and seriousness as was their original preparation for marriage. A pastoral group for new parents in the church, perhaps meeting once a month, could provide an atmosphere for discussing topics such as (1) the changing family in our culture, (2) biblical guidelines on such family issues as discipline, (3) how children learn about God, (4) the handicapped or exceptional child, and (5) the shared ministry of pastor and parents to children. Occasional films, visits at the birth of a child, sermons on appropriate family themes, pastoral letters, and provision of relevant literature in the church library—all reflect the church's concern for its families.

Parents-to-be need to prepare lovingly for a baby's coming so that there may be *psychic space* in the family's life for the new arrival. If there are other children, they may help to arrange the nursery at home and should be instructed about the baby's place in the rhythm of family life.[4] While the family does not build its daily routine and chief loyalty entirely around an infant, family members will need to pace their living according to the interior timing of the young child. In a poignant moment in an Old Testament family's journey a wise father responded to those who wanted him to travel faster: "I will lead on . . . according to the pace of the children" (Gen. 33:14). Pacing home activities and relations is a necessary aspect of the family's preparation for and acceptance of God's gift of new life.

Life's beginning provides specific occasions for an interprofes-

[4] Langstaff and Szasz have developed a pictorial booklet for parents' use in preparing children for the arrival of a baby in the home, *A Tiny Baby for You* (New York: Harcourt, Brace & World, 1955).

sional family ministry by members of the community's health team. Needs may arise at a child's birth which prompt the joint efforts of ministers, physicians, lawyers, and social workers. This is often the case with children born out of wedlock who need medical care and a temporary home before formal adoption. Co-ministry is also necessitated among professionals when childbirth involves a tragedy. Such was the case in the experience that follows.

Mr. and Mrs. Nelson Latham were members of a large church in which she had served for a time as a member of the staff. When it became evident that their first child was to be born she resigned the position and prepared for the child's coming. They had married late in life. Mrs. Latham was almost forty at the time of the child's birth. There had been no medical evidence of trouble during the woman's prenatal care, thus her physician was surprised when a hydrocephaloid son was born. He knew how difficult it would be when the couple learned that their child was deformed and would probably not survive. Thus he enlisted a minister who was receiving clinical pastoral training in the hospital at the time to talk to the couple with him. In this instance, an occasion of potential jubilation became a time of mourning when the deformed boy died.

The minister-in-training shared the couple's spontaneous sorrow, arranged for the child's burial at their request, and stood with them during that tragic period in their lives. He also notified the Lathams' pastor, so that they might have his spiritual ministry in the days ahead; and supported certain hospital staff members who had become involved emotionally with the couple during their loss and grief. Through appropriate pastoral care the Lathams were able to share some disturbing questions about their religious experience with the minister, to express their grief, and to face the future with new faith and devotion. In addition, the young minister learned that a physician was also a member of the human race and that their shared ministry had made the Lathams' tragic experience more tolerable to him.

The beginning of life involves varied kinds of experiences in pastoral work. Normally a child's birth is an occasion for rejoicing and for religious dedication of family members. My own free church tradition encourages the dedication of the *home* upon the occasion of a child's birth but rejects infant baptism because of the cardinal Baptist principle of the integrity of the individual in matters of religion. Churchmen of the sacramental tradition administer baptism to infants as a "rite of indentification" with the family's faith, name, and spiritual sponsorship.[5] Whatever the minister's particular faith, his chief obligation at life's beginning is to undergird parents for their new risks and responsibilities.

Certainly a minister will call upon a new mother after the safe arrival of her child in the hospital. Physicians remind us that nature permits her to "let down" a bit after an infant's delivery. Faced with new tasks, a mother may appear exhausted or depressed rather than exuberant during a postdelivery pastoral visit. Such is the case when multiple births—like twins or triplets—pose an economic crisis or grave burden to the new parents. In calling, the pastor will be alert to a young mother's mood as well as to her expressed concerns. Through appropriate scripture selections and prayer he will seek to inspire hope in God for life's new tasks and relationships.

Successful shepherding depends not only upon the pastor's intention but upon the new parents' receptivity or sense of need, and upon the gracious action of the Holy Spirit. The following conversation indicates that the shutter of each soul was open wide to God's help because of the existential situation. After learning that the Colvins' son was born with a slight orthopedic defect, pastor Bill Bateson called upon the couple in the maternity ward of a small-town clinic. The nurse assured him that things were clear for his call and noted that Mr. Colvin was with his wife at the time. They greeted each other as follows.

PASTOR: Well, good afternoon, folks (shook father's hand)! How's the new mother today?

MRS. C: Hi, Brother Bateson. Oh, I'm just fine (her voice was weak). We have that big boy we've been waiting for (smiles).

[5] Ernest A. Payne has written, "We are not born Christians, nor can we be made Christians by others, not even by the church. God has given us freedom, and salvation is by personal faith." See *The Free Church Tradition in the Life of England* (London: S.C.M. Press, 1951), p. 174. Also, cf. D. M. Baillie, *The Theology of the Sacraments* (New York: Charles Scribner's Sons, 1957), pp. 72-90.

PASTOR: Wonderful! What is his name?

MRS. C: We named him Mark, pastor. I've liked "Mark" for years, and it's a Bible name, too.

JOHN C: With a short name like Mark maybe he won't ever get a nickname like some of the kids in our family. We hope that everyone will just call him "Mark" (pause).

PASTOR: It's a big accomplishment to have a fine son here and to give him a good name. How is the young man doing since his arrival?

MRS. C: OK I guess. When they first brought him in here, having Mark beside me seemed almost too good to be true. We had waited for him so long. He hasn't cried a bit when he's been in here. The nurses say he's a good baby. (Her remarks revealed some strain and reserve.)

JOHN C (hesitantly): Did anyone tell you about Mark's feet, Brother Bateson?

PASTOR: About his feet?

JOHN C: Yeah, the doctor explained to us that his feet were turned around somehow from the way they should have been when Mark was born.

MRS. C: We noticed it the first time the nurse brought him in. Dr. Wills had already told us that his feet were turned wrong inside me.

PASTOR: Oh?

JOHN C: It's not too bad but they are turned around like this (demonstrated with his hands). Dr. Wills says that in a few months we will have to take him to St. Louis for orthopedic surgery. (Pause.) I don't know just how they do it, but he says they can be turned around straight in a couple of years. It's going to take several operations though.

MRS. C: He said that Mark will have to wear special shoes for a few years in order to support his ankles but that he ought to get along fine and will be able to run and play like other children.

The pastor felt their ambivalence—gladness in their first son's birth, yet sadness because of the bone defect. They did not reflect guilt or hostility toward God, merely concern about the child's welfare. Pastor Bateson sensed some undisclosed negative feelings and gave the Colvins an opportunity to express them. He knew that they were concerned and desired to lift up their concerns to God in prayer.

PASTOR: Well, you folks have experienced both a great blessing and a new concern in Mark's coming. We are fortunate to live in a day when surgery is available for the correction of such problems. This still doesn't eliminate your concern, however, does it?

MRS. C: We just hate to think that the little fellow will have to be in a cast most of the time for the next two years.

JOHN C: He'll probably be late in learning to walk. But we think he'll be all right (pause).

PASTOR: Jerri (took mother's hand) and John, may we pray together and ask God's guidance and strength for you. (He thanked God for Mark's safe arrival, for the doctor's wisdom in suggesting that the defect be corrected early, and asked for spiritual strength for the Colvins. His prayer caught the flavor of their mixed feelings, pointing them to God.)

Had the pastor been uninformed or called routinely with some quip about the Colvins' "bouncing baby boy," he might have missed their true feelings and failed to support them in their need. Again, he could have made too much of the matter, intensifying the couple's anxiety about what people might think or stirring hostility toward God. Instead, his acceptance, warm interest and genuine sharing of their pride and their plight helped the couple to think realistically and rely upon God's strength for events ahead.

Once children are born, churches will strengthen Christian homes in appropriate nurture and discipline of their offspring. As young parents try to rear children in personal and tolerant ways, based upon information rather than tradition, they are exposed to many conflicts and insecurities. Perceptions of one's child-rearing responsibilities come from a person's memories of his own childhood, from the models furnished by relatives and friends, from reading, discussion, personal mistakes, and the advice of professionals in our culture. Young adults are tempted occasionally to reject their own backgrounds and to turn against those who reared them. As immature parents reflect upon their elders' foibles they may secretly fear failure themselves and desire guidance from the church. Mistaken ideas change slowly through experience and new vision of truth.

Once a pastor called upon a family of newcomers in the community. As he approached the house he heard a child's cries during a spanking. When he rang the doorbell a young mother with a baby perched on one hip and a sobbing son at her knees came to the door. Obviously bothered, she explained the tearful situation and added: "Daddy always said, 'spare the rod and spoil the child.' But I always feel guilty when I whip Jimmy. He's not really a bad child, just meddlesome." The minister listened, then replied that he, too, was a parent and understood that there were no magic answers to child-rearing problems. He asked the mother if she had read anything on the subject of *discipline*. When she responded negatively he offered to lend her a booklet that might help.[6]

While young parents are not to be left to the mercy of every wind of doctrine, merely telling them what to do is not a cure-all either. Those who minister to young parents and through them to their children cannot expect perfection from the guardians of life's beginnings. Pastors can, however, assist parents to avoid some obvious dangers, can stand with them even in colossal failures and help them to achieve family serenity based upon a mature Christian faith.

II. THE RENEWAL OF LIFE

Pastors who share life's beginnings and growth may help to clarify the meaning of faith in childhood for parents and youth workers in the church. What, for example, can Christianity mean to the infant or young child who responds primarily to the touch of gentle hands and the tone of one's voice rather than to ideas? Robbie Trent's *Your Child and God* suggests numerous ways in which parents may guide a child's religious development at home.[7] Grownups mirror the meaning of God to youngsters first through relationships, then through example, and later through instruction. Children learn love through adults' timed responses to their frequent needs; later, through recognizing God's love for them.

Qualities of soul that parents incarnate, like faith, love, and hope,

---

[6] James L. Hymes, *Discipline* (New York: Bureau of Publications, Teachers College, Columbia University, 1949). See also, Dorothy Baruch, *New Ways in Discipline* (New York: McGraw-Hill Book Company, 1949).

[7] New York: Harper & Row, 1952.

as well as the spirit of the home, are caught by children and reflected in their maturing relationships. The studies of Erikson and
others indicate that a person's capacity for *basic trust* or mistrust
originates in early childhood.[8] Trust of oneself and others, beginning with an infant's dependence upon powerful providers, is
essential to both health and salvation in later development. A child
incorporates what he receives from his significant community into
his growing sense of selfhood. Some have likened religious experience in these early years to "Ten-Commandment Christianity" in
that numerous prohibitions are imposed upon children by adults. A
child's conscience develops as he internalizes the moral voice of his
parents, teachers, peers, and God. Also, he comes to think of himself as "good" or "bad" and to respect or disrespect himself according to the esteem in which he is held by his parents and other
significant persons. Home and church thus collaborate in pointing
youth to a personal faith in the living God.

*Pastors, parents, and church workers have the common aim of
leading young people to make a meaningful Christian commitment and to identify formally with the church at the appropriate
time in life.* Such Christian identification is timed to God's gracious
action and the individual's response. Conversion—the renewal of
life—is to be viewed dynamically in terms of the individual's spiritual sensitivity, emotional maturity, and sense of personal responsibility to God in Christ. The chronological *age* of Christian decision
is not uniform.[9] The general *stage* of development for Christian
commitment is timed to the individual's broadening relationships
with others, sense of need, and his personal response to Jesus Christ
as Savior.

Protestants generally view the renewal of life as the gracious
gift of God rather than as the achievement of an individual or his
family. Both divine and human determinants are involved in reli-

[8] Erikson, *op. cit.*, pp. 50-100.
[9] Allport observes that the individual's religious sentiment is not fully
developed until puberty. See *Becoming: Basic Considerations for a Psychology
of Personality* (New Haven: Yale University Press, 1955), pp. 93-97.   Cf.
Findley B. Edge's discussion of "Authentic Faith," *A Quest for Vitality in
Religion* (Nashville, Tenn.: Broadman Press, 1963), pp. 156-88; and Samuel
Southard, *Pastoral Evangelism* (Nashville, Tenn.: Broadman Press, 1962).

gious experience, whether the pattern is conversion in free churches or confirmation in those practicing infant baptism. The Christian faith must be at work in a youngster's home and community experiences before it becomes valid for him in life. Earl Loomis has written that the "member of a religious community must find his *faith and practice* a part of his total life if it is to 'take' with his children."[10] Salvation, while involving Christian education, is a transaction with God and can never be treated as a matter of nurture alone. However, a person does not jump out of the skin of his developmental history by means of a vast forgetfulness when he becomes a Christian. He still has a past, a present, and a future, but Christ enables him to face his own history and destiny with courage.

The family's indelible influence upon a person's religious experience is mirrored in the following conversation. A minister once called upon a young man who had presented himself for church membership but attended church only spasmodically thereafter. At first, the youth resisted the pastor's offer of interest and help.

PRESTON: There are some things that I have to get straightened out between me and my dad and my brother before I can give my heart wholly to God.

PASTOR: I don't know what you have reference to, but it may help to share this with someone.

PRESTON: I figure there are some things that a man has to do by himself.

PASTOR: Most things are better solved when you allow someone else to share them with you. (Pause.)

PRESTON: Well . . . it's my dad. Every time I need him, he just isn't there. It seems that things are just never right between us. Just about the time I think things are going all right my brother comes back and things are right back where they were before.

PASTOR: Is it that you want things to be right between your dad and yourself?

PRESTON: Yes, but he never takes my side. You know, I'm under a two-year suspended sentence for some trouble that I got into because of my brother.

[10] Earl A. Loomis, Jr., "Religion and Childhood," in *Religion in the Developing Personality* (New York: New York University Press, 1960), p. 32.

PASTOR: Someone told me that you were trying to protect your brother. (The youth told how he had stood trial for his brother, who had stolen a car and then fled to the West Coast.)

PRESTON: My lawyer advised me under the circumstances to plead guilty and throw myself on the mercy of the court. My dad didn't say a word for me. He just sat there. My aunt did say something for me, so did my mother. But nobody else believed me or stood up for me.

PASTOR: I know that it is hard for you to talk about things that mean so much and yet hurt so deeply.

PRESTON: I can try and try and do everything I can but I just can't seem to make things right between us. (He started crying at this point.)

PASTOR: Is this what you think has to be straightened out before you really give your heart to God?

PRESTON: Yes. I don't believe that I can live for God and feel this way toward my dad and my brother.

PASTOR: Preston, if you will let God help you, He will.

The minister longed to see Preston and his young wife serving God in the church and enjoying life together as a family. The youth, however, felt that his dad had failed him and that he could not have God's acceptance as long as he resented his father so deeply. Preston's God-relationship had been influenced indelibly by his relationships with an invalid mother and an inadequate father. Obviously, intensive pastoral work is required to lead such a person to Christian commitment and to active church membership.

George Sweazey has said that "the greatest weakness of the evangelism of the past was that it stopped too soon."[11] Religious instruction was neglected once a Christian commitment had been made. *The church's appropriate pastoral concern in life's renewal is that the individual be disciplined into a community of love and hope as well as into the content of the church's faith.* Pastoral work with those who have committed themselves to Christ includes: (1) Christian baptism, (2) a meaningful reception into the church membership, (3) instruction in discipleship, (4) strengthening their ties with God and men, and (5) providing opportunities for

[11] George E. Sweazey, *Effective Evangelism* (New York: Harper & Row, 1953), p. 206. Cf. pp. 206-43.

serviceable living through the church's ministry in the world. Caring for "life on the threshold" is thus a crucial aspect of evangelism.

Orientation or catechetical classes, meeting in four-or six-week series through the year, provide a strategic opportunity for the minister and new members to become acquainted personally. Literature has been designed for use in such classes by most Protestant groups.[12] By its very nature a discipleship class anticipates discussion of the *church's* history, beliefs, and organization, and of the individual *person's* questions, anxieties, and opportunities for additional education and service. Some churches expect all those coming into their fellowship to attend such a class. Others provide separate groups for children and adults when suitable teachers are available.

Answering questions of a doctrinal or personal nature is a vital aspect of pastoral care of the new member. Informed congregants act from inner strength and wisdom rather than from group conformity and shallow judgments alone. This is illustrated in the case of a woman who had presented herself for membership in a Baptist church. Following a worship service she asked the minister: "Am I going to have to get into *that* thing (pointing to the baptistry) and get myself all wet? Why do you folks dunk everybody under the water?"

The pastor explained that immersion is a symbolic and dramatic picture of one's Christian experience. "A person who links his life by faith to Christ is buried symbolically with him 'by baptism unto death.' The baptized believer thereby identifies himself with Christ's death and resurrection and pledges that thereafter he or she shall 'walk in newness of life.'"

Rather than rebuking the woman, the minister pictured immersion as her formal identification with Christ and with the church, and as a dramatic witness to her experience of eternal life (cf. Rom. 6:4-11; Gal. 3:27).

[12] In 1960, Judson Press (American Baptist) published an age-graded series of course guides for church membership classes. Guidebooks are provided for pupils and for teachers: (1) juniors, *Answering the Call;* (2) junior high, *On the Way;* (3) senior high, *It Costs Your Life;* and (4) adults and older students, *A Call to Discipleship.*

While new parishioners are pleased to receive a formal letter of welcome from the pastor, they need the personal touch of meaningful friendships and groups in the church. Children need to meet those who will teach their age groups in Sunday school and young people need the comradeship of others their age. Some persons, like Preston above, may require an extra investment of personal interest before they can thaw out and become involved meaningfully in church membership. In reality, the entire congregation is responsible for receiving new members into its fellowship. The minister helps by making such receptions personal, warm, and tangible.

III. THE CALLINGS OF LIFE

Like religious commitments, decisions concerning one's daily work are interrelated with the developing sense of identity in human personality. Some interpreters distinguish "calling" as God's gracious election through the gospel to the Christian life and "vocation" within his providence as both daily work and the " 'whole' of man's existence presupposed by God's 'calling.' "[13] I am aware of these distinctions but use the terms *calling* and *vocation* interchangably in this discussion. The church's interest in vocations is quite ancient; yet skillful vocational guidance is a recent development in pastoral practice.

Our culture anticipates that adults will be occupied with suitable work functions and frowns upon the man or woman who reveals chronic vocational instability. Meaningful work and play are essential to any individual's sense of spiritual and emotional well-being. Of the value of work Earl Loomis has noted: "Aside from its survival and utilitarian elements, it fulfills needed psychic functions of handling energy, of asserting and reinforcing personal identity, of reassuring one of personal worth, of allowing nonharmful expression of aggression toward material things and toward persons with whom one interacts."[14] Decisions concerning vocations are

[13] Otto Weber, *Karl Barth's Church Dogmatics,* trans. Arthur C. Cochrane (Philadelphia: Westminster Press, 1953), p. 248.
[14] Earl A. Loomis, Jr., *The Self in Pilgrimage* (New York: Harper & Row, 1960), p. 51.

made, changed, and remade during childhood and adolescence. The emergence of young adulthood is complicated by educational demands, vocational expectations, and family tasks or plans.

Clergymen may contribute to the vocational anxiety of some people by their failure to relate the Christian faith to problems of daily work. In the present century of mass production, automation, and depersonalized employment entirely new orders of occupations have been created. The technological revolution ushered in with the space age has created vast demands for workers with high-level skills of adjustment and thus for excellence in many educational fields. This advance in technology and the professional specialties has been accompanied by burgeoning labor organizations, growing government controls, and a vast migration of white and Negro workers to the West and North. The consequent rootlessness of families and economic and cultural adjustments of a vast segment of the American population call for skilled pastoral care today.

A concrete place for ministers to begin in vocational guidance is with the youth of the church. Adolescents, who are experiencing so many changes—physical, emotional, and social—are frequently receptive to sermons and personal counsel in the area of life's work. Boys manifest needs for appropriate male behavior and for satisfactory career selection. Their parents' judgments usually influence their job interests, though not in the nineteenth-century sense of identical family apprenticeships and work functions. A boy whose father has been successful in agriculture, for example, may not wish to remain on the farm. A banker's son may reject his father's vocation in preference for teaching, selling, or research. Erik Erikson has theorized that the special growth problem of late adolescence is the establishment of one's identity and that youth's special danger is "self-diffusion" or role diffusion. Arthur Miller's character, Biff, in *Death of a Salesman* reflected such work paralysis and identity diffusion: "I just can't take hold, Mom; I can't take hold of some kind of life." With boyhood past and the central core of personality confused, the growth crisis involved may require more than vocational guidance. Such instability may require professional treatment.

Adolescent girls are also deeply involved in a search for identity, meaning, and vocation in life. They are torn frequently between a personal desire to marry and establish a home and a parental demand that they select a suitable occupation and pursue additional education to that end. Some parents deny their daughters the opportunity of obtaining a college education. Other girls face uncertain futures.

A young lady once revealed her struggle with self-definition and life's direction to her minister.

PASTOR: This is your last year in high school isn't it? Where have you thought about going to college?

ALICE: Well, I really haven't done too much thinking about it. In fact, I don't imagine I'll be going to college at all. (Pause.) Mother and Daddy don't seem to be interested in my going to college.

PASTOR: You mean they don't care whether you go or not?

ALICE: I guess they care all right. It is just that they don't say one way or the other. I know they can afford it, but they won't say they want me to go. They just don't seem interested in a girl getting an education. I guess that's it anyway.

PASTOR: You think that because you are a girl they don't care if you go to college or not.

ALICE: Well, it's not just because I'm a girl. I just don't know. (Long pause.) I don't guess it's them all together. I'm really not sure I want to go to college. In fact, I don't want to get out of high school now.

PASTOR: You don't want to graduate?

ALICE: Oh yes, I want to graduate but I don't want to leave high school. I know it sounds funny. I know you think I'm silly.

PASTOR: You don't want to leave because of your friends there? (This was only an educated guess.)

ALICE: That's it partly. Another thing is that I'll have to make a decision about what I'm going to do.

PASTOR: You mean about whether or not to go to college?

ALICE: Yes, in a way. You know I've been going steady with Tim for about a year and a half now. (She looked at the floor.) Well, he wants to marry me when he gets through with college.

PASTOR: Oh?

ALICE: He plans to finish in three more years. I know that will be a long time and that I could go on to college during this time. But I'm afraid I won't get to live.

PASTOR: Get to live?

ALICE: Well, you know—have a family and a life, and all that. I've been going to school all my life and I don't want to waste three more years by just going to school. Anything could happen and I'd never get to do anything but go to school. Do you see what I mean?

PASTOR: Yes, I think I do understand.

Alice was described by her minister as a beautiful high school senior who had been elected to numerous honors by her fellow students. The school counselor told her pastor that, while Alice had great intellectual potential, her grades had been affected adversely by numerous extracurricular activities. Her ambivalence about finishing school and the future involved feelings about a woman's true vocation in the home, insecurity in having to make new friends and a new start at college, and the fear of possibly losing her boy friend.

Such conversations reveal that a young person's career concerns are many-faceted, frequently compounded by questions of basic identity and role function in life. Further, while Alice was growing up, she remained dependent and indecisive regarding some basic life concerns. Effecting a transition from immature dependence upon parents and others to a more secure self-reliance is a major aspect of vocational guidance. Young people need to trust their own feelings and deep convictions about a career while respecting the opinions of parents and judgments of others. Skilled information may be provided through tests in co-operation with public school guidance personnel and through literature supplying occupational information. Ultimately, a Christian's vocation is one aspect of his total stewardship of life unto God. As a young person seeks divine direction for his career, he may also be assured of God's guidance and providential care as he seeks to make a good vocational adjustment. The pastor may assure his people that man works "as unto God," not merely "for bread alone." The Christian workman "rejoices in hope" because of God's redemptive, creative work and the coming of his eternal kingdom.

Christian clergymen are called upon for guidance and counseling in several areas of vocational concern. The pastor serves as an interpreter when problems of work adjustment arise, particularly when interrelated family, personal, or religious problems are involved. Also, the pastor is uniquely qualified to counsel with persons who are interested in religious or church-related vocations. He can answer questions about educational requirements, job opportunities, the joys and hardships of religious occupations, and about the determinative quality of God's will in such vocational decisions. Some counselees will question their personality traits, wondering if they truly love people and are properly motivated for the Christian ministry.[15] Others feel handicapped because of a questionable past, a deprived emotional or educational background, or because of a previous job failure in another field.

A minister once talked with a young couple who were considering a church-related calling. The wife, Karen, was concerned about her husband's past.

KAREN: What about David's past?

PASTOR: What do you mean, Karen?

KAREN: Well, do you think his past will hurt if he is ever pastor of a church? What if somebody should find out about it?

PASTOR: I have heard that David has a "past," but I have never inquired about it. Nor do I feel that I need to know it, for to me it is just that—a *past.*

DAVID: I appreciate your attitude in this matter, but what about others? I'm always afraid it might hurt my work in a church. (The pastor suggested three ways a person might regard his past: parade it, hide it, or face it realistically as one forgiven by God and men.)

PASTOR: Perhaps the healthiest approach would be to regard this part of your life as past and over with, no longer to be recalled nor feared. It need not be paraded; nor should you be afraid of being found out.

DAVID: What would I say if somebody in a church asked me about it?

PASTOR: You might say, "Yes, that is the way I was before Christ came into my life. But now that I am forgiven I have a new life in Christ." If your people sense that you are not afraid of

[15] Helpful suggestions appear in Samuel Southard, *Counseling for Church Vocations* (Nashville, Tenn.: Broadman Press, 1957).

your past, then I doubt that they will be too concerned with it either.

Unresolved guilt can become an intolerable burden in a person's life. Doubtless the approaches to one's past suggested to this young couple were helpful. However, such a pastoral conversation may be the time for confession and affirmation rather than for premature reassurance. The young man had sought divine pardon for his past but was uncertain about human forgiveness. While David was covert about his guilt, his wife had the courage to open the subject for discussion and a possible solution. Or anxiety may have prompted her question. The pastor knew that healthy-mindedness moves beyond "what lies behind" and faces "what lies ahead" in life's journey (Phil. 3:13). Karen and David needed to experience this truth for themselves.

Charles Kemp has written of several areas of special need in *The Pastor and Vocational Counseling*.[16] The handicapped person, retarded youth, retired citizen, widows needing work, ex-convicts, alcoholics, and former mental patients need job opportunities and a meaningful existence. While such cases may not arise frequently, the needs are usually intense and complex when they do appear. How may the minister assist such individuals when they turn to the church for help? Kemp suggests that the pastor (1) obtain full information about the applicant; (2) co-operate with community agencies that exist for such purposes and with employers who help those in special need; (3) act with full honesty in each case; and (4) be a true pastor—a spiritual guide—to the person and his family.

iv. The Commitments of Life

Thus far the pastor's helping relationships have been examined in three significant areas: birth and childhood, religious experience, and vocational selection. The choice of a marriage companion is another primary moment of life in which church members look to their ministers for spiritual guidance and practical help. The term

[16] Charles F. Kemp, *The Pastor and Vocational Counseling* (St. Louis: Bethany Press, 1961), pp. 135-61.

"commitments of life" refers in this context to entering and sustaining the covenant of marriage. The *commitment* concept could be applied broadly to numerous covenants from forming personal friendships to business and civic relations. It is restricted here in order to examine the Christian minister's role in marriage—its origin, stresses, and success.

This discussion could conceivably proceed on the premise that every adult will be married some day, or at least hopes to marry. With the givens of America's population distribution in mind, however, marriage is not an option for some people. Numerous adults by choice or cimcumstance are committed to the single life. Accordingly, churches acknowledge their responsibility to unmarried adults such as professional students and career girls in urban centers. Life is not easy for the older unmarried person. Occasionally the community fails to understand why a certain man or woman remains single. Because of his or her difference and loneliness the single adult may feel left out of church plans and thus deserves special pastoral interest. Also, the widowed, unwed parents, the divorced, and handicapped adults in churches require skillful shepherding. Moreover, the church's youth merit spiritual direction and careful preparation in mate selection and marriage.

Preparation for marriage is a lifetime concern. Persons are prepared for marriage not only through technical sex education, sermons, reading, and formal pastoral interviews but through all of life's experiences. The capacity to love develops from infancy and has many facets: emotional, social, spiritual, and biological. Marriage preparation is thus another area for vital co-operation between homes, schools, and churches; between parents, teachers, and clergymen. Children and adolescents gain strength to love and inner serenity for the risks and responsibilities of marriage through all of life's relationships. They hope to be able to establish what H. S. Sullivan called a fully "human repertory of interpersonal relations," including marriage, in adulthood.

Divorce statistics indicate that many persons who intend to fulfill the requirements of marriage are either unwilling or unable to accept its claims, stresses, and challenges. Some potential marriage partners are unable to form secure relationships or covenants of trust with others. Giving such persons a "good talking to" rarely provides a solution for their maladjustments. Several counseling periods may be required prior to marriage in order to free aloof and insecure persons for successful marriage relationships. Much suffering between married couples and their families might be prevented by competent premarital counseling.

Ministers frequently hear laments from parents who have failed to prepare their children for adult family tasks. A mother whose teen-age son had eloped with his high-school sweetheart confessed to her minister: "John grew up before we realized it. His father and I haven't talked to him about these things like we should have." A couple whose only daughter had been permitted limited freedom in social relations and the selection of her friends were shocked when she married a divorcé nearly twice her age. "That marriage will never work out," the father said bitterly. "He is too old for Jane. Besides, he has no regular employment and is a heavy drinker." In time his prediction came true, but not before they had all experienced much grief and suffering. While repentance for omissions may assuage the grief of shaken parents, their postponements and permissiveness may permanently cripple their children's chances for a successful marriage. Family and church collaboration is not elective but essential in preparing persons for marriage.

What are some reasons for premarital conferences with couples planning marriage? What needs should the pastor perceive and prepare to face with the couple? First, many young people are immature. They are often guided by emotions rather than wise understanding when they agree to marry. Such persons need a Christian interpretation of marriage and of God's intentions for family life. As Henry A. Bowman suggested, "there must ... be ... an intent on the part of the couple to relate their marriage to God ... so that in so far as their abilities permit they make their marriage an expression of their relationship to God."[17] Again, some young people are not well-suited for each other because of radical

---

[17] Henry A. Bowman, *A Christian Interpretation of Marriage* (Philadelphia: Westminster Press, 1959), p. 21.

differences in age, interests, cultural background, race, and religious orientation. The more disparate they are in these basic areas of identity and life goals the more susceptible their marriage will be to conflict and deterioration. Adequate pastoral care will enable some persons to interpret such differences, to defer their plans, or to work through some maladjustments prior to marriage.

Third, divorced persons with a previous history of marital failure need to face their hurt, immaturity, and feelings of guilt, suspicion, and hostility before sealing marriage vows again. Many such persons will never remarry and must make the most of what life offers to them and their offspring.

In the fourth place, the Christian pastor and marital parties need to agree upon the ceremony to be used, the place for the service, rehearsal plans, and specific wedding procedures. As may be seen in the case that follows, religious ideals have great significance in the choice of a place for marriage and the kind of vows which shall be taken by a couple. Finally, there are special problems—such as pregnancy out of wedlock, extended educational plans, family objections, and illness or handicap—that must be considered prior to marriage. The pastor's attitudes, public statements, and personal success or failure as a family man will greatly affect his ministry in this vital area of need.

A specific occasion for pastoral consultation is indicated when persons of different faiths contemplate marriage. Such a case involving a Jewish youth, Gary, and a Presbyterian girl, Sue, was reported in a recent study of marriage counseling. Both Gary and Sue were warmly identified with their respective religious groups. They began to realize that, if they married, some important adjustments would have to be made. They elected to talk to Rev. George Blackham, Sue's minister, because he had developed a reputation as a reliable counselor in the community. Sketches from the case follow.

Neither of them had really thought through the importance of religion and its relationship to marriage and family living. . . . Gary told Reverend Blackham that both he and Sue enjoyed their own groups and certainly "a house divided would not bring unity within a family." Several possibilities were discussed but no final conclusions were reached.

. . . Sue was concerned not only with the place for the wedding and membership in different religious groups but also with the religious training of their future children. . . . Another problem they talked over with [the minister] was "What are the important spiritual values in living?" They were somewhat surprised to find as they talked with the minister individually and with each other that they wanted basically the same things. Through their discussions they detected real spiritual resources which they said should give them a firm foundation for marriage.

Various possibilities were pursued, but no conclusions were reached. . . . During the last interview Gary and Sue met together with Reverend Blackham, who made a few suggestions regarding reading materials, summarized some of their personal resources, problems, and potentialities, helped them understand better what marriage involves, and gave them a cordial invitation to return at any time. He also suggested that before final decisions were made they discuss their concerns with Gary's rabbi.[18]

We may note several things from this summary of a series of premarital interviews. In the first place, the couple's conversations with the pastor focused their significantly divergent backgrounds. Clearly, however, he respected their profound affection for each other and desire for marriage. The pastor did not ask them to deny their basic drive for marriage and family tasks. Rather, he helped them to see that they had been suppressing their religious backgrounds—a potential problem area in marriage.

Again, Mr. Blackham listened to the couple's concerns rather than listing his concerns for them. As Gary and Sue explored their positive feelings and negative attitudes they discovered what they really liked and disliked about themselves. Rather than marrying on the basis of blind emotion they examined their compatibilities and differences carefully. Third, the couple assumed ultimate responsibility for a suitable course of action. The minister did not force them into a superficial, conforming, or premature decision. Thereafter, they may have discontinued their courtship, deciding

[18] Rex A. Skidmore, Hulda Garrett, and C. Jay Skidmore, *Marriage Consulting: An Introduction to Marriage Counseling* (New York: Harper & Row, 1956), pp. 71-73.

to form relationships with more compatible mates. While the grief of a broken engagement is bitter it is also temporary. On the other hand, Gary and Sue may have married, conscious of their differences and needs for mutuality in the future.

Because preventive pastoral work can save persons much future heartache *most Protestant ministers ask couples considering marriage to meet with them for one or a series of premarital interviews.* They become better acquainted with those anticipating marriage in the church and plan for the ceremony together.[19] Young people can thus explore the adult roles of homemaking, child rearing, and investing in one's significant communities at work, at church, and in leisure. While parents have taught their children to walk, then to "walk away" in marriage, the minister can point the young couple to God, who planted the family in their essential natures.

Some ministers find that group conferences enable couples to experience their inner strengths and share the needs of others planning marriage. Personal inadequacies and blind spots prevent many parents from loving their children rightly and preparing them wisely for marriage. Shared experiences permit young people to face and forgive their parents' failures and to support each other for future family tasks. When young people comprehend their true feelings, attitudes, and motives in courtship they are able to face the demands of marriage more honestly. Preconceived notions about sex are exposed, and some fears may be dispelled.[20]

Following a Christian wedding ceremony the church's ministry should be continued through pastoral aftercare. Many adjustments are required of newly married persons—economic, physical, religious, and relational. What shall be their relationship to their parents and other relatives? Shall both of them continue in school or

[19] Marriage ceremonies appear in service manuals of the major denominations as well as in books of etiquette for brides. *Ethical note:* Ministers serve as representatives of both the church and the state in marriage and usually must have filed their ordination papers at the local county seat or at the state capital prior to performing a wedding ceremony. The minister should familiarize himself with such obligations upon his arrival in a new community.

[20] Cf. Lewin and Gilmore, *Sex Without Fear* (New York: Medical Research Press, 1950); Wm. Menninger, *How to Understand the Opposite Sex* (New York: Sterling Publishing Co., 1956); and Leland F. Wood, *Harmony in Marriage* (rev. ed.; New York: Round Table Press, 1961).

in their previous vocations? What plans shall they make for the coming of children into their lives? Who will they select as friends? What of the use of leisure time? Such questions have Christian answers and should be approached in a spirit of generous love. The couple should be visited by the pastor and included in the church's life. "The more the Church cares," says David Belgum, "the more the young couple will care." There is no greater ministry to be rendered to young families than helping their homes to be Christian.

Beyond counseling and calling *there are additional ways in which churches may prepare persons for marriage and strengthen Christian family life.* Family commitments are to be interpreted in a continuing process of religious education. Providing literature on family themes for engaged and young married couples strengthens the possibility of successful marriage. Books like David R. Mace, *Success in Marriage* (Abingdon Press, 1958); Capper and Williams, *Toward Christian Marriage* (Inter-Varsity Press, 1958); James Pike, *If You Marry Outside Your Faith* (Harper & Row, 1954); and Evelyn M. Duvall, *Love and the Facts of Life* (rev. ed. Association Press, 1963) provide a blueprint of husband-wife roles and obligations. An informed couple may avoid many pitfalls and work through crises in relationships when they arise.

Ministers should preach occasionally on some aspect of family life. Biographical texts on marriage, child rearing, and family life themes abound in the Scriptures. Illustrations of such sermons may be found in Theodore F. Adams, *Making Your Marriage Succeed* (Harper & Row, 1953); and John C. Wynn (ed.), *Sermons on Marriage and Family Life* (Abingdon Press, 1956). Some churches observe a Christian Family Week each year with discussion groups and worship devoted to family themes. Resource persons from varied professions may be enlisted for conference sessions with different age groups. Such periods of special emphasis enable families to face problems, to gain insight into solutions for areas of tension, and to seek improved relationships in the future.

The Christian pastor is in a unique position to guard the entrance into marriage and to undergird family life. He is not a "Marryin' Sam" who burbles sweet words for a fee. Rather, he is a principled man of God, sensitive to the sacredness and uniqueness of the marital relationship. As a representative of both the religious and civic communities, he will preside over the commitments of life with kindness, conviction, and courage.

v. THE DISCOVERY OF DEATH

Thus far we have considered the church's ministry in four major stages of the career of the human self: physical birth, religious conversion, vocational selection, and marriage. We have seen how people turn to the church in each of these stages of life and have viewed pastoral functions in the celebration of these great "rites of passage." The scope of this discussion prevents consideration of life's responsibilities during the creative years of maturity and during the process of aging. Ideally, adulthood is the period of personal and family fulfillment and old age is a time for simplification of status and functions in American culture. Beyond maturity in the human pilgrimage lies the experience of death and the life beyond. Death is life's last frontier. Each man must discover it for himself; no one escapes it.

The fact of one's own death is not discovered all at once. Scientists have demonstrated that we are always dying. The dying process is reflected in the gradual decline of all essential bodily functions and deterioration of vital organs. While instantaneous death is rare, persons do die suddenly in a variety of circumstances—drowning, fire, auto accidents, explosions, battle, or suicide. Others die gradually through infection, heart disease, accident wounds, cancer— in a hundred ways and more. "Death may come in infancy, youth, the prime of life, or old age. There is never a time when it should surprise us, and yet never a 'right' time for dying."[21]

Physicians have dispelled certain fears and illusions about life's termination. Medical research reveals that there is little perceptible pain in death, for the event provides its own anesthesia. In addition, medications reduce the pain of wounds or disease, nursing care is

[21] David Belgum, *The Church and Its Ministry* (Englewood Cliffs, N. J.: Prentice-Hall, 1963), p. 155.

increased during the gradual loss of consciousness, and mechanical devices ease stress on vital organs. Again, dying is usually peaceful at the last. There are no violent throes or convulsions, agony or resistance except in our imagination.

There is a time when the will to live and the fact of one's demise merge in human experience—the moment of dying. I recall the last words spoken by a dying youth who had been injured in an automobile accident. They were uttered in the form of prayer: "Don't cheat me, God. I want to live." Ultimately, each of us will face the final reality of death in the cold sweat of his own death-bed.

Mankind has known through the centuries that there is a time "to be born, and a time to die" (Eccles. 3:2; Heb. 9:27). The fact of one's death is written into his very nature, yet man is threatened by death. Modern culture has devised many ways of extending life, of prolonging vitality, of maintaining the illusion of earthly immortality. Yet the fact of a person's exodus from the world's stage remains life's ultimate certainty. The time awaits us all when we shall be called "the deceased," when our earthly estate will be settled in our absence, and we shall leave existence as we know it to be with God.

Paul Tillich has observed that man "always lives in the conscious or unconscious anxiety of having to die. Non-being is present in every moment of his being. Suffering, accidents, disease, loss of relations to nature and man, loneliness, insecurity, weakness, and error are always with him. Finally, the threat of having to die will become the reality of death."[22] What lies behind man's natural antipathy to dying? Biblical theology suggests that "the sting of death is sin" (I Cor. 15:56). The pain of human mortality is estrangement from God, not merely fear of the unknown. Those persons that die "in the Lord" may resent their "image of dust" though they are convinced of eternal life. The Christian man believes that "God has put all things in subjection under his feet." Through Christ's resurrection God destroyed "the last enemy" and has brought "life and

[22] Paul Tillich, "The Theology of Pastoral Care," *Pastoral Psychology*, X (Oct., 1959), 23.

immortality to light through the gospel" (I Cor. 15:20-58; II Tim. 1:10). While men dread death, the Christian faith affirms that "whether we live or whether we die, we are the Lord's" (Rom. 14:7-9). Accordingly, the church's primary concern is not how *long* a person lives but how *well* he lives with the years accorded him in God's kindly providence. Ministers thus prepare persons, not to die, but to live.

Ideally, a person's preparation for this last great "rite of passage" should begin long before the experience of dying. However, the process of death is almost imperceptible as retrogressive changes in the organism lead to old age. Sermons, group discussions, literature, personal conversations dealing with questions and doubt—all are resources for facing the reality of death. And when death comes the pastor can stand beside the dying individual, hear his or her confession, offer prayer for a peaceful journey into God's blessed presence, and comfort those left behind in bereavement.

I once shared a physician's ministry to a terminal cancer patient in her mid-thirties. Exploratory surgery had failed to reach a rapidly spreading tumor. A second major operation merely confirmed the certainty of her early death. The physician "leveled" with the young mother and her husband because he felt they could face reality better than uncertainty and anxiety. She was told that she had approximately six months to live. Cancer had decreed the death sentence. "But why?" she protested. "I have so much to live for." She enumerated her reasons for life and hope: her husband, her son, her church, her friends, desire to travel, unachieved goals, her love of life. As they talked quietly, the doctor reasoned, "You are 33, married; you've had one child, own a home, have traveled some. You've lived wisely and fully. Actually, Billie, every other experience from now on will be simply a repetition of the past. You have had a good life. You should be able to die with no regrets." His words were reasonable, spoken in love, but they did not reassure her.

In time the spectrum of Billie's activities, interests, and contacts narrowed to her bedroom, her family and a few close friends, and her constant pain. Her husband was a courageous sentinel, guarding his home against their bitter enemy—death. Yet the enemy approached as Billie grew weaker during passing weeks. Brief periods marked by concern for other persons and things were interspersed with long depressed periods of self-concern. Like liquid poured into a funnel, her glowing life narrowed to a trickle of interest in others.

As Billie was transferred to a hospital during her last days, sensations of other persons diminished slowly. She suffered intense pain. She was irritable and depressed, restless, unresponsive to her husband's soft words and the nurses' kind hands. The night she died her pastor was with the family in the hospital. Billie seemed to experience a vision in which the incoming waves of "that immortal sea" lapped first at her feet and then at her waist, finally overwhelming her in its surging power. She slipped quietly from safe moorings with her family and close friends and joined her Lord on the distant shore. As sense perception failed, circulation ceased and breathing stopped, it seemed that Billie had gone to sleep. Physicians tell us that, clinically, dying is like falling asleep.[23] For her, there was peace at the last, and for her family there was the knowledge that she would suffer no more.

Members of the health team do not agree on the matter of whether or not to tell a person that death is imminent. Some physicians feel that the patient gives up if he or she thinks death is near. Frequently a dying person senses a subtle change in his family's solicitude or in the words of the professional strangers who combat death with him. He may not mention death to his family, if he is conscious, for fear of upsetting them. Usually, however, a person who thinks that he or she is dying will share deep feelings with a minister. Billie, in the case above, talked to her pastor about death on several occasions. An elderly woman once confessed as she was dying: "I am not afraid. I am going to be with my Lord." A family, awaiting word from a clergyman who had entered their dying father's room, were relieved by his report. "Your dad says

[23] Cf. Herman Feifel (ed.), *The Meaning of Death* (New York: Blakiston Div., McGraw-Hill Book Co., 1959); and Kurt R. Eissler, *The Psychiatrist and the Dying Patient* (New York: International Universities Press, 1955).

that he has made his peace with God. He is ready to go." Separation is always sorrowful. The burden is lightened when a family has such Christian assurance.

The pastor's ministry to the dying person and to his or her family is mirrored in the following excerpt from a conversation with a woman whose husband was critically ill. The man had suffered a stroke and was in the intensive care unit of a hospital when the pastor called. Mrs. S had been at the hospital many hours; she was very tired and began to cry when she saw the minister.

MRS. S: If I did not have Christ I could not face this hour. I can't imagine what it would be like to go through this experience without him.

PASTOR: In times like this God becomes very real to us. We can feel his presence with us.

MRS. S: I can't imagine what life without Ralph (her husband) would be like. He's been sick before, and I have never given up. I just won't give up for him to die now. I just have to believe that he won't leave me (Silence followed as she wept.)

PASTOR (obviously he did not know what to say—he tried to reassure her with a reminder of the past): Now is the time to thank God for those thirty-seven years he gave you together. Remember telling me about those years—how wonderful they were?

MRS. S: Yes, I do remember. I know that I couldn't ask for anything more than God has given me. I suppose I must be concerned that his going be as peaceable as possible, since I know that he can never completely recover.

PASTOR: Giving up a loved one is hard to do. But we know that Christ has a place for all of us who trust him. . . . Now, we don't know what is going to happen but we do know that God will do what is right.

They read Psalm 23 and prayed together, standing near the helpless man's side. The pastor asked God's help for the man, for those that ministered to him, and his care for Mrs. S. As he left the room with its mood of death the woman said: "God is with us. We're fine. God will do what is right." The grieving process had begun. The pastor's faith had sparked her own. Evidently she had tasted "the fruit of the travail of [her] soul and [was] satisfied"

(Isa. 53:11). Even in the sorrowful pangs of death, Mrs. S was not afraid.

CONCLUSION

In the final chapter we shall consider the pastor's crisis ministry, including the crisis of grief. Here we have viewed his supportive role when death appears as a vital component of human experience. The Christian pastor shares his fellow pilgrims' plight of a fully human existence. He who shares the epochs of life, from birth to death, is subject to the peril of faithlessness. By God's grace and power the minister serves as a providential reminder of eternal life. Living in the cities of men, he lifts their vision to that "city which is to come."

SUGGESTED READING

Belgum, David. *The Church and Its Ministry.* Englewood Cliffs, N.J.: Prentice-Hall, 1963. A Lutheran pastoral theologian clarifies the church's ministry in life's common ventures and major crises.

Bowman, Henry A. *A Christian Interpretation of Marriage.* Philadelphia: Westminster Press, 1959. Brief treatment of basic topics by a Christian sociologist.

Johnson, Paul E. *Psychology of Pastoral Care.* Nashville, Tenn.: Abingdon Press, 1953. A basic work. Relates principles of interpersonal psychology and responsive counseling to all major areas of pastoral concern.

Kemp, Charles F. *The Pastor and Vocational Counseling.* St. Louis: Bethany Press, 1961. Interprets the guidance movement to churchmen as well as the pastor's role in vocational counseling.

Southard, Samuel. *Pastoral Evangelism.* Nashville, Tenn.: Broadman Press, 1962. A helpful interpretation of evangelism and church discipline based upon empirical investigation. Includes case studies.

Thielicke, Helmut. *The Ethics of Sex,* trans. John W. Doberstein. New York: Harper & Row, 1964. A profound study of sexual ethics by a German preacher and theologian who is well known in this country.

CHAPTER 9

❧❧

SUPPORTING PERSONS
IN LIFE'S CRISES

PASTORAL care was conceived in Chapter 8 as sensitive Christian response to personal and family needs at significant stages of change and growth in life. Influenced by Sherrill, Havighurst, Erikson, Duvall, Trueblood, and others, I designated birth, religious conversion, vocational selection, marriage, and death as "primary moments" in human experience. Life thrusts these *acts of being* upon mankind, requires major decisions in each epoch, and issues in some form of character growth or failure. Each of these experiences is crucial in that it involves appropriate spiritual response, i.e., responsible behavior, at the right time (*kairos*) in the course of one's pilgrimage (*chronos*). Such eras of change and growth may be regarded as creative crises when they prompt a person to place his life "in God's hands" (Ps. 31:15). Conversely, one who clutches life in his own hands is lost both to the human community and to the kingdom of God (Luke 9:24-25).

Disruptive crises, on the other hand, may arise at any stage of development, turning an ordinary experience into an unbearable situation. There are disasters, emergencies, and grave dysfunctions during which a person may be unable to bear his own burden. Such situations are multiplied *ad infinitum* in pastoral practice. At such times a person turns to a helping community for support, forgiveness, or companionship. The church, in turn, either accepts or refuses its responsibility to bear the burdens of the weak or injured individual and his family.

The word "crisis," from the Greek *krisis* or *krinein*, "to separate," implies a turning point or decisive moment in experience. A crisis, viewed medically, is that change in a disease process leading to either recovery or death. A crucial event or epoch in a nation's life may become a watershed, a shaping influence in its destiny. We are told that one Chinese dialect uses two characters, meaning "dangerous opportunity," to express this idea. Crisis experiences thus embody a dualism of possibility and danger. They denote a sudden turning of life's tide. Crucial situations become either decisively constructive or regressive experiences for persons, families, institutions, and nations. Crises are thus characterized by decisiveness, urgency, and a sense of ultimate concern.

Karl Jaspers, a contemporary philosopher, calls experiences when we come up against life or death "limit-situations" or "boundary-situations." They also may be viewed as revelatory moments, for in the New Testament a *krisis* implies God's immanence and judgment in the human situation. "No crucial situation is adequately lived through," writes Carl Michalson, "which does not take into consideration the dimension of the God-relation."[1] The fact of divine providence pervades every developmental crisis and failure in life's pilgrimage. The church's task, therefore, is to enable men to hear God's voice in human tragedy. Viewed in the light of this God-relation, crises not only test a person's spiritual resources, they challenge his growth and responsibility as well.

The purpose of this chapter is to distinguish the Christian helper's therapeutic ministry in three disruptive crises—guilt, illness, and grief. They typify a whole spectrum of crucial situations in pastoral work. Our knowledge of such crises is partial, for human feelings and states of soul are incredibly complex. Discussions like those in the recent work, *Constructive Aspects of Anxiety* (edited by Seward Hiltner and Karl Menninger, Abingdon Press, 1963),

[1] Carl Michalson, *Faith for Personal Crises* (New York: Charles Scribner's Sons, 1958), pp. 6-7.

should prompt us to probe the positive significance of anxiety states and crises. From the sufferer's point of view a crisis may be a foe from which he seeks help or protection. From the minister's perspective human extremities may become divine opportunities for health or salvation. Trouble isolates some persons but turns others to God and the church. It is hoped that, by means of a fellowship of concern, God himself may break through to kindle a person's faith and renew his life beyond tragedy.[2] Tillich calls this community a "shaping environment" that helps a person to interpret religious meaning in life's crucial situations.

I. THE CRISIS OF GUILT

The burden of guilt has been a problematic aspect of human personality from the earliest recorded experiences of man. We are told that Adam and Eve disobeyed God, then "hid themselves from the presence of the Lord" when he looked for them in the garden (Gen. 3:8). Their son Cain thought he was rid of his brother Abel after he had killed him. Yet the accusing finger of a guilty conscience marred his hollow victory. Undone by his blood-guilt, Cain was exiled as "a fugitive and a wanderer on the earth." Guilt thus provoked a crisis for him as its burden became unbearable. Cain found no place to hide in the "land of Wandering" and no promise of hope as he "went away from the presence of the Lord" (Gen. 4:8-16).

The complexity of guilt. Man alone of all God's creation experiences feelings of moral failure, painful reproaches of conscience, dread of eternal punishment, and hope through the gospel of Jesus Christ. Fashioned for fellowship with God, "a little lower than the angels," man has denied his true grandeur and become what Pascal called a "deposed king." Protestant theologians are generally agreed that man as sinner retains the capacity to perceive his life with intelligence and honesty. Consequently, man is the creature who

[2] James M. Gustafson reminds us that "it is not the action of the church that redeems a member of the community; it is God's action that is redemptive." See his introduction to H. Richard Niebuhr, *The Responsible Self* (New York: Harper & Row, 1963), p. 38.

feels the estrangement of guilt and requires continual forgiveness from God, others, and himself. He is never done with the need for confession, for he shares the guilt of a sinful world.

Personality is so constituted that some persons suffer an over-powering sense of shame about matters which others view lightly or overlook entirely. This complicates the matter of confession and resolution of guilt. While a person may be guilty of sinning against God or a neighbor (forensic guilt) he may or may not experience shame (feelings of guilt) about it. On the other hand, a person with an overburdened conscience may or may not be guilty of sin or moral error. The person with an intrapunitive conscience may be experiencing what psychologists call "neurotic guilt" and what some theologians call "anxious dread." Christian confessors, therefore, cannot assume that sin against God, others, or one-self always lies behind a person's guilt feelings in linear fashion. Nor is confession of sin the equivalent of "realized forgive-ness" in human experience. While God forgives freely, some per-sons cannot forgive themselves for past misdeeds. Accordingly, those who would assist others to live with integrity of heart need to understand the operation of guilt and forgiveness in human experience.

Perspectives on guilt and forgiveness. The impasse of man bound by his conscience is laid bare in biblical character sketches, in great literary works, in psychoanalytic theory, and in pastoral practice. Since guilt feelings may be handled in various ways, some of which are destructive, those who seek resolution of guilt should view it from every angle of possible help. Varied sources of wisdom have sounded a strangely similar note to contemporary man: "You are not what you think you are." Both theology and psychology, for example, hold that man has a far greater capacity for good and for evil than he thinks. Fortunately, the Christian shepherd sees man's ambiguous grandeur and misery silhouetted against the brilliant backdrop of the Christian faith (John 1:5).

From the biblical perspective guilt refers not only to a human *feeling* about disobedience, or a ruptured relationship with God or man; it is also a forensic term. It implies one's status of *being* guilty, of having one's guilt established under the divine law. Two terms translated "guilt" are used in the New Testament: (1) *hupodikos,* meaning "under judgment" or "liable to punishment"; and (2) *enochos,* meaning "guilty of anything, bound, under obligation, subject to" or responsible for something.[3] Both terms imply man's guilty status and condition as sinner before God (cf. Rom. 3:19; I Cor. 11:27; Jas. 2:10).

The experience of King David is a classic case of man's confinement in the bonds of guilt, sickness of his own secrets, and joy in confession and pardon. Nathan the prophet, who knew of David's sin against Uriah and Bathsheba, became his brother's keeper by relating a parable to the king. Portraying an economic evil—a rich man taking a poor man's one ewe lamb—he aroused the king's sense of justice. "As the Lord lives," vowed David, "the man who has done this deserves to die . . ." When confronted with reality: "You are the man!" David's stricken conscience prompted his admission: "I have sinned against the Lord" (II Sam. 12:1-15). His confessional prayers, Psalms 32 and 51, reveal man's anxious longing for divine cleansing and renewal. As long as his moral fault remained unconfessed David experienced great distress. "When I declared not my sin, my body wasted away . . . for day and night thy hand was heavy upon me . . ." (Ps. 32:3-4). Yet when he implored: "Create in me a clean heart, O God, and put a new . . . spirit within me," David experienced forgiveness and release from bondage in guilt.

Shakespeare's characters frequently mirror human guilt and desire for pardon. Lady Macbeth's poignant cry "Out, damned spot!" is a dramatic paradigm of all human longing for freedom from the stain of guilt. In Manuel Kimroff's story, *The Death of Judas,* Lazarus encounters Judas following the crucifixion. Lazarus, feeling implicated in the crime against Christ, accuses Judas: "Your face has become loathsome." Judas replies, "The face of every murderer is loathsome. This is God's imprint, the hot iron brand, so that all mankind may know what guilt looks like." But note

---

[3] J. H. Thayer, *A Greek-English Lexicon of the New Testament* (rev. ed.; New York: American Book Co., 1886), pp. 217, 643.

what happened. Lazarus actually admitted that he had failed
Jesus Christ by accusing Judas.[4] He took his own guilt out on the
betrayer, a mechanism called *projection* by modern psychology.
The biblical account of the betrayal, however, reports that Judas
Iscariot was so remorseful about his misdeed that he returned the
blood money, then hanged himself (Matt. 27:3-5). Unresolved guilt,
unfreely revealed, led Judas from self-accusation to self-destruction.

Psychoanalysts such as Sigmund Freud, Alfred Adler, Carl Jung,
and Erich Fromm have reaffirmed the destructiveness of guilt and
provided new theoretical knowledge about the inner life of man.
In 1923 Freud recorded certain discoveries from his psychoanalytic
practice in *The Ego and the Id*. Not only did his patients experience
a "normal conscious sense of guilt (conscience)," wrote Freud, but
some of them disclosed destructive guilt feelings at unconscious
levels of existence. Repressed guilt found "atonement in illness"
so that some of his patients refused to "give up the penalty of
suffering." This resistance to analysis, reported Freud, put "the
most powerful obstacles in the way of recovery."[5] While he thought
that a great part of man's sense of guilt remained inaccessible,
Freud recognized improvement in patients who experienced
catharsis and insight through therapy. By various methods the
patient was enabled to recognize his hidden drives and emotions,
to elevate them to conscious levels, and to place them under ego
control.

Carl Jung, Freud's contemporary, moved beyond his former colleague's biological formulations of psychoanalysis and took man's
cultural environment into systematic consideration. For example,
Freud thought that guilt neuroses developed from the superego's
function as a vindictive vehicle—"a punitive inner agency of 'blind'
morality."[6] He conceived no norms, no objective moral standards,
for human behavior. He was concerned not with objective (factual)
guilt but with a patient's neurotic guilt feelings. Jung, on the other

---

[4] Quoted in Michalson, *op. cit.*, p. 63.
[5] John Richman (ed.), *A General Selection from the Works of Sigmund
Freud* (Garden City, N.Y.: Doubleday & Co., 1957), pp. 228-30 *et passim*.
[6] See Erik H. Erikson, *Identity and the Life Cycle* (New York: International
Universities Press, 1959), p. 148.

hand, advanced a theory of cultural archetypes by which society provides models of morality and encourages the development of conscience—an inner sense of obligation. When an individual violated his internalized moral standards Jung held that any consequent guilt feelings should be confessed. Otherwise, a person might experience psychic conflict to the point of physical or mental illness. "To cherish secrets and to restrain emotions," wrote Jung, "are psychic misdemeanors for which nature finally visits us with sickness . . ."[7] He felt that psychic concealment alienated an individual from himself, his family, and a helping community.

While such practitioners have reminded us afresh of the need for confession and forgiveness, their studies have yielded inconclusive hypotheses. Recent claims by a research psychologist, O. Hobart Mowrer, that neither Freud nor faith can resolve guilt have provoked great debate among scientists and churchmen.[8] In *The Crisis in Psychiatry and Religion* Mowrer has advanced a guilt theory of psychopathology. He accuses ministers of offering "cheap grace" through easy forgiveness and attacks Freudians for replacing guilt with "guilt feelings." He proposes confession of real guilt to another person, penitential acts, and amendment of life as a formula for psychic healing. His theory, developed from personal experience, is being researched in several mental hospital settings.

Theologians, with few exceptions, have been preoccupied with abstract categories of sin and redemption rather than with the clinical reality of man's guilt and forgiveness. David Belgum has

---

[7] Carl G. Jung, *Modern Man in Search of a Soul,* trans. W. S. Dell and C. F. Baynes (London: Paul, Trench, Trubner & Co., 1933), p. 39.

[8] O. Hobart Mowrer, *The Crisis in Psychiatry and Religion* (Princeton, N.J.: D. Van Nostrand Co., 1961); John G. McKenzie, *Guilt: Its Meaning and Significance* (Nashville, Tenn.: Abingdon Press, 1962); and Paul Tournier, *Guilt and Grace,* trans. A. W. Heathcote (New York: Harper & Row, 1962). Though these writers worked independently they have attacked many of the same problems.

My criticism of Mowrer arises at two crucial points: (1) his oversimplification of the components of guilt and (2) his superficial view of Christian forgiveness. He places primary responsibility for healing upon man's confession, rather than upon God's action as Reconciler. Also, his "new group therapy" overlooks the significance of the church as the fellowship of confession and forgiveness. Mowrer is both right and wrong. He certainly does not go far enough, yet his criticisms may be salutary for both theologians and therapists.

challenged the silence of churchmen on this subject in a recent work—*Guilt: Where Psychology and Religion Meet*.[9] Influenced by Mowrer, with whom he studied, Belgum sees a positive correlation between specific antisocial acts (sins) and mental disease. He does not distinguish between *sin* as rebellion against God and *sins* as evil practices against oneself or others. His thesis is that sickness is often the "amplified voice of conscience" and that resolution of many forms of mental disorder follows repentance, confession, and amendment of life.

Christian pastors, meanwhile, are compelled to forego the luxury of theoretical tilting because of their practical efforts to make divine forgiveness effective in human experience. Interestingly, the skilled shepherd understands models of sin advanced by both theologians and psychologists. He knows that the human heart is a rebel against God. Yet the counseling pastor discovers sin in terms of (1) bondage to urges one cannot master, (2) alienation through broken relationships, (3) rebellion against authority, (4) guilt for breaking the laws of God or the human community, and (5) unworthiness because of a feeling of nastiness, of being soiled inside. And for resolution of guilt the pastor turns from such unacceptable models as (a) classic psychoanalysis, (b) the Catholic sacrament of penance, and (c) Mowrer's "new group therapy" to biblical realities of grace, faith, repentance, forgiveness, and responsibility before God.[10]

The resolution of guilt. Guilt does not always prompt a crisis in human experience. The responsible person handles his or her guilt constructively by facing its sources, confessing it to God, appropriating forgiveness, then forgetting it. Thus what Calvin called

[9] Alan Richardson's *A Theological Word Book of the Bible* (New York: The Macmillan Co., 1960), omits the topic of "guilt." While *A Handbook of Christian Theology* discusses "forgiveness," the topic of "guilt" is omitted (New York: Meridian Books, 1958). David Belgum serves as apostle for Mowrer's theses in *Guilt: Where Psychology and Religion Meet* (Englewood Cliffs, N.J.: Prentice-Hall, 1963). One may hope that more objective and penetrating studies, including carefully appraised clinical pastoral work with guilty persons, will appear in the future.

[10] Some of these ideas were developed in discussion with Paul Pruyser of the Menninger Foundation during a conference at Princeton Theological Seminary, April 22, 1963.

"inward integrity of heart" is renewed before God and the human community. Again, some persons do not feel a sense of guilt toward men nor sin toward God. Such sociopathic personalities shrug off moral defections with a "So what!" attitude because of an insulated or devitalized conscience. Paul Lehmann laments the fact that we have witnessed the "decline and fall of conscience in the Western ethical tradition."[11] He calls for a renewed "theonomous (God-centered) conscience" within the context of the Christian *koinōnia*. Creating constructive pressure on congregants so that they will "walk in the Spirit" is not easy, however. In fact, some ministers' perfectionistic preaching and repressive conversations actually compound their church members' guilt feelings. Such men offer little hope for "realized forgiveness" in human experience.

How may a Protestant congregation function as a fellowship of confession and reconciliation for persons who *are* guilty? To those bowed beneath the weight of sin, shame, and guilt the church offers the opportunity of corporate confession through public worship and private confession through prayer. Each member of the church, in turn, is to be a confessor to his brethren and to those in the world for whom Christ died. Ideally, each member of the corporate priesthood is to be an agent of reconciliation. At times, as in the following instance, a congregant confesses to God through a minister.

A middle-aged spinster, whom we shall know as Miss White, once made an appointment with the minister of a village church. Before their meeting the pastor knew that Miss White (1) lived with her widowed mother, for he had visited them; (2) had secured a temporary leave from her teaching position because of ill health; and (3) was seeing a psychiatrist who had advised her to forego church attendance temporarily. Miss White asked for an evening appointment in order that adequate time might be given to her story. She also requested that her mother and the minister's wife be present during the interview. This was arranged. Their face-to-face meeting in the pastor's home had the flavor of a confessional conversation.

[11] Paul Lehmann, *Ethics in a Christian Context* (New York: Harper & Row, 1963), p. 361.

The counselee explained the compulsive symptoms that had kept her away from church in recent months and revealed much insight into their cause. One involved a strong psychosexual attraction to a certain businessman in the community. She wanted to talk with the man each time she saw him and controlled this urge with great difficulty. Moreover, Miss White felt compelled to confess her past misdeeds publicly to the entire congregation each time she attended worship services. Her absence from church was explained as an effort to cope with this compulsion to repeat a confessional act. She indicated that neither prayer to God nor sessions with her psychiatrist had relieved her overpowering sense of guilt.

Miss White quoted a familiar Bible passage: "I know that God forgives us, for he has said, 'If we confess our sins, he is faithful and just, and will forgive our sins and cleanse us from all unrighteousness' (I John 1:9). But, Pastor, I have confessed again and again and still feel dirty inside. I know that God hears my prayers; he will forgive, but I don't *feel* forgiven." She felt that her sin was unforgivable.

Voluntarily, she confessed that years before she had engaged in an illicit love affair with a man whom she planned to wed. Their marriage plans failed however. Since that clandestine affair she had masturbated over a period of many years and felt very guilty about it. Each lonely episode resulted in feelings of disgust with herself and of unworthiness before God. Finally, a depressive reaction had set in and she had turned to a psychiatrist for help. She had "cleared" with him about talking with her minister.

The pastor indicated that he knew something of how hard it was to live in the past and to carry one's past into the present and future. They talked of God's forgiveness in Christ and of the *demands* of that forgiveness—that one both "own and disown" his sin. This had been only a *paper faith* for Miss White in the past since she had mishandled her guilt by (1) projecting it onto others, (2) suffering psychic illness, and (3) withdrawing from every potential community of help save one, her psychiatrist. She needed volitional strength in order to turn from her destructive sexual inversion to constructive social pursuits. She also needed to *accept* God's acceptance of her and to forgive herself. A pastoral prayer focused the counselee's feelings of helplessness, need for forgiveness, and desire to live again. Her confession and desired amendment of life were viewed as positive steps by the group. They agreed to meet periodically, since Miss White needed reassurance in redirecting the course of her life.

Several clues to shepherding guilty persons may be noted from this experience. (1) The stated problem is rarely the true source of a person's guilt. Miss White spoke first of her absenteeism from worship services, for she felt guilty about that. But *that* was not all! In time she revealed uncontrollable urges, shame for past misdeeds, and morbid guilt. (2) The burden of guilt is both isolating and depressing. A deeply depressed person is capable of suicide as a final act of atonement. Therefore, the minister suggested that Miss White remain in her doctor's care until he dismissed her. (3) The confessional group pledged themselves to confidentiality, for the counselee did not want to be betrayed to the community. Fear of betrayal to those who may not understand is involved in all confessional situations. (4) Confession may be a meaningless, compulsive act until a person achieves insight into the sources of his or her guilt and exerts volitional control through amendment of life. (5) To count one's sin as "unpardonable," instead of placing its burden in God's hands, may be a subtle form of pride. "Hardness of heart" is a component in some pseudo confessions, particularly when a person gains some gratification through his or her behavior. Such a disturbed person may cling to his symptoms in order to win others to his position or to gain sympathy.

Miss White's psychiatrist had advised therapeutic activities, such as needlework and gardening, to help her regain self-esteem. (6) While therapeutic activity may restore lost esteem, there is no substitute for God's gracious forgiveness in human experience. (7) As Christians confess their faults "one to another" and forgive each other *to the degree* that Christ forgives them, divine pardon becomes more real to them. (8) The only true criterion for release from bondage in guilt is not confession but character change. Alteration of conduct follows such inner amendment of life. Finally, confession is intensely personal. As one minister reminded his flock: "Only you can confess your sin to God and receive his forgiveness."

II. THE CRISIS OF ILLNESS

Accidents, hospitalized illnesses, and surgical procedures disrupt life's serenity and threaten the security of persons and their families. Hospitalization creates a crisis as the ill or injured person experiences his own finitude, suffers pain, and copes with alien forces and persons. He leaves the familiar routine of work, home, and leisure for the unfamiliar schedule, sterile procedures, complex equipment, and uncertain future of a medical setting. Illness is a depersonalizing crisis, disrupting relationships and draining physical and financial resources. A businessman who develops a heart ailment, for example, temporarily loses his vocational identity and status in a hospital setting. His life-situation becomes more complex. Normal anxiety is intensified as he becomes a shut-in and the world outside functions without him.

That a parishioner has become a *patient* does not alter the fact that he remains a *person* needing understanding, affection, and support. Organic distress, whether its source be accident, aging, stress, or infection, is accompanied by emotional distress. Flanders Dunbar and other pioneers in the field of psychosomatic medicine have demonstrated that emotions are frequently causative factors in illness. Accordingly, persons suffering physical or mental illness need spiritual as well as medical care. Studies by Jerome Frank, M.D., of Johns Hopkins Medical School and by Richard Young and Albert Meiburg, chaplains at North Carolina Baptist Hospital, have demonstrated the role of faith in the healing process.[12] Clinical case studies validate the psalmist's testimony: "My flesh and my heart may fail, but God is the strength of my heart and my portion for ever" (Ps. 73:26).

The first requisite of those calling upon life's wounded and weak

[12] Jerome D. Frank, *Persuasion and Healing* (Baltimore: Johns Hopkins Press, 1961), and Richard K. Young and Albert L. Meiburg, *Spiritual Therapy* (New York: Harper & Row, 1960).

citizens, therefore, is that they be wise men of faith. The Christian pastor represents God's healing power to patients by his quiet trust, steadfast love, and undiscouraged hope. He cares wisely by joining the medical community in providing appropriate conditions for God's healing forces to work in a patient's life. The shepherd of the sick will also be alert to the patient's private world. Rarely will he find people so stripped of pretense and pride. Illness humbles individuals and prompts "teachable moments" in life. "When I was down," confessed a man who had broken his back, "there was no way to look but *up*." Through conversation, suggestion, and prayer God's servant becomes a healing agent in the crisis of illness.

Visiting the hospitalized patient. Since the appearance of Cabot and Dicks' *The Art of Ministering to the Sick* in 1936, numerous books have been written in this specialized area of pastoral care.[13] While I am presupposing the reader's acquaintance with such literature, some practical suggestions are germane to this discussion.

When moving to a new locality a clergyman should acquaint himself with the medical facilities and personnel of that city or region, including physicians, hospital administrators, and chaplains. As to the question of whom to visit, the pastor will call upon his own congregants, upon those whom he is requested to visit, and upon anyone for whom he feels pastoral concern. Some hospital residents have no church affiliation, yet they need a minister. Others are from out of town with no pastor available unless the hospital employs a chaplain. As a general rule he should visit members of another church only at the request of a fellow pastor or family member.

[13] See Russell L. Dicks, *Toward Health and Wholeness* (New York: The Macmillan Co., 1960); Joseph Fletcher, *Morals and Medicine* (Princeton, N.J.: Princeton University Press, 1954; paperback ed., Boston: Beacon Press, 1960); Wm. A. Lauterbach, *Ministering to the Sick* (St. Louis: Concordia, 1955); Wayne E. Oates, *Religious Factors in Mental Illness* (New York: Association Press, 1954); Edith Stern, *Mental Illness: A Guide for the Family* (rev. ed.; New York: Harper & Row, 1957); Richard K. Young, *The Pastor's Hospital Ministry* (Nashville, Tenn.: Broadman Press, 1954); and Granger Westberg, *Minister and Doctor Meet* (New York: Harper & Row, 1961).

As he seeks to personalize his visits with each patient the minister should inquire at the nursing station about the person's general condition. As a colleague in the helping professions he knows that the patient's welfare is the hospital's first concern. *Any Christian caller* should remember that, while he represents God and life's central values in the sickroom, *he is not indispensable to the patient's recovery.* In protecting the patient's welfare, hospital visitors will be guided by the following principles.

1. Regard signs on the door such as: Isolation, X-ray, No Visitors, and the call light. Knock before entering. The visitor should introduce himself as he is received into the sickroom.

2. Call back later when a patient's meal is being served, when his or her physician appears, or when several visitors are present in the room.

3. Be sensitive to God's presence and identify with the patient's situation. It is easy for a caller unconsciously to assume a patronizing air of looking down upon the sick.

4. Address others in the room but, where possible, concentrate upon a face-to-face ministry to the patient. Stand or sit in the patient's line of vision. Avoid leaning on the bed or jarring equipment like an infusion flask or an oxygen tent. If the patient is unconscious, asleep, or too ill to talk, visit briefly with family members.

5. The call should be conducted in a spirit of prayer (Matt. 18:20). It is best not to talk or laugh boisterously, since a quiet mood generally pervades the sickroom. When a scripture selection and verbal prayer are employed, the patient should feel that his concerns are being met. Spontaneous use of these resources is more effective than canned phrases offered as a pious gesture.[14]

6. It is impossible to say how long a visit should be. Its duration will vary according to the level of relationship—social, supportive, confessional, and so on—achieved with the patient. The presence of others in the room, interruptions, and the patient's condition and responsiveness also influence a visit's length.

[14] See Wayne E. Oates, *The Bible in Pastoral Care* (Philadelphia: Westminster Press, 1953).

Psalm 90 or 91 [handwritten marginal note]

Be especially concerned about spending time with the patients in intensive care. Have concern for the time you spend there. [handwritten note]

Entering the patient's private world. A pastoral visit, like a sermon, proceeds from an introduction through the body of the call to a conclusion. Each patient is unique. Thus the same technique will not work in every case. Factors such as the person's age, sex, physical condition, cultural background, religious heritage, emotional state, and relationship patterns condition the call. *Why* the person is there provides a clue to the degree of anxiety he or she may feel. Has he been hospitalized for an examination, an injury, emotional disorder, acute infection, surgical procedure, chronic infirmity, or catastrophic illness? An individual may be experiencing any one of a whole gamut of feelings: shock, guilt, depression, weakness, pain, hostility, separation anxiety, fear of death, or anxious longing for health.

Primarily by *listening*, the shepherd enters the patient's private world in order to determine what his real needs are. Through that channel he receives from the Holy Spirit what he is to say to each sufferer (Matt. 10:19). Prefabricated responses are a poor substitute for a genuine relationship. The following conversation illustrates how a minister entered a patient's world by listening and incarnated God's grace in time of need. This was the first meeting between Mr. Coleman, a newly admitted patient, and a general hospital chaplain.

CHAPLAIN (introductions had been exchanged): Mr. Coleman, you've just come into the hospital?

COLEMAN: Yes, I came in yesterday afternoon. The doctor is giving me some tests (very soft voice).

CHAPLAIN: You say that you are in for some tests?

COLEMAN: Yes, the doctor thinks that I may have a brain tumor or something. Dr. Y wants me to get my head X-rayed and get a spinal tap. They'll probably get a brain-wave test, too.

CHAPLAIN: He thinks it may be a tumor?

COLEMAN: Uh-huh. See, I've been having these blackout spells. I've had three of 'em. Sometime I just get rigid—like this—(demonstrated) and I can't even talk. The doctor thinks it may be a pressure on my brain. (Pause.) When they tap my spine, that may take off some of the pressure. I sure hope so.

CHAPLAIN: I'm sure you do. You've probably been pretty concerned about yourself.

COLEMAN: I'll say! Why, the other day—about three weeks ago now—I just fell on my face on a concrete floor. (He rubbed his face.) I cut it up here, and here, and here. It's a wonder I hadn't of broken it up.

CHAPLAIN: That must have been a frightening experience!

The patient related other blackout experiences. Once, while driving, he froze at the wheel and ran into a parked car. Also, he said that his nerves interfered with little things around the house where a fellow needed steady hands.

CHAPLAIN: So your family has noticed this, too.

COLEMAN: I guess you'd say they have. (Pause.) See, my wife and I have been separated for six months now. I love my wife and my two boys, but we don't live together any more (real grief and depression were apparent—he implied that she had been unfaithful to their marriage vows). Man, this has been the hardest thing I ever ran into in my life. I love her and the boys. I just couldn't believe it at first. I trusted her completely.

CHAPLAIN: This must have come as a terrible shock.

COLEMAN: It has nearly killed me (he explained how he learned of her infidelity and had talked to her "boyfriend"). He didn't deny it. In fact, he just made one request—that I shouldn't tell his wife. And I haven't. My home has been wrecked. I don't see any reason for seeing theirs busted, too.

CHAPLAIN: So you've been under this pressure for about six months?

COLEMAN: I'd never been sick a day in my life till this happened.

CHAPLAIN: You'd never been sick before . . . never been a patient in a hospital like this?

COLEMAN: Not till about three months ago when I started having these blackouts spells. The doctor said that it *could* be my nerves. He said I'd been through enough to make 'em bad and I guess I have. I'm real shaky.

CHAPLAIN: You feel then that there may be some connection between your broken home and your blackout spells?

COLEMAN: Yes . . . I guess I do.

CHAPLAIN: While the doctors check every possibility with you, Mr. Coleman, to see if there is some physical cause behind the blackouts, I want to be your pastor here in the hospital. Spiritual and medical skill can work together to improve your health, and perhaps to save your home as well.

COLEMAN: I sure hope so. (A nurse entered and gave Mr. C a tablet.)

CHAPLAIN: Your doctor can give you a tablet to ease the pain in your head. Your minister represents the living God who can ease the pain in your heart. (Pause.) Mr. Coleman, I shall see you again after the tests.

We may observe *first* that the chaplain identified with the patient and tried to understand his plight. Obviously, Mr. Coleman felt (1) grief in the loss of his wife's love and hostility because of her rejection and infidelity. He carried (2) an unresolved grudge against the man who had shattered the serenity of his home. Perhaps Mr. Coleman had unconsciously turned this destructive hostility in upon himself through somatic symptoms. (3) The blackouts compounded his suffering but had prompted little sympathy (secondary gain) from others. The patient was experiencing real depression. He felt cut off "from the land of the living." At one point he admitted, "It has nearly killed me." (4) Mr. Coleman had discovered what it means to be lonely. He carried a great burden and spoke hopefully of one medical procedure: "That may take off some of the pressure. I sure hope so." (5) His status as a man was threatened. Secretly, he may have preferred death to suffering continual defeat as a man, husband, and father.

Second, not all sick persons suffer such stress and anxiety. The casualness of an ordinary call, however, would have been inappropriate in Mr. Coleman's case.

Third, note that the chaplain refrained from reassuring the patient prematurely. All the facts were not in hand. He might have a brain tumor. The advantage of a thorough diagnostic work-up on such a patient lies in checking every possible source of difficulty. The minister has no right to tell such a patient that everything will be fine or that his trouble is only emotional. While sin and guilt are concomitants in illness, the chaplain in this case did not blame Coleman's trouble on sin. Assessing blame is often an "out," not a remedy.

Fourth, both Mr. Coleman and the chaplain were realistic about what they expected to accomplish in one interview. They did not expect an instant cure from one pastoral conversation. Rather, they opened themselves to the healing presence and daily providence of God. The hospital pastor pledged continued concern during the tests and promised to return soon. He realized that Mr. Coleman's eyes were open to several possible causes of illness and that he had taken a small, yet significant, step in the right direction during their visit. He was trusting God and man for healing.

Pastoral responsibility in illness. The Christian pastor supports persons and their families in numerous kinds of physical and mental illness. The family as the unit of illness may require more time and skill than does the patient. Families of accident victims or heart patients, for example, experience anticipatory grief prior to the event of death. In cases of emergency surgery, a psychiatric illness, cerebral hemorrhage, attempted suicide, and so forth a pastor stands with a family that is experiencing shock, grief, and anxiety.

After being with her hospitalized husband many days, a parishioner confessed to her minister, "I think I'm coming apart at the seams. I asked the doctor for a prescription for myself—something for my nerves. I've taken some of the capsules in order to rest at night. I just have to be here with Jim during the day." A religious ministry to a patient *and* his family is essential during the crisis of illness.

Because of the magnitude of this ministry the pastor should enlist and train his congregants in a shared service to the sick and their families. In smaller congregations a member's illness actually constitutes a crisis for the entire congregation. Parisioners share such caring responsibilities as child care, financial support, providing companionship, food, or transportation; visitation, and prayer support. A person may require nursing care, housekeeping assistance, and interest from a congregation during convalescence at home. The church's rehabilitative ministry of receiving former psychiatric patients, alcoholics, and so forth into its fellowship is also significant. Even as God hides a person's past "behind his back," church members should help former patients to forget the past and face the future with confident faith.

III. THE CRISIS OF GRIEF

If things go the other way in a prolonged illness, or when death is imminent, pastoral understanding and comfort should be extended by every possible means. There will be times when the minister will not know how to pray with someone who is dying. No words of assurance seem appropriate. When the dying and those who stand with them are speechless, "the Spirit himself intercedes for us with sighs too deep for words" (Rom. 8:26). There will be occasions—suicide, or accidental and tragic deaths—when no explanation will suffice for the bereft. When hearts are broken persons do not need explanations. They need the healing presence of God, who in everything "works for good with those who love him, who are called according to his purpose" (Rom. 8:28).

Guidance, old and new, is available for those who would faithfully represent the "God of all comfort" in the crisis of grief (II Cor. 1:3). Christ's ministry with acutely bereaved persons, as with Mary and Martha of Bethany, reminds us that he still enters into man's experiences of grief (John 11:1-44). God himself is the bereaved person's true burden-bearer, not those of us who minister for his sake (Heb. 4:14-15). Little has been written by pastors, beyond sermons and devotional helps, regarding the use of religious resources during bereavement. Edgar N. Jackson's *Understanding Grief* is the most ambitious attempt by a parish minister to trace the dynamics and resolution of grief situations.[15] The work is an adaption from psychiatric studies of grief for clergymen rather than a clinical investigation within the context of the church. Such studies offer valuable wisdom to all churchmen who would help bereft persons to experience what Granger Westberg appropriately terms "good grief."

While ministers deal primarily with acutely bereaved persons, psychiatrists see exaggerations of behavior in delayed and distorted grief reactions. In recent years the behavior of bereft persons following injury, separation, or loss by death has been the

[15] Edgar N. Jackson, *Understanding Grief* (Nashville, Tenn.: Abingdon Press, 1957).

subject of extensive scientific investigation. Two of the most widely read reports of research in pathological grief behavior are Freud's "Mourning and Melancholia," and Erich Lindemann's studies of grief following the Cocoanut Grove night-club fire in Boston.[16] Some of their observations regarding pathological grief processes offer valuable wisdom to those who minister in normal bereavement situations. We know, for example, that *grief work* involves a whole spectrum of emotions and reactions that "deserve respect and reverence." Though we speak of bereavement "as an experience," writes psychiatrist Clemens E. Benda, "we understand that human beings will react in many different ways."[17] Accordingly, no one method of comfort will work in all cases of loss, for each grief experience is clothed in its own unique circumstances.

Grief situations in life. There are grief situations in life that are often more disruptive and painful than the loss imposed by death. (1) The birth of a physically deformed or mentally defective child (about 6 per cent of all births in the United States are abnormal) is a bewildering experience for most parents. Prior planning is shattered with feelings of doubt or guilt and with questions about the future. (2) Some persons, including clergymen, are misunderstood in a community and suffer grievous psychic injury through unjust criticism and rejection. The likelihood of such misunderstanding is much greater in a small town than in a city where persons may live as strangers most of their lives. For example, a woman who had been falsely accused of infidelity almost lost her sanity before her husband agreed to move from their rural home to a nearby city. She found acceptance in the new situation and an opportunity to start life over again.

The family (3) whose only daughter marries secretly or becomes an unwed mother suffers deeply. While parents may forgive a delinquent child, whatever the nature of his or her misdeed, the

---

[16] See Sigmund Freud, "Mourning and Melancholia," *Collected Papers* (London: Hogarth Press, 1949), IV, 152-70; and Erich Lindemann, "Symptomatology and Management of Acute Grief," *American Journal of Psychiatry*, CI (Sept, 1944), 141-48. (Reprinted in *Journal of Pastoral Care*, V [Fall, 1951], 19-31.)

[17] Clemens E. Benda, "Bereavement and Grief Work," *Journal of Pastoral Care*, XVI (Spring, 1962), 2.

scars may never disappear. (4) A social stigma is often attached to the family of an alcoholic or mentally ill person which compounds their grief and guilt. In such an event the pastor's role as interpreter of illness to the community is a necessary aspect of his healing ministry with the person and his family. (5) Betrayal of trust may prompt any of a whole gamut of grief reactions—from depression or drunkenness to suicide. A shattered courtship, a disloyal marriage partner, a dishonest business associate, or any broken covenant may precipitate a serious crisis. (6) Events such as the loss of home and friends by removal from a community, failure in school, or an undesired transfer at work may isolate an individual and mar his life with grief.

In discussing the anxiety of grief Wayne Oates has written: "Grief by death cuts with a sharp edge like unto a razor; grief [in life] cuts with the jaggedness of a saw."[18] Grief situations in life are frequently unrecognized. There has been no death to call Christian helpers to the sufferer's side. Persons grieved in life often have "tears for food day and night" because they are left to bear their burdens alone. What shall be said of supporting those bereaved by death applies generally to persons suffering losses in life as well.

Considerations in grief work. A person's earliest grief experiences occur through the losses of childhood. A small girl's doll is mutilated by a mischievous brother. A treasured pet is killed by a passing car in the street. The family moves and a child loses his or her best playmate or a favorite teacher. Grief prompted by a close relative's death may require parents to serve their children as ministers of comfort and instruction. Yet some parents feel ill-equipped to face life's losses with their children. It is not atypical to hear a mother say, "I never want my child to attend a funeral." Such unrealism, while avoiding morbid circumstances temporarily, does not prepare youth for future grief work. Experience indicates that children generally accept and adjust to life's losses more easily than do adults. Early grief experiences become a training ground for more severe losses in the future. When life's events warrant

[18] Wayne E. Oates, *Anxiety in Christian Experience* (Philadelphia: Westminster Press, 1955), p. 49.

tears, parents should not be ashamed to display grief before their children. Also, when a relative or friend dies, grownups should not distort the truth to children. The mother might say, for example, "Grandmother is dead. She has gone to be with God and we shall miss her very much." Children's questions about death should be answered honestly in terms that they understand.

Another consideration is a person's reaction to loss *in the normal process of grief work*. Reactions to an accident, amputation, divorce, or death, for example, are remarkably similar. The process of grief work was evidenced by a man whose foot had been crushed in an industrial accident. He was thrust into a forced decision after being hospitalized several weeks. His surgeon said that he could keep the maimed, useless limb but advised an amputation and installation of a useful prosthesis. When the news of amputation came it plunged the man into shocked grief and depression. The day he received the report he confessed tearfully to a friend: "I have prayed so long and suffered so much that, sometimes, all I do is say His name. I know that God will not place more on me than I am able to bear, but I never thought one person could suffer so much." In ensuing days his grief proceeded with decreasing intensity from (1) shock and physical distress symptoms, such as vomiting; to (2) acts of mourning for the anticipated loss by tears, talking, and restlessness; (3) mild depression and expectant dread; and (4) adjustment to the limb's loss by renewed interest in hospital rituals, concern for his family's welfare, and plans for future employment. The wound of grief has been called "the illness that heals itself." Bereavement properly becomes *grief work* when a person, rather than avoiding reality: (a) accepts his loss and the suffering that goes with it, (b) consolidates memories of the past with future plans, and (c) reassumes responsibility for life's new demands. Comforters of those that mourn should understand the nature of grief work so that its developmental stages may be met with appropriate resources. Normal expressions of grief—shock, protests, tears, rote behavior, numbed dependence, and impulsive talking about the deceased—permit a creative catharsis of emotions.

Some churchmen mistakenly imply that a true Christian person should "prove his faith" by remaining dry-eyed and composed during a funeral service and thereafter. Their repressive statements and reassuring actions may prompt guilt feelings in a person who displays strong emotional reactions to loss. Thus some people conduct the business of funeral arrangements and attend the memorial service with a masked composure that hides their true state of mind. "Good grief" permits the bereft person to reveal his true feelings openly, according to his cultural, racial, and religious background. When grief has its work, life must go on.

Further, studies by Lindemann and others suggest that "comfort alone does not provide adequate assistance in the [bereaved person's] grief work."[19] A minister cannot assume, as did the Rev. Paul Baker in the case cited in the Introduction, that a few words will heal a wound inflicted by a loved one's death. The Christian pastor should rely upon several resources in assisting congregants to work through grief.

1. *The Christian funeral* undergirds the bereft family with its strengthening fellowship of friends, hymns of consolation, inspiration from God's Word, and hope of the resurrection. There is a growing conviction that the church itself, rather than a commercial funeral chapel, is the most appropriate setting for a Christian funeral service. The final "rites of passage" accompanying the burial of the dead are not devices to avoid facing the fact of death.[20] Neither are they meant to elevate the deceased to an idolatrous substitute for God. Rather the Christian funeral is designed to comfort the mourners through the hope of the resurrection provided in Jesus Christ. The service provides a community of understanding and occasion for the expression of grief and affirmation of the Christian hope.

2. Prior to and following the funeral, *the church fellowship incarnates God's comforting grace* to those pained by bereavement. Local customs and traditions in a community will influence the congregation's services of meal preparation, child care, financial

---

[19] Lindemann, *op. cit.*, p. 147. Cf. Wm. F. Rogers, *Ye Shall Be Comforted* (Philadelphia: Westminster Press, 1950).

[20] See Paul T. Irion, *The Funeral and the Mourners* (Nashville, Tenn.: Abingdon Press, 1954).

aid, and provision of companionship temporarily for bereft persons.

3. *The pastor's work does not end with the funeral.* Through follow-up calls and continuing friendship, he assists the person to undertake life's responsibilities again. His traditional resources of comfort—prayer, Bible readings, suggestion, and reassurance—may be supplemented with biographical or devotional literature. Along with relatives and friends, he becomes a "primer," assisting the bereaved person to resume life's roles and relationships.

4. Finally, Christian comforters need to be alert to *abnormal manifestations of grief.* Rather than effecting a smooth transition through stages of mourning to new life patterns, a person may fixate or regress to an earlier emotional state. A person who is relatively insecure, guilty, or hostile, for example, may go all to pieces following a loss. He or she may "act out" a neurotic grief pattern through flight from reality or by aggressive talk or behavior. Of course, guilt may be present in so-called normal grief as well, manifested by excessive funeral expense, and so on.

One such distorted grief manifestation is the *deification of the deceased* relative. The survivor, in an unconscious act of idolatry, elevates the dead person to a state of saintly perfection. The survivor may adopt the deceased's phrases, gestures, church affiliation, or life philosophy; or assume his business role and obligations. Or the dead person's room may remain undisturbed. Things have to stay the way the child or relative left them "for the last time." One family whose son had been killed in an auto accident erected a statue of the lad on their lawn. A garden spot was developed around the statue which became a shrine for their continual mourning for the deceased son.

Distortions of conduct or relationships which appear immediately or even years after a loved one's death are often abnormal grief reactions. A man once cried at his wife's open grave: "I can't let her go down there alone. I can't let her go! I'm going to get down there with her." His shocked minister asked the funeral director, "What shall we do?" "Let him get down in there if he wants to," came the calm reply. Later the minister learned that the man had been unfaithful to his wife. The funeral director and several persons in the community knew about his infidelity. It was not grief but guilt that drove him to such extreme behavior.

An elderly man once related to me how he had kept his deceased mother's clothing through the years. Occasionally, he said, it helped him to dress in her clothing and to sit in the old rocking chair that she had used across the years. Such bizarre behavior may require more than acceptance. In extreme cases it may require therapy in a medical setting.

A person may develop a *deep depression* in which he feels that he cannot continue life without the deceased. A clue may appear when the depressed person seeks to drown his trouble with alcohol. A woman whose mother had died of cancer at the age of forty-nine *developed the same symptoms* her mother had manifested in her last illness. The symptoms were purely psychosomatic, according to physicians, yet she *had* cancer as far as she was concerned. When a person manifests abnormal behavior following a grief situation the minister should consult with both the person's family and a physician. Temporary hospitalization may be indicated in such a crisis. A medical moratorium from intrapsychic strife may help the person to regain inner serenity and regroup resources for life's tasks again.

Conclusion

In this final chapter we have considered the pastoral action of the church during three disruptive crises—guilt, illness, and grief. Beyond human skill and understanding, those who serve in such crises must "pray at all times in the Spirit," seeking to be "strong in the Lord and in the strength of his might." The results of their labors are in God's hands for time and eternity. Paul's admonition to the Ephesian Christians provides an appropriate epilogue to this treatise concerning "pastoral care in the church." "As servants of Christ, [do] the will of God from the heart, rendering service with a good will as to the Lord and not to men, knowing that whatever good any one does, he will receive the same again from the Lord" (Eph. 6:6-8).

SUGGESTED READING

Bachmann, C. Charles. *Ministering to the Grief Sufferer*. Englewood Cliffs, N.J.: Prentice-Hall, 1954. A Protestant hospital chaplain examines the church's responsibility for persons experiencing bereavement.

Belgum, David. *Guilt: Where Psychology and Religion Meet*. Englewood Cliffs, N.J.: Prentice-Hall, 1963. An introduction to the problem of guilt by a Lutheran pastoral theologian.

Jackson, Edgar N. *Understanding Grief*. Nashville, Tenn.: Abingdon Press, 1957. A comprehensive work, addressed chiefly to ministers.

Oates, Wayne E. *The Bible in Pastoral Care* and *Anxiety in Christian Experience*. Philadelphia: Westminster Press, 1953 and 1955. Source books for pastoral ministry in varied crises.

Westberg, Granger. *Minister and Doctor Meet*. New York: Harper & Row, 1961. Also Young, Richard K. and Meiburg, Albert L. *Spiritual Therapy*. New York: Harper & Row, 1960. Team treatment approaches to hospitalized illness.

INDEX OF NAMES

INDEX OF SUBJECTS